The Philosophy of TV Noir

THE PHILOSOPHY OF POPULAR CULTURE

The books published in the Philosophy of Popular Culture series will illuminate and explore philosophical themes and ideas that occur in popular culture. The goal of this series is to demonstrate how philosophical inquiry has been reinvigorated by increased scholarly interest in the intersection of popular culture and philosophy, as well as to explore through philosophical analysis beloved modes of entertainment, such as movies, TV shows, and music. Philosophical concepts will be made accessible to the general reader through examples in popular culture. This series seeks to publish both established and emerging scholars who will engage a major area of popular culture for philosophical interpretation and examine the philosophical underpinnings of its themes. Eschewing ephemeral trends of philosophical and cultural theory, authors will establish and elaborate on connections between traditional philosophical ideas from important thinkers and the ever-expanding world of popular culture.

Series Editor
Mark T. Conard, Marymount Manhattan College, NY

Books in the Series
The Philosophy of Stanley Kubrick, edited by Jerold J. Abrams
The Philosophy of Film Noir, edited by Mark T. Conard
The Philosophy of Martin Scorsese, edited by Mark T. Conard
The Philosophy of Neo-Noir, edited by Mark T. Conard
The Philosophy of The X-Files, edited by Dean A. Kowalski
The Philosophy of Science Fiction Film, edited by Steven M. Sanders
The Philosophy of TV Noir, edited by Steven M. Sanders and Aeon J. Skoble
Basketball and Philosophy: Thinking Outside the Paint, edited by Jerry L. Walls and Gregory Bassham

THE PHILOSOPHY OF
TV NOIR

Edited by
Steven M. Sanders
and Aeon J. Skoble

THE UNIVERSITY PRESS OF KENTUCKY

Publication of this volume was made possible in part by a grant from the National Endowment for the Humanities.

Scholarly publisher for the Commonwealth, serving Bellarmine University, Berea College, Centre College of Kentucky, Eastern Kentucky University, The Filson Historical Society, Georgetown College, Kentucky Historical Society, Kentucky State University, Morehead State University, Murray State University, Northern Kentucky University, Transylvania University, University of Kentucky, University of Louisville, and Western Kentucky University.

Editorial and Sales Offices: The University Press of Kentucky
663 South Limestone Street, Lexington, Kentucky 40508-4008
www.kentuckypress.com

12 11 10 09 08   5 4 3 2 1

Library of Congress Cataloging-in-Publication Data

The philosophy of TV noir / edited by Steven M. Sanders and Aeon J. Skoble.
    p. cm. — (The philosophy of popular culture)
  Includes bibliographical references and index.
  ISBN 978-0-8131-2449-0 (hardcover : alk. paper)
  1. Detective and mystery television programs—United States—History and criticism.
2. Fantasy television programs—United States—History and criticism. 3. Film noir—United States—History and criticism. I. Sanders, Steven, 1945–   II. Skoble, Aeon J.
  PN1992.8.D48P45 2008
  791.45'61—dc22   2007029906

This book is printed on acid-free recycled paper meeting the requirements of the American National Standard for Permanence in Paper for Printed Library Materials.

∞ ✱

Manufactured in the United States of America.

Member of the Association of
American University Presses

Contents

Preface and Acknowledgments

The Philosophy of TV Noir was designed to present original essays on the most important noir television series, from *Dragnet* and *Naked City* to *The Sopranos* and *24*. Though sufficient as a stand-alone contribution to the study of philosophy, popular culture, and media studies, our book complements the two volumes on film noir in the University Press of Kentucky series on the Philosophy of Popular Culture, *The Philosophy of Film Noir* (2006) and *The Philosophy of Neo-Noir* (2007), both edited by Mark T. Conard.

The thematic arrangement of essays is designed to illuminate philosophical aspects of TV noir and to introduce readers to some of the problems and arguments of philosophy. Part 1 takes up issues of realism, relativism, and moral ambiguity in *Dragnet*, *Naked City*, *Secret Agent*, and *The Fugitive*. Part 2 discusses existentialism, nihilism, and the meaning of life as treated in *Miami Vice*, *24*, *Carnivàle*, and *The Sopranos*. Part 3 examines crime-scene investigation and the logic of detection in *CSI* and *The X-Files*. Part 4 considers autonomy, selfhood, and interpretation as they are explored in *The X-Files* and *Millennium*, *The Prisoner*, and *Twin Peaks*.

Several criteria guided our preparation of this volume. First, we sought essays that dealt with distinctively noir television programs. (What constitutes noir, in both film and television, is discussed by Steven M. Sanders in the introductory essay.) Second, we wanted a collection of essays that reflected the broad scope of noir television, from the classic series of the late 1950s and 1960s to the newest noir. Third, we asked for essays that would treat the philosophical themes in noir programming in a way that did not presuppose a knowledge of the history, problems, and methods of philosophy. Indeed, our contributors include not only philosophers but also film historians and other scholars whose essays give the volume an interdisciplinary dimension. Adherence to the first criterion compelled us to exclude essays on programs that we judged to be only marginally noir or not noir at all. Adherence to the second criterion led us to include essays on nonstandard noir programming, including mixed genre programs and noir science fiction. Adherence to the third criterion made demands that our contributors have met with skill and imagination.

This may be the place to warn readers that both the introductory essay and the contributor essays that follow disclose plots, points of suspense, and endings. Those who are not yet caught up on one or more of these series may want to take this spoiler alert to heart.

As with most books on film studies, citations include director and year the first time a film is mentioned. Film historians typically date films by year of release (as set by the Academy of Motion Picture Arts and Sciences), though there is no consensus on this method, which explains why *Ministry of Fear*, for example, can be dated 1944 in David Thomson's indispensable *New Biographical Dictionary of Film* (New York: Alfred A. Knopf, 1975; expanded and updated edition, 2004) and 1945 in the equally indispensable *Film Noir: An Encyclopedic Reference to the American Style*, edited by Alain Silver and Elizabeth Ward (Woodstock, NY: Overlook Press, 1979; revised and expanded edition, 1992). We made no attempt to require our contributors to adopt a uniform method for dating the films they refer to in their essays.

The noir television programs that are the subjects of the essays in this volume are the products of creative collaboration. We are grateful to the writers, producers, directors, actors, and production crews who made the television fare we are calling TV noir possible in the first place. We would like to thank our contributors, who combined resourcefulness with intelligence and who have written so well to illuminate the aesthetic impulse and philosophical import of TV noir. Steve Wrinn, director at the University Press of Kentucky; Mark T. Conard, editor of the Philosophy of Popular Culture series; Anne Dean Watkins, assistant to the director of the press; and the rest of the press staff have given us valuable encouragement and support. Steven M. Sanders would like to thank Christeen Clemens for her essential research assistance. Aeon J. Skoble would like to thank Lisa Bahnemann for her help and support.

An Introduction to the Philosophy of TV Noir

Steven M. Sanders

Television is the definitive medium of popular culture. With its mass audience, TV has become indispensable for transmitting the legacy of film noir and producing new forms of noir. *The Philosophy of TV Noir* was conceived in the belief that the themes, styles, and sensibilities of film noir are preserved even as they are transformed in a variety of television series from the mid-1950s to the present.

No doubt readers can identify the principal characters and describe numerous episodes of many of the television series discussed in this book. But while one's knowledge of TV noir may be extensive in this respect, it may be less so when it comes to understanding the philosophical ideas presupposed and reflected by such programming. For, in addition to its importance as a cultural phenomenon, noir television is particularly valuable in dramatizing situations and experiences that raise philosophical questions about how to live, what kind of person one should be, and what, if anything, gives meaning to life. This is where philosophical explanations are most helpful. The essays in this volume were written to stimulate and engage intelligent nonspecialist readers and to enliven discussion about such themes as alienation, nihilism, personal identity, and autonomy. These topics will be timely as long as crime, freedom, heroism, and anxiety are part of the human condition. In this introductory essay I want to discuss the nature, scope, exemplary instances, and philosophical dimensions of TV noir and to provide an overview of the volume.

From Film Noir to TV Noir

Television noir is historically and conceptually related to *film* noir, and it has long been a matter of dispute whether the latter is best described as a remarkable cycle that began in the early 1940s and lasted until nearly the end of the 1950s, a distinctive visual style with roots in German expression-ist cinema and French surrealism, a highly fatalistic sensibility and point of view reflecting American hard-boiled fiction, or all of these. Various "noir wars" or controversies over the definition of film noir have dominated academic discussions for decades, and the concept of TV noir itself bears the inherited scars of this battle over noir's elucidation.[1] Obviously, if there are disagreements about the concept of film noir, they will to some extent infiltrate what contributors to this volume say about the application of that concept to television. TV noir does not constitute a period or movement in the way that classic film noir does. Nor is it simply a programming trend like reality television. Instead, it represents an ever-changing adaptation and extension of the themes and styles of its influential film predecessors, updated, to be sure, by technological innovations. Its multiple associations with police procedurals, crime dramas, private detective series, psychological thrillers, espionage and foreign intrigue serials, and science fiction programs prevent a reduction to a single genre.

Much of the style and many of the themes of the TV noir programs discussed by philosophers, film historians, and other scholars in this volume have a source in, and trace out the implications of, those noir movies from the classic period of the 1940s and '50s that introduced us to a postwar world of crime and violence, alienation, estrangement, and existential crisis. Angst, absurdity, dread, and death—these were central to the existentialist philosophy that swept across Europe and came to America in the aftermath of World War II, and to the noir filmmakers, many of whom (like Billy Wilder, Otto Preminger, and Fritz Lang) were Austrian or German émigrés. They went into the studio and produced gripping dramas with a psychological edge and at least some element of crime, either actual or imagined.[2] Some were meditations on anguish; others, like *The Asphalt Jungle* (John Huston, 1950) and *The Killing* (Stanley Kubrick, 1956), chronicled robberies, heists, criminal capers, and big scores; still others provided an anatomy of those shadow figures of the noir demimonde: the killers and con artists, misfits and outsiders, femme fatales, corrupt cops, and bought-and-paid-for politicians, the criminal types who menaced, and the police detectives and private eyes who tracked them down.

By the 1960s, American filmmaking was increasingly involved "in creating the unique or spectacular," writes R. Barton Palmer. "One of the casualties of this revisionism was the film noir." Nevertheless, "popular taste for noir narrative has never waned since its advent in the 1940s."[3] Some of the more noteworthy achievements of the neo-noir period dating from the late 1960s include films as dissimilar from one another as *Bonnie and Clyde* (Arthur Penn, 1967), *Point Blank* (John Boorman, 1967), and the unjustly neglected *Pretty Poison* (Noel Black, 1968). These and other neo-noir films modulated classic noir themes into new frequencies. *Chinatown* (Roman Polanski, 1974), *The Conversation* (Francis Ford Coppola, 1974), and *Night Moves* (Penn, 1975), three of the most accomplished examples of the mid-1970s phase of neo-noir, externalized the violence and turned up the volume. Subsequent phases, beginning in the late 1980s, include *Blue Velvet* (David Lynch, 1986) and *Mulholland Drive* (Lynch, 2001), *Reservoir Dogs* (Quentin Tarantino, 1994), *Pulp Fiction* (Tarantino, 1995), and *L.A. Confidential* (Curtis Hanson, 1997). What is evident in these productions is that the elements of the human condition that provided the classic noir novelists and filmmakers with their philosophical grounding were still aesthetically viable, whether they were period pieces, as in *Chinatown*, updated remakes of noir classics, such as *No Way Out* (Roger Donaldson, 1987), a remake of *The Big Clock* (John Farrow, 1948), or reappraisals of familiar noir characters, as Robert Altman's deconstructed Philip Marlowe in *The Long Goodbye* (1973).

Film noir functions as a counterweight to the Hollywood blockbuster mentality that reached its apotheosis in the 1970s with the *Star Wars* franchise and is with us still, with big-budget films and massive marketing campaigns. The fact that film noir, a modest movement or genre, managed in its barely fifteen-year cycle to become what Alain Silver and Elizabeth Ward have called "the American Style" speaks to an extraordinary legacy.[4] That legacy can be found not only in the neo-noir productions to which it gave rise but also in the TV noir of today

The Through-Line of Film Noir

Film noir was always about more than tilted camera angles, chiaroscuro lighting, voice-over narration, and flashbacks, though the presence and significance of these elements of visual and narrative style cannot be denied. Certainly the pervasive theme of crime—its planning, execution, investigation, and consequences—figures prominently in both film and TV noir, as do the themes of the influence of the past on the motivations and actions of the principal characters, and the familiar made unfamiliar through the point of view of the noir antihero, whose alienation invariably reflects his estrangement and distorts the narrative. Noir is distinguished as well by its discontinuities, its distancing from conventional norms and sensibilities. TV noir's use of style in the service of point of view reflects a dedication to the "through-line of film noir," in the words of Philip Gaines, without overlooking the importance of storytelling and the constraints of a weekly format.[5]

After classic film noir had run its course, producers, directors, and scriptwriters, including those who had already made important contributions to movies and would continue to do so, like Blake Edwards, Robert Aldrich, and Don Siegel, turned to television. The classic TV noir programs were broadcast from the mid-1950s to the late 1960s, and included police procedurals (*Dragnet*), urban melodramas (*Naked City*), suspense stories (*The Fugitive*), and tales of espionage and foreign intrigue (as in the British import, *Danger Man,* known in the United States as *Secret Agent*). In the 1970s, television noir was rare; it did not come into its own again until the mid-1980s, with *Miami Vice* and *Crime Story.*[6] From the 1990s to date, noir narratives and visual styles have appeared in a wide variety of genres and forms, from weekly series to the made-for-television movie format.

TV noir, like film noir, is patterned with so many shadings of ambiguity, criminal violence, alienation, and paranoia that no single generalization about its nature is likely to do justice to its multiple dimensions. TV noir represents a match of style with dark and psychologically compelling themes. But since each of these has numerous facets, there can be significant variation from noir program to noir program. For example, *Secret Agent* points to political hypocrisy and corruption, whereas *The Fugitive* does not, and the visual style of *Miami Vice* is appropriate for a program shot in South Florida in the 1980s but would be curiously at odds with other types of noir television programs with their own narrative needs. Even within a single program there are dramatic alterations in style and theme. Virtually all the examples of TV noir discussed in this volume reflect variations, modifications, and innovations made necessary by changes in both the cultural climate and the medium itself. As the essays demonstrate, the transition from film noir to TV noir is not merely an extension of classic noir to the small screen. Rather, the noir television series themselves establish the autonomy of TV noir as an art form in its own right.

The extensive range in television noir programs represented in this volume by more than a dozen contributors with their own ideas about noir means the imposition of a single definition is out of the question. Nevertheless, distinctive stylistic and thematic elements permeate TV noir, and contributors have found it helpful to stress these in their explanations of how they understand TV noir. Typically, they have identified salient features of film noir and noted the presence of these features in the TV series they are discussing. For example, characters in film noir are often thrown into crisis by unresolved conflicts in their troubled pasts. We can find this thematic element in such noir classics as *The Strange Love of Martha Ivers* (Lewis Milestone, 1946), *Out of the Past* (Jacques Tourneur, 1947), and *The Third Man* (Carol Reed, 1949). One can then argue, as Kevin L. Stoehr does in *"The Sopranos, Film Noir, and Nihilism,"* as Eric Bronson does in *"Carnivàle* Knowledge: Give Me That Old-Time Noir Religion," and as I do in *"Noir et Blanc* in Color: Existentialism and *Miami Vice,"* that key episodes of *The Sopranos, Carnivàle,* and *Miami Vice,* respectively, illustrate this pervasive noir theme, making them good examples of TV noir. Throughout, contributors show how thematic elements and stylistic patterns found in exemplary models of film noir turn up in television genres as unlike one another as police procedurals, espionage dramas, and science fiction, and this provides an indication of how well noir has stood up in the nearly seventy years since the first noir films began to appear. To be sure, all this film noir material is *aufgehoben,* as the great nineteenth-century German philosopher Hegel might have said: preserved and transcended in TV noir, but not negated. The pervasiveness of noir themes, styles, and moods in noir television indicates that film noir managed to transcend its own time even as it mirrored it. Like its film predecessors, TV noir is edgy and unsettling and communicates something of philosophical substance about ourselves and the condition of our lives.

Realism and Relativism

The technique of bringing both foreground and background objects into focus contributed to the realism of classic film noir by allowing the audience to see actors and their reactions in a single frame. Without this technique—called "deep focus" and associated with Greg Toland, the cinematographer on *Citizen Kane* (Orson Welles, 1940), a film whose noir style is found in countless subsequent films—the camera had to show one actor, then cut to another for a reaction shot, then cut back to the first. With deep focus, filmmaking achieved greater realism, reproducing the way we actually perceive space and heightening the emotional impact of whatever was depicted. This technique, together with the tendency among noir filmmakers to emphasize canted angles and low-key lighting in which grays and darks predominate, and the irregular, off-center placement of figures in the frame, greatly enhanced the means of visualizing those emotions so characteristic of the noir world. In the words of the film critic Andre Bazin, "the stretching of the image in depth . . . produces . . . an impression of tension and conflict," while the walls, window frames, ceilings, and other narrowing imagery emphasize confinement and entrapment and preclude any escape, an important noir motif.[7] With the use of handheld-camera techniques in the late 1960s to convey realism, immediacy, and spontaneity, however, deep focus fell out of favor, an indication of a significant departure of neo-noir and TV noir from classic film noir. And with its fast cutting, television departed even further from the more fluid style of many classic film noir directors.

This may be the place to point out that a television series is by its very nature a collaborative enterprise. Its unique character is rarely, if ever, attributable to a single individual. One might mention Jack Webb, Michael Mann, Chris Carter, and David Chase as auteurs who put their distinctive stamps upon the influential and highly successful series *Dragnet, Miami Vice, The X-Files,* and *The Sopranos,* respectively. Even here, however, their inspiration required many hands (writers, directors, editors, set designers, and actors) to turn their visions into program realities. For this reason, contributors to this volume for the most part have not taken an auteurist approach to the discussion of TV noir.

These contributors include distinguished veterans of the academic noir wars to which I referred above, as well as emerging scholars who have begun what promise to be outstanding careers. They combine an appreciation of noir television with the expertise to explore issues in ethics, aesthetics, metaphysics, theory of knowledge, and social and political philosophy raised by TV noir programs. Their philosophical approaches are primarily interpretive and analytical, though they by no means overlook the importance of the historical development of noir television. In "*Dragnet,* Film Noir, and Postwar Realism," R. Barton Palmer provides a richly allusive account of the landmark TV noir series and its film noir lineage. His essay is particularly useful for its depiction of the postwar context out of which *Dragnet* and other noir television programs emerged in the 1950s. Palmer illustrates important ways in which TV noir reversed polarities, as it were, placing noir protagonists, especially in police procedurals but also in private detective dramas, on the side of law and order, unlike many of their film noir analogues at the margins. Of course, Sam Spade, Philip Marlowe, and Jake Gittes had codes of honor by which they lived. If Joe Friday, Sonny Crockett, and Gil Grissom are not idealists and dreamers, neither are they amoralists or nihilists.

Nor are they moral relativists, though, as Robert E. Fitzgibbons argues in "*Naked City:* The Relativist Turn in TV Noir," the transition from the moral absolutism of 1940s film noir to the relativism that characterized the cinema and television of the 1960s and 1970s can be seen in various episodes of *Naked City.* In relativism, one finds a fatal conflation of the notions of moral and immoral with those of normal and abnormal. Once one equates the two or assimilates behavior that is commonly thought to be immoral to behavior that is said to be (merely) abnormal, the former is drained of its normative import, as the passages from the anthropologist Ruth Benedict cited by Fitzgibbons confirm. Viewers of television programs in which this equation occurred were then left to question whether any behavior really was morally wrong because morality became identified in many viewers' minds with socially approved habits, and such matters are relative to culture. Thus, Fitzgibbons writes, by the end of many of *Naked City*'s episodes one was left to wonder whether a person's choices—which were wrong, judging by conventional moral standards—"might not have been right in some way. This conflation of the normal with the abnormal, of the moral with the immoral, and the promotion of relativism, permeated *Naked City.*"

Questions of diagnosis aside, Fitzgibbons advances an interpretation at odds with conventional thinking about both film noir and noir television in two respects. First, there is his idea that a strain of absolutism permeated much of classic film noir. This would be denied by those critics who claim to find ambivalence, ambiguity, disorientation, and radical ideas and techniques in film noir. Second, there is the sense, well expressed by James Ursini, that in television shows "safe bourgeois values most often emerged victorious by the final frames no matter what had preceded." As Ursini points out, such subjects of controversy as sex, drug addiction, corruption in institutions, and violence in American culture "had to be soft-pedaled in order to gain the omnipotent advertiser's imprimatur."[8] Fitzgibbons's analysis, however, suggests that subtle ways of undermining these constraints were at work in *Naked City.*

As for the relativist position itself, this has been a concern of philosophers since at least the time of Plato. Whether contemporary relativism is a defensible position depends in part on how successful relativists are in formulating a version of the view that avoids the many objections that have been raised against it, including those in Fitzgibbons's essay.

An Unreasoning Annihilation

Film noir protagonists often seem to fear mere existence itself, which, as Schopenhauer says, makes each of us a victim of the metaphysical force he calls the will to live. The classic noir protagonist is, in the words of James Ursini, "bound by his compulsions."[9] The grim determinism against which the existentialists, for example, were in open revolt was a dominant motif in classic film noir in the form of a preoccupation with the troubled pasts of its protagonists, who often felt doomed to repeat the very mistakes that had given rise to their troubles in the first place. The remnants of a fated destiny hang over events in film noir like a dense fog from which one cannot emerge without being unalterably changed. This accounts for the haunted character of so many noir protagonists in their doomed quests. Exaggerated lighting effects, ominous soundtracks, and cynical one-liners convey the noir atmosphere of desperate characters too occluded by anxiety to seize the opportunity to get past the disruptions in their lives. If we look back to classic film noir and try to identify a noir protagonist who achieves personal transformation in which his fractured, fragmented identity is rendered whole, his self unified, we may be surprised at the lack of plausible candidates. Not the Robert Mitchum characters in *Out of the Past* or *Where Danger Lives* (John Farrow, 1950), William Holden in *Sunset Boulevard* (Billy Wilder, 1950), or James Stewart in *Vertigo* (Alfred Hitchcock, 1958). Not Fred MacMurray in *Double Indemnity* (Wilder, 1944), and not Humphrey Bogart in *In a Lonely Place* (Nicholas Ray, 1950).

Film noir features convoluted and often bizarre plots, symbols and shadows, urban angst, and cat-and-mouse dialogue. The special art of noir is a style that delivers us from the contortions of plot and makes us care as much about individual characters as the relations between them, which are in any case often revealed in voice-over narration and flashback and thus subject to all the distortions in the consciousness of the troubled protagonist. Often our interest is less in understanding than in observing the protagonist's descent into crisis or immersion in dread. The most uncompromising film within the classic noir tradition to exhibit this theme is *D.O.A.* (Rudolph Maté, 1950). As R. Barton Palmer has noted, *D.O.A.* suggests that "the real problem life poses is . . . that an unreasoning annihilation may crush dreams and hopes at any moment."[10] No TV noir protagonist suffers a fate quite as extraordinary as that film's doomed Frank Bigelow, who faces imminent death from luminous poison slipped into his highball at a waterfront jazz club in San Francisco. But *The Fugitive*'s Richard Kimble, in his quest to establish his innocence and get out from under the death sentence that hangs over his head, runs him a close second. So does *The Prisoner*'s Number 6, who struggles to understand where he is, why he is being held captive in the Village, and who is responsible for bringing him there.

Alienation and Moral Ambiguity

Tales of alienated antiheroes can be found in numerous noir television series. Mike Hammer (*Mickey Spillane's Mike Hammer,* 1956–1959), Johnny Staccato (*Johnny Staccato,* 1959–1960), Fox Mulder (*The X-Files,* 1993–2002), Mike Torello (*Crime Story,* 1986–1988), Sonny Crockett and Ricardo Tubbs (*Miami Vice,* 1984–1989), and Jack Bauer (*24,* 2001–) recapitulate the dark destinies of their classic film noir forbears. Music, realistic location footage, and flashbacks are used to establish the disconnection between the otherwise mundane lives of the noir protagonists and the emotionally wrenching nature of their predicaments.[11]

Classic noir espionage films such as *Ministry of Fear* (Fritz Lang, 1944) and *The Third Man* are precursors to TV noir espionage series whose most conspicuous and distinguished example is *Secret Agent.* The mid-1960s series pits British agent John Drake, an independent-minded antihero who masquerades as artist, writer, travel agent, and milquetoast teacher against spies, terrorists, blackmailers, and assorted denizens of the international criminal underworld. Its black-and-white episodes were stylishly directed (some by Peter Yates, who would go on to direct the noir textured Steve McQueen hit *Bullitt* [1968], and others by Don Chaffey, who would also direct episodes of *The Prisoner*). Sets simulating such locales as Paris, Vienna, Singapore, Beirut, and Hong Kong achieved verisimilitude with admirable economy.

Sander Lee argues in his essay, "John Drake in Greeneland: Noir Themes in *Secret Agent,*" that moral ambiguity characterizes many of the situations Drake must face, including one in which it appears that Drake has been betrayed by an arm of the government whose actions are morally equivalent to those of its own adversaries. Another situation involves a typical noir couple, pulled into a web of duplicity and betrayal by the complexities of Cold War politics that Drake is powerless to alter. The episode titled "Colony

Three" prefigures the dilemma of the British espionage agent depicted in *The Prisoner* and highlights the cynical and sinister side of an intelligence agency of the British government. The psychological territory of *Secret Agent* is thus, in Lee's words, a landscape "void of meaning, haphazard, and morally indifferent."

In "Action and Integrity in *The Fugitive*," this volume's coeditor, Aeon J. Skoble, takes a close look at the noir protagonist type with his confusion, bewilderment, and paranoia, his vulnerability in a hostile and often violent environment. Skoble's focus is the popular 1960s series starring David Janssen, whose other TV noir roles include private detectives Richard Diamond (*Richard Diamond,* 1959–1961) and Harry Orwell (*Harry O,* 1974–1976). Skoble challenges the standard view of noir as involving moral ambivalence and ambiguity. The characterization of film noir and its protagonists by terms such as "ambivalence," "morally ambiguous," and "amoral" can be found in the early and highly influential work of critics Raymond Borde and Etienne Chaumeton and is repeated by subsequent commentators on film noir. For example, Jeremy G. Butler writes that moral ambiguity is one of the three principal themes in film noir.[12] This familiar refrain is also expressed by Mark T. Conard, who speaks of "the inversion of traditional values and the corresponding moral ambivalence" in film noir, by Jason Holt, who writes that "one of the most distinctively realistic features of noir is the role (or lack thereof) that values play in the characters' lives" which are depicted on a continuum that goes "from the morally ambiguous to the completely amoral" and by the present author, who writes that "film noir presents us with moral ambiguity, shifting identities, and impending doom."[13]

Skoble argues that *The Fugitive* is a counterexample to this standard view: it demonstrates moral clarity insofar as Richard Kimble "is consistently shown making tough decisions about what (to him) are clearly defined standards of right and wrong." Kimble's actions should be seen as expressions of his moral integrity and assertion of himself while at the same time he seeks to preserve his safety.

Given a certain amount of vagueness in the key notions, and a characteristic looseness in their employment, it is not altogether clear that there is a substantive disagreement between those who maintain and those who deny that moral ambiguity characterizes noir cinema and television. No doubt there are moral realist features of the noir protagonist that even the staunchest partisan of noir's ambiguity would not deny, and even scholars use terms like "ambivalence" and "ambiguity" somewhat loosely, so we should not be surprised to find some imprecision in their application. But the theme of the noir protagonist's predicament and the use of visual motifs (low-key lighting, unconventional angles, dark and narrow interiors, night-for-night exterior photography) together convey the idea that appearances are deceptive and mask a highly unstable reality. In TV noir, ambiguity is typically found in the morally compromised position of its protagonists, from the police detective who fails to inform the subject he is interrogating of his right to an attorney, to the undercover cop who is implicated in unlawful activity in order to achieve his goals. The principal characters of *Miami Vice, Crime Story,* and *24,* for example, often use morally questionable measures to gain information. Although these tactics are designed to expose those whose factual guilt is a foregone conclusion, viewers are sometimes left wondering whether their loyalties should lie with the law enforcement official who is carried away by such zeal. In the most complex and interesting cases, uncertainty about a character's guilt as well as the shifting identities, oblique loyalties, and tenuous alliances contribute to the sense of ambiguity found frequently in both film and TV noir. Whether there is an irreducible core of moral ambiguity in noir and whether this is in some sense definitive of noir remain open questions.

Morally ambivalent or not, there is an important difference between the angst-ridden antiheroes of classic film noir and the TV noir protagonists of the present day. As Jeremy G. Butler argues, "Broadcast television's lack of [narrative] closure undercuts" the "arch fatalism" of film noir. "Narrative closure is critical to *film noir* because it fulfills the doom that is prophesied implicitly at the film's start."[14] Since a television series typically requires recurring principal characters, it can never achieve complete narrative closure until the series finale. Even then, the need to make the series an appealing prospect for syndication can dictate an upbeat ending or at least an ambiguous one (as in the case of *The Fugitive, The Prisoner,* and *Miami Vice*) that permits interpretation along vaguely optimistic lines.

Sunshine Noir

From classic film noir, television took over the idea of the noir city. A noir subtext runs through the depiction of Los Angeles in *Dragnet* and New York in *Naked City,* where sequences are filmed on location in the city streets, whose authentic character is enhanced by documentary-style photography. By the time we get to *Law & Order* and *CSI,* the representations, often using the increasingly popular handheld camera style, implicate the cities themselves as buzzing hives of criminality and corruption, places whose disruptive and destructive elements can only be partially contained but not avoided.

For a time in the 1960s, site-specific programs were the vogue, in the manner of *77 Sunset Strip* (Los Angeles), *Hawaiian Eye* (Honolulu), *Surfside Six* (Miami Beach), and *Bourbon Street Beat* (New Orleans). When *Miami Vice* premiered in 1984, this format returned to television with an array of stunning visuals, cinematic production values, a scintillating soundtrack, and a noir sensibility I have called "sunshine noir."[15] The series showcased Miami as the paradigmatic sunshine noir city, evoking images of tieless men in guayaberas and pastel art deco hotels on Ocean Drive. After several decades of viewing cops in ill-fitting suits driving undistinguished government-issue cars, it was an unexpected pleasure to see Sonny Crockett in T-shirts and linen jackets, at the wheel of what was soon to become a TV noir icon, his black Ferrari Daytona Spyder.[16] An acute chronicle, *Miami Vice* captured the mid-1980s Miami milieu of tropical location sites, New Urbanism architecture, Grand Prix race-car driving, Cigarette boats, and jai alai.

But Miami is also a place where criminal activity is carried out on a massive scale, with the accompanying danger and fear that effectively contrast with the beautiful location photography. Many episodes of *Miami Vice* exhibit the characteristic existential motifs that Robert Porfirio has found in film noir, including alienated antiheroes who must perforce confront the absurdity and meaninglessness of life.[17] Paranoia is present throughout, owing to the need of its two principal characters to maintain their undercover identities. Yet even the most outlandish plotlines of its paranoid episodes are dramatized in ways that lend themselves to a disconcerting realism—as, for example, when Crockett and Tubbs investigate a Haitian master criminal with a penchant for the occult in "Tale of the Goat." Political conspiracy paranoia can be found in episodes such as "No Exit" and "Baseballs of Death," which appear to suggest that law enforcement's war on drugs in fact consolidates the power of the South American drug cartels because it was planned that way. And the linkage between drug trafficking and corporate interests is disclosed when Crockett and Tubbs are told in no uncertain terms by a New York City banking executive that there is no way that he and his colleagues in the financial community are going to let the South American governments default on their massive loans, even if that means turning a blind eye to their largest cash crop, cocaine.

Existentialism, Crisis, and Revolt

Questions about the meaning of life and doubts about its point enter into the central preoccupations of many of TV noir's principal characters, even if they themselves do not always articulate their concerns this way. These questions reflect and are reflected by existentialist philosophy.

The existentialists were by temperament and life choice not only philosophers but also authors of essays, novels, and plays upon which much of their reputation depends. Kierkegaard and Nietzsche, precursors of the existentialist movement, had already produced works of literary distinction a century before Albert Camus and Jean-Paul Sartre won Nobel Prizes for literature with work that was, as philosopher Hazel E. Barnes would put it in a book of the same title, a "literature of possibility."[18]

Their status as novelists and playwrights as well as members of the Resistance against the German occupation of France during World War II gave Sartre and Camus undeniable cachet. Both men were concerned with questions of what to do and how to live in an absurd world. The most philosophically significant aspect of the human condition and the one to which both Sartre and Camus give pride of place is our experience of freedom. Accordingly, they place great emphasis on spontaneity, chance, and contingency, as well as the more somber experiences of absurdity and revolt. For both thinkers, the existential recognition of the contingency and absurdity of life by no means involves a passive acceptance of its limits, accompanied by disillusion and defeat. On the contrary, it calls for engagement (Sartre) and defiance (Camus), thereby illustrating how various styles of existentialism contrast with the typical passivity of the classic noir protagonist. Camus, however, emphasizes the centrality of revolt in a less strident and radical way than Sartre, who called for the use of revolutionary violence in the Algerian war of independence from France. Camus, far more conciliatory and moderate, was an ardent champion of social justice without, however, the rhetoric of the firebrand.

The essays by Jennifer McMahon and Eric Bronson as well as my own offer interpretations of three of TV noir's existentially oriented programs. In "*Noir et Blanc* in Color: Existentialism and *Miami Vice,*" I discuss episodes that dramatize Sonny Crockett's existential crisis. In the final season of the series, Crockett's identity has been merged with his undercover persona, Sonny Burnett, and Crockett must come face to face with the killer inside him. I introduce the views of Kierkegaard and Sartre in the interpretation of such existentialist ideas as freedom, crisis, and recognition. In addition, I discuss two episodes in which Bruce Willis and Ed O'Neill, in guest-starring roles, portray noir protagonists whose predicaments illustrate familiar existentialist themes.

In "*24* and the Existential Man of Revolt," Jennifer McMahon subjects Jack Bauer, the protagonist of the long-running series *24,* to an analysis of the protagonist as existential hero using categories from the writings of Camus. McMahon highlights the theme of absurdity in Bauer's attempts to deal with critical challenges to order and stability, and subsequent fears of loss of meaning, caused by terrorist threats. In terms of the qualities of character found in the existential hero, she argues that Jack Bauer, particularly by virtue of his lucidity and courage, fills the bill as a Camusian man of revolt.

In response to these essays, however, it may be questioned whether existentialism, at least as it was espoused by Sartre and Camus, is any longer a viable political philosophy or prescription for action, or, for that matter, even a reliable diagnosis of the human condition. Understood in Sartrean terms, existentialism places an almost perverse emphasis on the darkest and most conflicted aspects of human relationships and holds these up as representative of the whole. This may account for the affinity between existentialism and film noir, but by reducing human relationships to sadism, masochism, or indifference, it is difficult to avoid concluding that Sartre has reduced the position to absurdity. Sartre himself, it should be noted, virtually abandoned existentialism when he embraced Marxism in his *Critique of Dialectical Reason* (1960).

Whatever else may be said for it, the moderation of Camus has not in fact been the way oppressed peoples have responded to their felt political and economic desperation, which of course makes its small influence all the more lamentable. In thinking about the absurd, Camus writes that "there is no fate that cannot be surmounted by scorn."[19] But it might be argued that he does not give entirely convincing grounds for recommending this attitude toward the absurdity of our lives. As the philosopher Thomas Nagel writes: "absurdity is one of the most human things about us: a manifestation of our most advanced and interesting characteristics." If it is true that nothing matters, then the fact that life is absurd does not matter either, and, in Nagel's words, "we can approach our absurd lives with irony instead of heroism and despair."[20]

Many viewers were surprised when they turned to *Carnivàle* to hear Brother Justin, a defrocked Methodist minister, despairingly say: "I lost my

God." The series proceeded to dramatize all the moral ambiguity, existential angst, and unresolved struggle associated with film noir but presented from a traditional Christian framework. In "*Carnivàle* Knowledge: Give Me That Old-Time Noir Religion," Eric Bronson cites both *Diary of a Country Priest* and *The Third Man* as films noirs that use old-time religion to highlight classic noir conflicts and struggles, to which we might add *Red Light* (Roy Del Ruth, 1950), whose film noir elements atypically accommodate a religious message.[21] Situating *Carnivàle* in this tradition, Bronson writes that *Carnivàle*'s "spiritually foreboding storylines appeal to viewers not because they seek easy answers but because it asks them difficult questions."

Nihilism, Noir, and *The Sopranos*

The nearly irremediable darkness of *The Sopranos* is redeemed by moments of piercing light into the moral psychology of its recurring characters. Its darkness comes from its nihilism. Film noir and, by extension, TV noir, is anchored in nihilism, a "values-denying and life-negating vision" that has cast its shadow upon modern Western culture since at least the nineteenth century and most conspicuously in the postwar years of the twentieth century. The view that nothing matters, that meaning and value have collapsed, is given dramatic expression in the activities of the show's protagonist, Tony Soprano, and his henchmen in organized crime. In the essay "*The Sopranos*, Film Noir, and Nihilism" (from which this characterization of nihilism comes), Kevin L. Stoehr sees perspectivism as the cause or ground of our loss of belief in objective truth. "The idea of perspectivism, the belief that all knowledge and experience results from our subjective and personal viewpoints," he writes, "leads to a subsequent rejection of our belief in objective, universal truths and our conviction in values that are intrinsic or valid in themselves, apart from merely subjective interests and preferences." Of course, the adoption of perspectivist views of meaning, truth, and value may be a consequence of the loss of belief in universal truths and objective values, and not the other way around. That is to say, the acceptance of perspectivism may be the effect rather than the cause of our declining belief in universal truth and objective values. What is more, the perspectivist thesis itself can be brought under closer scrutiny. For even if perspectivism is the cause of the loss of belief in objective reality and values, we still want to know whether the perspectivist position is itself justified. Is it just another position that might be rejected in favor of a non-perspectivist one? This complex question lies at the heart of recent philosophical discussions of relativism and objectivity.

Of even greater interest in the present context is the question of whether nihilism and perspectivism are even coherent positions. If to say that something matters is to express one's concern with that thing, then to say that "nothing matters" is presumably to express one's unconcern about absolutely everything. To say, with the nihilist, that "nothing matters, not even oneself" would seem to express one's unconcern with everything, including those merely subjective interests and preferences that give content to the perspectivist approach in the first place. Tony Soprano is not a nihilist in this sense, for he is very much concerned with his own interests and preferences: he wants power and the respect that power brings; he wants success in his criminal enterprises; and he wants the pleasures of good food and sex. This is by no means all there is to Tony's complex psychological makeup, as Stoehr shows in his illuminating section on animals and animosity. But on any ordinary construal of meaning and value, the annihilation of values has not happened to Tony Soprano.[22]

Postmodernism and *Crime Story*

As *Miami Vice, 24, Carnivàle,* and *The Sopranos* illustrate, a number of the styles and themes found in TV noir extend the models found in classic film noir in their indebtedness to existentialism. But *Miami Vice* also departs from the existentialist model and can be classed with other series that are determinedly subversive because they owe something to the influence of postmodernist philosophies.[23] And just as *Miami Vice* is noteworthy for its visual realization, showcasing a tropical deco palette in its wardrobe and set design, *Crime Story* (1986–1988), a series not covered in the essays included in this volume, vividly recalls early-1960s Chicago and Las Vegas. *Crime Story* combines its site-specific format with a radical postmodernist critique of government power and corruption. The series begins its first season in Chicago where police detective Mike Torello battles his own demons and his personal nemesis, Ray Luca. The master narrative of *Crime Story* is a Manichean one of the struggle between the forces of criminal darkness and of law and order. The forces of criminal darkness are represented by Luca, a low-level Chicago thug who has earned a reputation for his success at putting down scores. As he works his way up through the organized crime subculture, his ruthlessness and uncompromising approach earn him the attention of mob bosses and the undying enmity of Torello. Luca is answerable to no one except Miami-based mob boss Manny Weisbord, a fictional character modeled on alleged organized crime figure Meyer Lansky. Once Luca leaves Chicago and moves to Las Vegas, Torello and his team form a federal task force whose sole mission is to regroup in a demonic Las Vegas, no longer merely vulgar and trashy, kitschy and campy, and set up surveillance on Luca with the objective of putting him out of business once and for all. But time and again, Luca bests Torello and his task force.

Crime Story can be viewed on one level as a series that hews rather closely to reassuringly conventional American values. In a contest between good and evil, the former prevails, at least in the sense that criminal violence is shown to have enormous personal and social costs. On this viewing, *Crime Story* has not surrendered its commitment to American values: not everyone is a criminal sociopath like Ray Luca; not all human relationships are marked by exploitation and betrayal; not all institutions are corrupt. But on another level, *Crime Story* is deeply subversive in the way the foundational rules and systemic practices that give shape to American institutions and values are exposed as being nothing more than disguised expressions of criminal and governmental power, often operating in tandem. It is this philosophical critique, associated with postmodernist thinkers such as Foucault and Lyotard, that gives *Crime Story* its purchase on post-1980s developments in TV noir.[24]

The dominant narrative for film noir was a hard-boiled sensibility that projected itself into stories about those misfits, losers, loners, and marginal figures in the shadows who are moved by envy or ambition on the cheap.[25] This constellation of sensibilities and themes was itself the product of the political and cultural assumptions of the early hard-boiled novelists who accorded a certain moral superiority to the oppressed. These assumptions can be found in many episodes of *Crime Story,* especially those set in Chicago, where the corruption of institutions and the social ills of poverty and racism are dramatized. Of course, one does not need to accept the politics of the postmodern left to follow the events that take place in *Crime Story.* But it clearly helps to know that its creators are intent on doing more than telling a story. They are also delving into the power relations that constitute the network of acknowledgments of organized crime in Las Vegas in the early 1960s. In one sense, Manny Weisbord and the mob control the grand narrative: individuals are required to follow the party line of the mob, to whom all loyalty is owed. By the end of the decade, however, the mob's stranglehold over the casinos, the profit-making sectors of the Vegas resorts, has collapsed. As some postmodern theorists would argue, with the weakening of the old grand narrative comes a new authoritarian grand narrative of the multinational corporation. *Crime Story*, however, takes this conspiracy-oriented approach one step further, forging links among Ray Luca, the U.S. government, and an ambitious Mexican *generalissimo* who stays in power at the dispensation of a cocaine cartel. When Luca travels south to oversee his massive international drug operation and Torello and his crew go after him, the corrupt nature of U.S. involvement is in danger of being exposed, and Torello must go.

The significance of *Crime Story* lies in its restaging of classic film noir's conventions and preoccupations on the foundations of capitalism and government power as a means of exposing the dark and corrupt side of the United States, depicted as a racist, imperialist state with ambitions of empire. The censorious reception that *Crime Story* must have met in the executive boardroom at NBC may help to explain why the series was cancelled at the end of its second season, leaving the principal characters quite literally up in the air in an abrupt cliffhanger with many loose ends. As noir as anything one could find on network television at the time, *Crime Story* established a benchmark of what TV noir could achieve but rarely did.

Paranoia, Detection, and Crime Scene Investigation

In film noir, paranoia is part of the atmosphere and everyone takes it in, like the air they breathe. But paranoia is more than a mood. It is also a way of thinking, and it helps to explain why so many noir protagonists give expression to the thought that "whichever way you turn, Fate sticks out a foot to trip you up" (*Detour* [Edgar G. Ulmer, 1945]). Paranoia takes other forms as well, but in film noir it is typically combined with, or a component of, this notion of fate or determinism that is central to the conception of a fragmented, divided, and therefore inefficacious agency or will. The ineffective will, the inability to prevail against something from out of the past that exerts a kind of constraint, is a noir idea because the response to the dark force against which all attempts are doomed to failure is to fear it, and such fear can become paranoid.[26] In this respect, TV noir series as apparently unlike one another as *The Fugitive, The Prisoner, Crime Story,* and *The X-Files* share the noir paranoia of dark forces, whether they are the one-armed man, Number 1, Ray Luca (as in "Lucifer"), or the vast conspiracy to conceal the truth about extraterrestrials. There is a significant difference, however, between the paranoia of fate in film noir and its TV noir analogue, in which paranoia can be mitigated by modern technology. The dark forces of TV noir can be studied empirically. They can be investigated.

The television crime investigation franchise programs, such as *CSI* and *Law & Order,* pick up some of those features of noir cited by French critics who emphasized the indebtedness of film noir to surrealism with its concept of *amour fou.* However, the eroticized treatment of violence in *CSI* and *Law & Order: CI,* for example, should not, however, lead us to overemphasize their affinity with surrealism-based film noir. There is, significantly, enough dramatic closure in each of the episodes in these series to ensure a measure of coherence or narrative rationality that was anathema to the surrealists. And the emphasis on death in surrealism is, for the most part, not the raison d'être of most of these programs. Unlike the surrealists, who saw film noir as turning bourgeois values and morality upside down, there is a fairly conventional sense of right and wrong among the principal characters in *CSI* and *Law & Order.* These programs also tend to emphasize the investigations themselves. The backgrounds and characters of the detectives, forensic scientists, and district attorneys who investigate the crimes and bring the guilty to justice are often merely narrative conveniences on which to hang the plot or storyline. With this updating of the police procedural, noir television gives us a closer look at the methodology of crime scene investigation, portrayed in all its clinical detail in *CSI.*

Two essays about key philosophical issues in the methodology and epistemic status of detection and crime-scene investigation provide invaluable guides. The original *CSI* is itself investigated in "*CSI* and the Art of Forensic Detection" by Deborah Knight and George McKnight. Their essay addresses the film-historical roots of, continuities with, and departures from, classic film noir and neo-noir. They argue that the process of reading the evidence is part of a strategy of constructing a convincing explanatory narrative of the motives and actions of suspects. According to Knight and McKnight, "detection works from evidence to narrative explanation by means of good guesswork and the testing of competing hypotheses." Their essay can be seen as an attempt to give some content to the notion of explanation, and as such it raises questions about "explanatory bestness." The crime-scene investigators in *CSI* presumably seek the best explanation, the one that accounts for as much of the evidence as possible and ties up loose ends that are otherwise inexplicable. But in the end, what is it for one explanation to be the best explanation? Philosophers have given alternative and even conflicting answers to this question, reflecting ongoing philosophical debates.

In their essay, "Detection and the Logic of Abduction in *The X-Files*," Jerold J. Abrams and Elizabeth Cooke describe and develop "the logic of guessing," what the founder of pragmatism, C. S. Peirce, called "abduction," and what most philosophers refer to as inference to the best explanation. This process is epitomized by the procedure of FBI agents Fox Mulder and Dana Scully, who investigate cases of the paranormal. There is an ambivalent attitude in *The X-Files* over Mulder's convictions and inspired guesses about the paranormal versus Scully's equally insistent rationalism, and this ambivalence is explored in this essay. Abrams and Cooke quote Mulder approvingly when he asks Scully: "You tell me I'm not being scientifically rigorous and that I'm off my nut and then in the end who turns out to be right like 98.9 percent of the time?" But they also say that "Mulder, in his search for truth, needs Scully and her . . . extreme caution in the search for the evidence." Is this the program's attempt to have it both ways? If Mulder really is right almost all of the time and if Scully sees, in their words, "with her own eyes hard evidence of the truth that Mulder has long known about aliens, conspiracy, and the end of the world," it is difficult to see what contribution Scully's extreme caution makes to Mulder's nonscientific way of knowing. Of course, Mulder does not *know* but only guesses, and the fact that his guesses often turn out to be right does not establish the legitimacy of guessing, since the fix is in thanks to the scriptwriters for *The X-Files*. If Mulder comes up with an explanation that turns out to be better than Scully's, that is because the scripts are written so that he does. We should no more accept this as proof of the superiority of his methods than we should conclude that Columbo is a brilliant detective because he always manages to entrap the murderer no matter how cunning and resourceful the murderer is.

Espionage, Science Fiction, and Realism

Some of the most creative efforts within TV noir have extended the noir sensibility beyond the stock images of Chandleresque private detectives, urban architecture, and shadow-filled streets into the less familiar vicinity of espionage, science fiction, and mixed genre series. It is instructive, of course, to watch the oneiric episodes "The Ubiquitous Mr. Lovegrove" from *Secret Agent,* with its noir iconography of doors, windows, staircases, mirrors, and clocks, "Shadow in the Dark" from *Miami Vice,* and "Pauli Taglia's

Dream" from *Crime Story*. These idiosyncratic instances within their respective series are earlier examples of the multifarious forms TV noir took and how it manifested itself in unexpected and sometimes bizarre ways. But the viewer who wants to see more recent TV noir in some of its nonstandard forms must look beyond the private detective series and police procedurals to see the ways noir bleeds into other genres. Much of what is extant as TV noir reconfigures noir elements in what Andrew Spicer calls a "complex generic mix."[27] This should come as no surprise. It would be simplistic to identify TV noir with just one genre, the police procedural, for example, or the detective series. Going back to classic film noir, the noir sensibility can be found in a variety of genres, including melodrama, horror, espionage, and science fiction.[28] As *The Prisoner, The X-Files,* and *Twin Peaks* show, the development of TV noir extends to programs that share an affinity with these forms found in classic film noir.

Three key questions epitomize the enigmas at the core of three nonstandard TV noir programs: "Who is Number 1?" (*The Prisoner*), "Who can I trust?" (*The X-Files*), and "Who killed Laura Palmer?" (*Twin Peaks*). With reference to these questions, each of the series is radically underdetermined, for there is more than one answer with which its episodes are consistent. In fact, each series ends on a highly ambiguous note.

NOIR AND THE WORLD ORDER

The fact that noir style is value-free means that it can show up in almost any genre and can serve just about any ideological interest, from the anticapitalist critique of material values of *The Asphalt Jungle, Night and the City* (Jules Dassin, 1950), and *The Prowler* (Joseph Losey, 1951) to the affirmation of conventional values of *T-Men* (Anthony Mann, 1948) and the Cold War anticommunism of the science fiction noir *Invasion of the Body Snatchers* (Don Siegel, 1956).[29] Nevertheless, it may seem more than coincidental that progressive themes find natural expression in noir films. In its determinism and depiction of the squalor of predatory capitalism, the prewar, Depression-era proletarian writers (James M. Cain, Dashiel Hammett, Horace McCoy) and their postwar literary legatees (Jim Thompson, Charles Willeford) portrayed a sordid life unredeemed by initiative or action.[30] Many of the hard-boiled novelists from whose material noir films derived were critics of bourgeois values in general and capitalist America in particular. Still, politics in TV noir takes many forms, from the law-and-order conservatism of *Dragnet* to the libertarianism of *Millennium* to the leftist postmodernism of *Crime Story* to the paranoid/conspiracy extremism of *The X-Files* and *24*.

In the same way that *Ministry of Fear* and *The Third Man* lie somewhere in the prehistory of *Secret Agent*, *The Prisoner* is a precursor to *The X-Files*. This is not because of any supernaturalist motif in the former, but, rather, it is because the thread of anxiety that runs through these films and series reflects the conviction that the authenticity of life can be affirmed only by dramatizing our desperations and dreads, our deepest fears of loss of identity, autonomy, and individual liberty. Michael Valdez Moses treats these themes in detail in "Kingdom of Darkness: Autonomy and Conspiracy in *The X-Files* and *Millennium*." With its use of some of classic liberalism's most important philosophers, Moses's essay provides theoretical grounding for the all-important question of autonomy in an age of conspiracy and crisis. In the course of their investigations, Fox Mulder, Dana Scully, and Frank Black come face to face with conspiracies that undermine their confidence that the agents of good and evil—whether these are governments, business organizations, religious institutions, or even supernatural forces—can be either practically or theoretically distinguished. All they can be sure of is that such forces of darkness pose an unprecedented threat to individual freedom, autonomy, and democracy.

The law enforcement noir protagonist's isolation and estrangement that, in *"Noir et Blanc* in Color," I attributed to the cultural vacuum in which he works and lives, is explained by Moses in a somewhat different fashion, but the two accounts are complementary. The principal characters of *The X-Files* and *Millennium* show those indications of alienation so typical of the noir protagonist because this is the price that must be paid by those who seek truth and justice in the modern state. This conclusion was also strongly suggested in the discussion of *Crime Story* in this essay. But is it obvious that those who seek truth and justice must wind up this way? Is the state necessarily to blame for their alienation and isolation? Readers who cannot come up with counterexamples of those who have at least a neutral, if not a benevolent, relationship with the state may have to concede that Moses is on to something.[31]

The problem of reconciling government's protection of national security with individual autonomy has led many theorists in our own time (on both the political right and left) to prefer clear rules with few exceptions for fear that civil liberties will suffer severe erosion if government is given a freer hand. Still others prefer a procedure where some such reconciliation ideally should achieve some sort of balance between the expansion of security and the contraction of individual liberty. Events in the United States dating from September 11, 2001 can be seen as object lessons in the complexity and importance of debates over individual liberties in an age of international terrorism.

INFLECTIONS OF MEANINGLESSNESS

Can one develop a noir television series around inflections of meaninglessness?[32] *The Prisoner, The X-Files,* and *Millennium* answer this question affirmatively, each in its own way. From *Metropolis* (Fritz Lang, 1926) to *Invaders from Mars* (William Cameron Menzies, 1953) and *Invasion of the Body Snatchers,* the theme of personal identity and its fragmentation, partial recovery, and ultimate loss is crucial to film noir and is given new expression in TV noir series where the effect of science and technology—to say nothing of visitations from extraterrestrials—on human identity has terrifying results. Science fiction series like *The X-Files* and *The Prisoner* complement noir visuals with literate dialogue to dramatize the experiences of the angst-ridden Fox Mulder and the alienated Number 6. They consistently deploy noir themes: paranoia in *The X-Files,* as Mulder and Scully investigate paranormal phenomena and seek confirmation of a national conspiracy; the precariousness of autonomy and personal identity in *The Prisoner* as Number 6 struggles with his incarceration in "the Village" and attempts to discover the identity of his captor, Number 1.

In *The Prisoner,* a man—unnamed but widely believed by devotees of the series to be John Drake from *Secret Agent*—resigns from a high-level government job, passes out when he is gassed by an unidentified abductor, and wakens in a hermetic community known only as "the Village." He is given the moniker "Number 6" and housed in a bungalow that duplicates his London flat down to the last detail. He spends seventeen episodes trying to escape from the Village and to determine the identity of Number 1, while alternating Number 2s and their accomplices make every effort to find out why Number 6 resigned. Each episode finds Number 6 back at the Village, a return that signifies the inescapable Village-as-prison aspect of his existence. Try as he may, for sixteen episodes he never learns the identity of Number 1 or succeeds in escaping without being recaptured. In the series finale, "Fall Out," the mysterious Number 1 turns out to be, to all appearances, himself! The prisoner's role in his own narrative of imprisonment is thus rendered far more ambiguous, to say the least.

Having ended in narrative chaos, the final episode supports, and perhaps even requires, a variety of interpretations. Given the heavy emphasis in film noir on the need for redemption, a noir interpretation of "Fall Out" might take a theological form: Number 1 is God, and Number 6's discovery of His identity is a discovery of that aspect of Him in himself. If the Village is seen as the place to which the sinner, John Drake, has been consigned while he works out his redemption, Number 6's struggle to learn the identity of Number 1 is his struggle to come to know God, and in the end he returns to London, a redeemed man. On the other hand, it can be argued, no doubt even more plausibly, that *The Prisoner* shows that totalitarian systems cannot have a redemptive effect through their attempts to radically transform human nature.

Whatever the merit of such approaches, Shai Biderman and William Devlin are well aware that the surrealistic finale is a massive obstacle to anyone who tries to provide a unified interpretation of *The Prisoner*, theological, political, or otherwise, as their essay "*The Prisoner* and Self-Imprisonment" makes clear. Rather than attempt to paper over this difficulty, Biderman and Devlin confront it head-on with a bold reinterpretation of the series, exploiting the French postmodernist philosopher Michel Foucault's notion of the socially constructed self. Since the series examines the psychology and moral character of a British agent within the constraining atmosphere of a place with all the devices of a sophisticated prison, Biderman and Devlin apply Foucault's parallelism between prisons and society and the mechanisms for surveillance and control employed by each. A central feature of the Village is that one is always being watched by a type of Orwellian Big Brother. Against such a background, the standard Village expression, "Be seeing you," takes on an ominous meaning. Biderman and Devlin call attention to some of the central ways the administrators of the Village, chiefly Number 2, use confusion, apprehension, and ambiguity—themselves features of the noir world—to break Number 6's resistance. Conversely, they illustrate Number 6's use of wit, sarcasm, and irony as defense strategies. But they are determined not to reduce Number 6 to a symbol through sheer allegorical ardor, and they ask: What is the correct thing to say about selfhood in *The Prisoner*, once we know that Number 6 and Number 1 are the same person? They argue that "there is no completely independent individual; rather, people are dependent upon society in forming their personal identity." However, this seems to leave the main issue begging for an answer. The fact that one forms his or her identity in relation to others does not mean that one does not have an individual personal identity; additional premises are required to establish that point. Ultimately, the Foucauldian position adopted by Biderman and Devlin raises a difficult question that readers must ask themselves: Is the supposition that the Prisoner is Number 1 coherent in any literal sense? If it is not, then the vehicle of that incoherence, the script by Patrick McGoohan—or the episode that instantiates it—is an unforgettable but nonetheless undeniable travesty.

A KIND OF REALISM

As a mixed genre program, *Twin Peaks* inevitably takes on some of the characteristics of its constituent genres. If it is not unadulterated noir, it nevertheless can be characterized as noiresque with its darkness and corruption on full display, convoluted plot and subplots, grotesque minor characters, and a protagonist, FBI special agent Dale Cooper, with a troubled past. For these reasons, *Twin Peaks* qualifies as near-noir if not full-fledged noir, and in the end we may be inclined to accept the bizarre series as something old (a crime drama), something new (a Lynchian postmodernism), something borrowed (its noir source material can be traced to the self-parody of *His Kind of Woman* [John Farrow, 1951]), and something blue (as in Lynch's disturbing neo-noir film *Blue Velvet*).

Construed as a philosophical meditation on interpretation, with *Twin Peaks* his paradigm example, Jason Holt argues in "*Twin Peaks*, Noir, and Open Interpretation" that to classify *Twin Peaks* as noir may actually limit its aesthetic possibilities. In this connection, Holt argues that because noir is a type of realism, to designate a series "noir" is to limit the possibilities that are interpretively open to it. He claims that the central question of *Twin Peaks*—"Who killed Laura Palmer?—is interpretively closed to several alternative answers if we take the series to be a kind of realism. To argue, as some do, that the killer is BOB, necessitates a departure from the very realism that lies at the heart of noir. Nevertheless, Holt makes a case for the aesthetic desirability of radically open interpretations—of *Twin Peaks* and anything else worthy of the honorific "art."

The reader may wish to ask whether Holt's characterization of interpretive openness applies not only to the case of *Twin Peaks* but to others as well. Holt himself applies it insightfully to both *The Maltese Falcon* and *The Prisoner*, but in doing so he may have inadvertently weakened his own case. For if we accept his claim that the motivations of Sam Spade are multiply interpretable, what are we to make of his earlier claims of Spade's "underlying nobility," that he is a "noble hero"? That seems to assume that various debatable matters about Spade's character are already settled. There is also Holt's claim that the interpretive openness of *The Prisoner* enhances rather than compromises the aesthetic appeal of the series, making it more, not less, aesthetically rewarding. This may come as a surprise to the angry viewers who jammed the network switchboards following the broadcast of "Fall Out" in 1968, but Holt might reply that an aesthetically rewarding experience is not always a psychologically comforting one.

The Ambiguous Perspective on Life

This volume traverses the distance from the realism of *Dragnet* and *Naked City* through the existentialism of *Miami Vice* and the nihilism of *The Sopranos* to the realms of darkness and the unknown of *The X-Files* and *Millennium*. In the end, the noir way of looking at things translates into a way of being in the world, and as such it implies, at the very least, vulnerability if not actual jeopardy. The philosopher and film theorist Irving Singer writes, "The price one pays for the ambiguous perspective on life is a lack of security, recurrent doubt about one's mettle and the goodness of what one has achieved."[33] The ability of producers, writers, directors, and the rest to create the noir television series that the essays in this volume address almost certainly reflects their awareness of this ambiguous view of the human condition.

It would be folly to attempt to predict the future of TV noir. But its pervasiveness and the tenacity of its hold on the imagination suggest the vitality of what might be called the noir dimension of human experience and the relevance of that dimension to questions of who we are and how we are to live.

Notes

I would like to thank the authors of the essays in this volume whose correspondence contributed so much to my understanding of the issues with which this introductory essay deals. I am particularly grateful to Aeon J. Skoble and Christeen Clemens for our many conversations about philosophy, film noir, and TV noir.

1. *The Philosophy of Film Noir* (Lexington: University Press of Kentucky, 2006) and *The Philosophy of Neo-Noir* (Lexington: University Press of Kentucky, 2007), both edited by Mark T. Conard, clarify and extend these controversies and also challenge key

assumptions about the meaning and nature of film noir, as do many of the essays found in Alain Silver and James Ursini, ed., *Film Noir Reader* (New York: Limelight, 1996) and *Film Noir Reader 2* (New York: Limelight, 1999).

2. See Robert Porfirio, "No Way Out: Existential Motifs in the *Film Noir*," in Silver and Ursini, *Film Noir Reader*, 78.

3. R. Barton Palmer, *Hollywood's Dark Cinema: The American Film Noir* (New York: Twayne, 1994), 167, 168.

4. Alain Silver and Elizabeth Ward, ed., *Film Noir: An Encyclopedic Reference to the American Style* rev. and exp. ed. (1979; Woodstock, NY: Overlook, 1992).

5. Philip Gaines, "Noir 101," in Silver and Ursini, *Film Noir Reader 2*, 341.

6. James Ursini, "Angst at Sixty Fields per Second," in Silver and Ursini, *Film Noir Reader*, 286–87.

7. A valuable, nontechnical discussion of the contributions of Gregg Toland to cinematography can be found in Hilton Als, "The Cameraman," *New Yorker* (June 19, 2006): 46–51. The Bazin quote is from Andre Bazin, *Orson Welles: A Critical View* (Los Angeles: Acrobat, 1991), 74–75. The significance of noir visual motifs is given succinct explanation by Palmer, *Hollywood's Dark Cinema*, 38–39.

8. James Ursini, "Angst at Sixty Fields per Second," 275.

9. See Irving Singer, *Three Philosophical Filmmakers* (Cambridge: MIT Press, 2004), 230–31; James Ursini, "*Noir* Science," in Silver and Ursini, *Film Noir Reader 2*, 227.

10. Palmer, *Hollywood's Dark Cinema*, 87.

11. On this and other aspects of the noir protagonist, see R. Barton Palmer's perceptive account of *D.O.A.* in *Hollywood's Dark Cinema*, 83–92.

12. Jeremy G. Butler, "*Miami Vice:* The Legacy of *Film Noir*," in Silver and Ursini, *Film Noir Reader*, 289.

13. The relevant essays by Raymond Borde and Etienne Chaumeton, Robert Porfirio, and Jeremy G. Butler can be found in Silver and Ursini, *Film Noir Reader*, 17–25, 77–93, and 289–305, respectively. The quotes from Conard, Holt, and Sanders are taken from essays in Conard, *The Philosophy of Film Noir*, 1, 24–25, and 92, respectively.

14. Butler, "*Miami Vice*," in *Film Noir Reader*, 296.

15. I use the term to refer to crime drama that combines a noir sensibility with South Florida locales and high-toned production values.

16. "The car, for instance, has virtually lost its capacity to convey nuances of character and event, to participate in anything like the sleek ripple and jagged surge of the old *noir* textures." See Richard T. Jameson, "Son of *Noir*," in Silver and Ursini, *Film Noir Reader 2*, 200. Crockett's black Ferrari was destroyed by a shoulder-launched stinger missile in the first episode of season 3 and eventually replaced by a white Testarossa.

17. Porfirio, "No Way Out," 83–86.

18. Hazel E. Barnes, *The Literature of Possibility: A Study in Humanistic Existentialism* (Lincoln: University of Nebraska Press, 1959).

19. Albert Camus, *The Myth of Sisyphus,* trans. Justin O'Brien (New York: Vintage Books, 1955), 90.

20. Thomas Nagel, "The Absurd" (1971), reprinted in Nagel's *Mortal Questions* (Cambridge: Cambridge University Press, 1979), 23.

21. See the entry on *Red Light* by Bob Porfirio in Silver and Ward, *Film Noir,* 241.

22. R. M. Hare provides an interesting account of the impossibility of "the annihilation of values" in "'Nothing Matters,'" reprinted in his *Applications of Moral Philosophy* (Berkeley: University of California Press, 1972), 32–47.

23. In "Sunshine Noir: Postmodernism and *Miami Vice,*" in Conard, *The Philosophy of Neo-Noir,* I provide a postmodernist interpretation of three episodes, including "Heart of Darkness," which I interpret existentially in my essay in this volume. This is not inconsistent, since I am not *endorsing* alternative conflicting interpretations, but rather putting them forward for the reader's consideration.

24. Michel Foucault's appeal to intuition rather than analysis, his emphasis on dream experience, and, in the words of Allan Megill, his "call for a descent into the 'infernal' depths of human psychology" have an obvious affinity with noir themes and motifs. Allan Megill, *Prophets of Extremity: Nietzsche, Heidegger, Foucault, Derrida* (Berkeley: University of California Press, 1985), 221.

25. As James Naremore puts it, "No doubt movies of the noir type have always appealed strongly—but not exclusively—to middle-class white males who project themselves into stories about loners, losers, outlaws, and flawed idealists at the margins of society." Naremore, *More Than Night, Film Noir in Its Contexts* (Berkeley: University of California Press, 1998), 276.

26. Isaiah Berlin, *The Roots of Romanticism* (Princeton: Princeton University Press, 1999), 108.

27. Andrew Spicer, *Film Noir* (Harlow, England: Pearson Education, 2002), 150.

28. For noir science fiction, see James Ursini, "Noir Science," in Silver and Ursini, *Film Noir Reader 2,* 223–41. For noir horror films, see Eric Somer, "The Noir-Horror of *Cat People,*" in *Film Noir Reader 4,* ed. Alain Silver and James Ursini (New York: Limelight, 2004): 191–205. For the noir western, see Ursini, "Noir Westerns," and Robin Wood, "*Rancho Notorious* (1952): A Noir Western in Color," in Silver and Ursini, *Film Noir Reader 4,* 247–59 and 261–75, respectively.

29. Interpretation and discussion of films on various points of the political spectrum can be found in Grant Tracey, "*Film Noir* and Samuel Fuller's Tabloid Cinema: Red (Action), White (Exposition) and Blue (Romance)," in Silver and Ursini, *Film Noir Reader 2,* 159–75, and Reynold Humphries, "The Politics of Crime and the Crime of Politics: Postwar Noir, the Liberal Consensus and the Hollywood Left," in Silver and Ursini, *Film Noir Reader 4,* 227–45.

30. See David Cochran's absorbing discussion of Thompson and Willeford in

America Noir: Underground Writers and Filmmakers of the Postwar Era (Washington, DC: Smithsonian Institution Press, 2000), 19–52.

31. I am grateful to Aeon J. Skoble for suggesting this point.

32. I am unable to identify the source of this phrase, but I suspect that it comes from the art critic Robert Hughes or the film critic Stanley Kauffmann.

33. Singer, *Three Philosophical Filmmakers,* 234.

Part 1

REALISM, RELATIVISM, AND MORAL AMBIGUITY

DRAGNET, FILM NOIR, AND POSTWAR REALISM

R. Barton Palmer

Conceived by radio actor Jack Webb, who also starred and directed, *Dragnet* was one of the longest-running and most critically acclaimed dramatic series of 1950s American television, with a phenomenal total of 263 episodes broadcast from 1952–1959 and a reprise (for which there was little precedent in the industry) in 1967–1970 that generated a hundred more programs. No doubt Webb's police drama dominated the airwaves in the earlier decade. The initial version of the show was designed for radio, first airing in 1949 and continuing for 318 weekly episodes until 1955. Not only did the two series run concurrently for three years; they were intimately connected, with the radio scripts providing most, if not all, of the material for subsequent tele-visual production and broadcast. Once Webb made the move to television, his decision to film episodes rather than broadcast them live ensured that *Dragnet* would, because of syndication, be a continuing presence for years afterward on the small screen. In its radio and television forms, *Dragnet* left an indelible mark on American popular culture, inspiring a host of popular imitations in its own time (*The Lineup, Highway Patrol, M-Squad,* and *The Untouchables* chief among them) and establishing conventions for police action programming that have been followed by the most successful series of the last three decades, including *Law & Order,* whose producer, Dick Wolf, acknowledges, "*Dragnet* is the father of us all."[1]

As critics remarked at the time, what made *Dragnet* distinctive, and popular, was its deep commitment to a form of realism that Webb borrowed, if in a substantially modified form, from the cinema, where, as a young actor, he had begun to make a name for himself in such hard-edged films as Fred Zinnemann's *The Men* (1950), Billy Wilder's *Sunset Boulevard* (1950), and

Lewis Allen's *Appointment with Danger* (1951). Albert Werker's *He Walked by Night* (1949), in which Webb played a small role as a detective, exerted an especially powerful influence on his developing conception of a police procedural series, which would derive its name from the initial response to a bloody murder detailed in the film, the dragnet that brings dubious characters and the usual suspects into temporary custody for questioning. The realism *Dragnet* introduced to television violated many industry conventions, as *Variety* effusively observed when the television series was first broadcast in 1952: "There was no wasted motion, establishing the theme swiftly with racy, realistic dialog and deft locale transition. More important, there was no violence or blood-letting, and none of the artificially contrived clichés to achieve suspense."[2]

While the connection between *He Walked by Night* and Webb's radio/ television series has been generally recognized, what has hitherto received little attention is the particular form of realism that Webb developed from it. Werker's film certainly could not be said to avoid "violence or blood-letting" or eschew "artificially contrived clichés to achieve suspense." It seems, instead, that Webb's desire was, as a literary critic once remarked of realist and naturalist novelists, "to resurrect the complete illusion of real life, *using the things characteristic of real life*" (emphasis mine).[3] Despite borrowings from the real, all fictional realisms, of course, depend on conventions, not on some special access to actuality denied to other representational traditions. The sense of lived rather than fictional experience that Webb created in *Dragnet* proves no exception. We may grant that here too is a confection largely dependent on techniques and consciously repeated devices that—providing the consistent stylization necessary for a long-running series to be produced on a limited budget—could easily be, and often were, effectively parodied. More interesting, however, is that Webb's break from the well-established traditions of radio and screen crime drama, as well as his desire to make use of the "things characteristic of real life," was consonant with the critical protocols that elite critics of the age, enamored of the Italian neo-realist films then such a sensational presence on the silver screen, were using to judge Hollywood movies and the various forms of television drama as well.

Successfully embodying a realistic aesthetic, *Dragnet* established its significant difference from ordinary television series, a difference ratified by its continuing popularity and appeal to the critics. A quality program, with artistic connections through its realism to the celebrated live televisual drama of the age, *Dragnet* challenges the conventional paradigm of the industry's early years of development. According to this view, the decisive break in the early history of the medium was the abandonment of single-sponsor programming in favor of network licensed shows for which advertising time was sold to various sponsors. The so-called Golden Age of live drama thus made way for an era of Hollywood-produced filmed programming, which, critic William Boddy suggests, meant

> a repudiation of the aesthetic values promoted by prominent television critics and writers earlier in the decade. Via journalistic reviewing, technical handbooks, and general sociological criticism, writers on television in the early 1950s constructed an unusually explicit and widely shared normative aesthetics of television drama. To these critics and writers, the program changes in the mid-1950s signaled a retreat by the industry from an earlier commitment to aesthetic experimentation, program balance, and free expression.[4]

Dragnet, I would argue, complicates this simple narrative of flourishing and decline. Developed during an age of aesthetic commitment and single-sponsor financing, the series inaugurated a tradition of quality that did not end when the financing and production practices of the industry altered. Instead, its particular brand of realism, though reflecting the artistic values and cultural concerns of the late 1940s, has found a continuing home in the medium nearly half a century on. And that aesthetic, though partly inspired by noir films with a documentary style and feel, effects a genuine break with cinematic tradition, taking the fictional representation of criminal activity and police investigation in quite another direction.

Realism and Documentary in the Film Noir

The immediate postwar era in Hollywood witnessed the sudden emergence of a generic hybrid: what critics of a later age have called the noir semi-documentary. Earlier entries in the hitherto somewhat slowly developing noir series had been largely based on the American roman noir, the high voltage fiction of James M. Cain, Raymond Chandler, Cornell Woolrich, and others whose work was beginning to appeal to a broadly middle-class audience.[5] These stories of seedy private investigators and murderous adulterers had been realized on screen by a visual style that owed much to the German

expressionism brought to Hollywood by a talented group of émigré directors. Films such as *Murder My Sweet* (Edward Dmytryk, 1944) and *Double
Indemnity* (Billy Wilder, 1944) offered a break from the previous canons
of Hollywood realism, with sequences dominated by chiaroscuro lighting,
strangely angled or distorted framings and an imprisoning mise-en-scène
that served as the external correlatives of the existential dead ends to which
these fatalistic narratives usually delivered their unsympathetic characters,
whose world-weary cynicism found its voice in a highly stylized argot far
removed from everyday speech.

Henry Hathaway's *The House on 92nd Street,* released in September 1945,
a little more than a month after final victory in the Pacific, moved film noir in
a substantially different direction. This wartime thriller, fictional only in the
sense that it expands its spare story with some imagined scenes and confected
dialogue, combines the visual style and formal conventions of documentary
filmmaking with the exaggerated naturalism of the film noir, especially the
genre's probing of hitherto off-limits themes and its Zolaesque preoccupation
with the seedier side of contemporary American life. Produced by Louis de
Rochemont, whose *March of Time* newsreels had become accustomed fare
in American cinemas during the war, *The House on 92nd Street* is true, or
at least so its authoritative narrator declares; the film reenacts a real case of
German espionage foiled during the early stages of World War II by timely
and expert police work. FBI files were made available to the screenwriters.
Many sequences were shot in locations around the New York City area, where
the plot to steal nuclear secrets was discovered and foiled, and in Washington, D.C., at the FBI complex, where much of the investigative work on the
case was done. Much of this footage is straightforwardly documentary in
its apparently unstaged recording of police activities and its dispassionate
description of law-enforcement procedure. Nonprofessional actors were
used in minor parts (with some of the roles being played by actual police
personnel). Sequences shot silent are explained by the self-assured and
omniscient narrator (Reed Hadley, in a role he would repeat many times in
subsequent films and on television).

And yet *The House on 92nd Street* is more than a re-creation of a true
case. The film's narrative focus is uneasily split between the Nazi agents, those
fascinating perpetrators of an unfathomable and perverse evil, and their
pursuers, whose unalloyed and rather flat virtue proves much less appealing, even though it naturally emerges victorious in a finale that celebrates
the invincibility of American institutions. A neutral, unglamorized visual

style attests to the film's accurate reenactment of the official response to the discovered threat, but the sequences detailing the machinations of the reptilian villains strain to evoke a different atmosphere. These sequences are overly theatrical, barely contained by Hathaway's otherwise subdued and objective approach to his material. Subsequent entrants in the noir semi-documentary manifest the same unstable melding of two opposed story worlds: the well-organized modern state, knowable as well as knowing, its irregularities surveilled and corrected by government agencies of enormous power that are always put in service of the public good; and an underworld of the maladjusted and dissatisfied, whose transgressions, moral and legal, are not only self-defeating but otherwise easily disposed of by an unchallengeable authority.

He Walked by Night

Because of its influence through *Dragnet* on the development and subsequent history of American television in the 1950s, the most important noir semi-documentary is *He Walked by Night,* which is based on an actual case: the killing of two policemen by a fellow member of their own Pasadena, California, department who worked in the fingerprint records division. In the hands of screenwriters John C. Higgins and Crane Wilbur, this rather mundane criminal becomes a self-taught and sociopathic genius, who not only is adept at designing innovative electronic equipment but is not above stealing what others have invented and selling it as his own. Roy Martin (Richard Basehart), unlike the pathetically inept German agents in *The House on 92nd Street,* is a cunning adversary. After he somewhat rashly kills a policeman who spots him about to burglarize an electronics shop, Martin eludes capture with his amazing knowledge of police technique. Moreover, he is brazen enough to shoot it out with detectives who have staked out the businessman to whom he sells his inventions and stolen property. Wounded in the encounter, Martin is even possessed of the necessary sangfroid to operate successfully on himself. The police discover his hideout, yet this time he escapes through the Los Angeles sewer system, whose intricate twists and turnings he has made not only a private path of attack and retreat but a hideout as well. Only a lucky chance enables the police to corner and kill him. Having once again foiled his pursuers, Martin is about to escape to the dark city above when a car happens to park on the manhole cover he needs to lift. The shotgun and stores of ammunition he had previously cached underground do him no good, as he cannot triumph in a shootout against a gang of determined policemen.

He Walked by Night offers much of the same documentary stylization as does *The House on 92nd Street,* even though the "case" in this film is no more than superficially based on actual events. A written title somewhat misleadingly proclaims: "This is a true story. It is known to the Police Department of one of our largest cities as the most difficult homicide case in its experience, principally because of the diabolical cleverness, intelligence and cunning of a completely unknown killer. . . . The record is set down here factually—as it happened. Only the names are changed, to protect the innocent." These words are echoed by the narrator, who, as shots of Los Angeles and its police department play on the screen, provides an overview of the nation's largest urban area, whose cosmopolitanism and mixed, transient population, so he avers, provide a challenge for law enforcement. Somewhat wryly, he concludes that "the work of the police, like that of woman, is never done. The facts are told here as they happened." Many of the sequences in the film that detail police work are in every sense documentary, having been filmed inside the headquarters (an imposing building shot from a low angle to emphasize its embodiment of well-organized power) and furnished with an appropriate voice-over commentary. The staged sequences are carefully stylized to match the reality footage. Producers Robert Kane and Bryan Foy were so eager for authenticity that they asked the Los Angeles Police Department for a technical advisor. Sergeant Marty Wynn, who was eager to have the film avoid the distorting clichés that had dominated Hollywood treatment of crime detection, provided much valuable information about police procedure; under Wynn's tutelage, the screenwriters and performers learned the jargon of the trade, including the abbreviated language of police radio calls and the specialized vocabulary of evidence gathering and testing.

Yet it is important to note that the film, in detailing what it confesses is for the LAPD "the most difficult homicide case in its experience," commits itself to focusing on the extraordinary rather than the everyday aspects of police work. Influenced by film noir's preoccupation with the bizarre and the perverse, Werker and the screenwriters not surprisingly developed Roy Martin, the diabolical genius, as a kind of monster who, in fact, cannot be identified and collared by ordinary police procedure. Instead, in a movement of the plot that intriguingly anticipates the spectacular finale of a more celebrated contemporary thriller, Carol Reed's *The Third Man* (1949), Martin must be hunted down and exterminated in his filthy underground lair. Werker and cinematographer John Alton, famous for his expressionistic setups and visual stylization in such noir classics as *The Big Combo* (Joseph H. Lewis, 1955), *Mystery Street* (John Sturgis, 1950), and *The Hollow Triumph* (Steve Sekely, 1948), put Martin in control of a shadowy alternative world, a place of darkness, anomie, and reckless self-assertion that the police enter only to their peril. Detective Sergeant Marty Brennan (Scott Brady) is foiled repeatedly by Martin, who seems to know police procedure better than the policeman themselves, while the criminal survives and prospers by his wits and considerable derring-do. Certainly the film's most striking scene shows the gunshot Martin removing a bullet himself without the benefit of either an anesthetic or medical advice. Brennan is a colorless character in comparison. Scott Brady's low-key performance in the role makes him much less dashing, energetic, and resourceful than the man he seeks, played by the charismatic and attractive Richard Basehart. In fact, Brennan's failure to capture Martin after an abortive stakeout that results in the wounding of one of his partners earns him an early dismissal from the case. Only a sudden flash of inspiration persuades his chief to let him rejoin the investigation.

Martin confounds police procedure by changing what the narrator calls his "modus operandi," transforming himself from a burglar to a robber. In his new incarnation, Martin terrorizes the city with a series of daring liquor store robberies. The man's intimate knowledge of how the police work suggests that he is a rogue cop. His cunning duplicity revealed by police lab work (bullets fired from the cop killer's gun are shown to match one fired from the robber's), the killer is eventually, in a striking sequence, given a face by police artists, who assemble the robbery victims to construct a group portrait. The patient and time-consuming check of leads provides yet another breakthrough. Martin is identified by Brennan, who wearily troops from one area police station to another looking for a match to the composite sketch. Surrounded a second time, however, the resourceful Martin manages to escape the police cordon into his sewer hideout. There he can only be stopped by his own bad luck (the blocked manhole cover) and the heroic—but group—action of the police.

The unfortunate criminal is gunned down in a shootout reminiscent of the western and the classic gangster film (such as *Public Enemy* [William Wellman, 1931], *High Sierra* [Raoul Walsh, 1941], or *White Heat* [Walsh, 1949]). This climactic sequence provides Martin with a dramatic apotheosis, as his bullet-ridden body tumbles from a ladder into the sewage below; he suffers a literal fall from power and control. Significantly, there is no closing

narration to fix the meaning of this event, no celebration of the successful pursuit of a dangerous felon. The law triumphs, but that victory is not
documented; it is neither brought into the public realm to be adjudicated
nor stylized as real. The surveilling and enforcement powers of the police
may prove superior (if only barely) to Martin's monstrousness, but in the
clash of representational traditions the expressionism of film noir, and not
the naturalism of classic documentary, furnishes the film with its summa-
tive image.

As does the noir semi-documentary more generally, *He Walked by Night*
juxtaposes a city of light (populated by citizens going about their business
and surveilled by the benevolent police) and a city of darkness (a criminal
underworld that, metaphorized by the darkness and night that enfold it,
does not easily admit the knowing, official gaze). Like the film's narrative
and visual structure, the sound track is schizophrenic, split between the
heavy, grim romantic theme that plays over Martin lurking in the shadows and the upbeat, almost military air that accompanies the work of
the police, the grinding routine according to the book, which eventually
identifies the criminal. The city is the focus of productive communal life
(as the opening montage of shots depicting everyday life emphasizes), but
its anonymous spaces shield those who, in their exceptionality, would live
in defiance of officially imposed law and order. The two worlds found in
the contemporary American metropolis seem utterly opposed, but they
are actually strangely connected: Martin *is* a former employee of a local
police department.

And Martin is hardly, at least at the outset, a career criminal, nor is his
lawbreaking to be explained sociologically. The underworld he inhabits
is never figured in either economic or class terms. It seems, instead, the
underside of bourgeois normality. Martin's thefts of electronic equipment
are meant to further a career of invention and self-promotion for which his
extraordinary mental abilities would certainly qualify him. Because he is
never interrogated by the police, Martin's abandonment of a career in law
enforcement remains a mystery. His former employer reveals that he left in
1942 for the military, after his discharge refusing any offer to rejoin the department. This much is clear. Eager to make a mark for himself in a postwar
world driven by technological advance, inured to violence, and disposing
of technical knowledge and skill gained from government service, Martin
is yet another version of the returning soldier who cannot fit easily into a
changed world despite his exceptional talents and energies.

The veteran mysteriously damaged by wartime service is a stock character of film noir, an essential element of the nightmare vision of American life offered in this antiestablishmentarian Hollywood series. *He Walked by Night,* as its title suggests, is finally more interested in exploring, if not explaining, this enigmatic figure (Martin's moral nature is evoked but little through dialogue and mostly, in the expressionist manner, by visual style and mise-en-scène). Despite its opening avowal of truth-telling and the narrator's commitment to setting out the facts "as they happened," the film is much more than a straightforward chronicle of the infallible methods, the irresistible institutional power, and the quietly heroic dedication of the police to identifying and capturing criminals.

And yet it was just such a chronicle Jack Webb intended to produce in *Dragnet* (named, significantly enough, for an investigating technique, not a monstrous villain). *He Walked by Night* provided him with a model for a police series, but Webb carefully eliminated the film's double focus on dedicated public servants and psychopathic killers, rejecting both the expressionist stylization of film noir and the wisecracking dialogue of hard-boiled fiction.

Dragnet: A Different Kind of Realism

Webb's development of *Dragnet* is a case, to put it in Darwinian terms, of ontogeny repeating phylogeny, or, in plain language, an instance of the development of the individual replicating that of its species or type. Under the influence of the worldwide postwar fashion for realist film, noir underwent a rapprochement of sorts with the other Hollywood genres that could more fully accommodate themselves to this new aesthetic. The types most affected by this new taste for and evaluation of realism were the social problem film (such as *The Men,* which treated the readjustment to civilian life of maimed veterans) or the "small" film, which is most importantly exemplified by *Marty* [Delbert Mann, 1955], a kind of anti-Hollywood romance. Webb's developing artistic interests show something of the same pattern of development. His first two radio dramas were firmly in the tradition of hard-boiled fiction and the classic film noir: *Pat Novak for Hire* and *Johnny Madero, Pier 13* were private eye dramas in which he played a tough guy detective with an attitude who vented his disdain for both crooks and cops with an unending stream of elaborate wisecracks.[6]

As he often told the tale, Webb's experience on the set of *He Walked by*

Night gave him a new career direction. Police officer Marty Wynn suggested that he could provide Webb with access to actual police files.[7] Webb rejected the idea at first but soon called Wynn, who let him ride around in his police prowler for several nights, responding to calls. Provided by Wynn and his partner with a good deal of information about police procedures and jargon, Webb decided to make authenticity the watchword of the new series, which Wynn suggested could easily find its materials in the public record (names and other particulars, of course, would need to be changed in order to avoid lawsuits). In other words, the realism he was after (which could be pursued more deeply in the television version of the show) would depend not only, in the manner of Hollywood, on creating an effect of plausibility, with a view toward convincing the viewer to suspend disbelief. As we will see in detail below, Webb's realism would also be characterized by imitative precision, by the extent to which the fiction might exactly limn the contours of the real. The focus would be on the police rather than on the criminal, and the main character would be, as Webb described him, "a quiet, dedicated policeman who, as in real life, was just one little cog in a great enforcement machine. I wanted him to be an honest, decent, home-loving guy—the image of fifty thousand peace officers."[8] His Sergeant Friday was a man without much of a present or a past, whose only life was his work (a halfhearted attempt to provide him with a love interest was quickly abandoned). Certainly the access afforded by Wynn (and, later, an entire grateful and supportive LAPD) to the hitherto somewhat mysterious world of police work influenced Webb substantially in his desire to tell the "real" story of criminal investigation. But the young actor turned director and producer was likely responding as well to the critical and intellectual climate of the times. Certainly the particular fictional devices and techniques Webb selected (including a particular naturalist style of acting) owe little to what he learned from Wynn.

We have already remarked about the effect on the film noir of the wave of Italian neo-realist films that flooded the American exhibition market in the late 1940s and early 1950s. With their limited budgets and almost hand-made quality, these productions, as two noted film historians have remarked, "displayed a grasp of the human condition that made Hollywood pictures seem slick and stylized." They were "filled with harsh detail" and showed "ordinary lives twisted by events and social forces beyond their control."[9] Neo-realist films were generally shot on location and with available light; they addressed topical subjects, often focusing on the experiences of those in the lower orders; plots were simple, emphasizing everyday events and avoiding both melodrama and spectacle; and unglamorous or nonprofessional actors were cast in featured roles, making an important connection between real and film worlds. Reviewing Roberto Rossellini's *Open City* (1946), Bosley Crowther of the *New York Times* (perhaps the era's most influential critic) praised the film for its "overpowering realism." *Open City,* Crowther wrote, has "the windblown look of a film shot from actualities, with the camera providentially on the scene." In part, such an aesthetic resulted from the conditions of production: "The stringent necessity for economy compelled the producers to make a film that has all the appearance and flavor of a straight documentary." More important, the neo-realist film rejects the narrative conventions of Hollywood cinema: "The heroes in *Open City* are not conscious of being such. Nor are the artists who conceived them. They are simple people doing what they think is right. The story of the film is literal . . . and is said to have been based on actual facts. . . . All these details are presented in a most frank and uncompromising way which is likely to prove somewhat shocking to sheltered American audiences . . . yet the total effect of the picture is a sense of real experience."[10] Crowther also found much to praise in Vittorio De Sica's *The Bicycle Thief* (1949), a film "sharply imaged in simple and realistic terms." Here also the elaborate, Aristotelian designs of Hollywood narrative are absent, for the "story is lean and literal, completely unburdened with 'plot.'" Absent too is the customary spectacle of commercial cinema: "The natural and the real are emphasized, with the film largely shot in actual settings and played by a nonprofessional cast."[11]

Among the directors who demonstrated that this kind of film could be made and marketed successfully in Hollywood was Fred Zinnemann. Jack Webb played an important supporting role in his *The Men,* a chronicle of paraplegic veterans receiving treatment in a VA hospital, which was independently produced by Stanley Kramer. Crowther praised Zinnemann and Kramer for creating such a "firm, forthright, realistic study of a group of paralyzed men." He found it noteworthy that "much of this picture was photographed and practically all of it was derived at the Birmingham Veterans Hospital near Los Angeles." Kramer and screenwriter Carl Foreman spent several weeks at the hospital, studying both the methods of treatment employed and the experiences of the patients, a number of whom were recruited to play minor roles in the film (the credits express gratitude to some forty-five of "the men"). The result is that there is a "striking and authentic documentary quality . . . imparted to the whole film in every detail, attitude, and word."[12]

"The Story You Are about to See Is True"

Like Kramer, Zinnemann, and Foreman, Webb, transferring his program from radio to television, incorporated within *Dragnet* those "things characteristic of real life," creating a fictional world that had not been seen before on the small screen, where crime shows had meant hard-boiled dramas such as *The Adventures of Ellery Queen, Martin Kane, Private Eye,* and *Lights Out: Men against Crime,* all of which were quite obviously directly descended either from the film noir, especially in its B-movie form, or the detective serial. Using actual cases for story material guaranteed authenticity, especially since Webb avoided exceptional crimes for the most part and eschewed violent action. In the first episode, "The Human Bomb" (aired December 16, 1951), Friday and his partner prove able, in the nick of time, to prevent a bomber from destroying City Hall, but this episode was a teaser whose adrenaline-pumping plot was seldom to be repeated. Subsequent episodes, though they were all titled "The Big ——" (thus recalling notable films noirs such as *The Big Clock* [John Farrow, 1948]), seldom depended on either fast-paced action or a deadly threat of some kind to provide audience interest even when violent criminals were being sought. Instead, the subject matter is often quite mundane, even deliberately undramatic. "The Big Cast" (aired February 14, 1952) traces the hunt for a missing man who, once he turns up, reveals his fascination for pulp detective fiction. In "The Big Phone Call" (aired May 22, 1952), Friday and his partner quickly corral the criminal; the bulk of the episode details their explanation to him of the police methods that led to his capture. As in the neo-realist film, the emphasis is less on a compelling narrative (even though a conventional story provides the structure for each episode) and more on the representation of the rarely viewed world of criminal investigation. Webb had no interest in creating suspenseful action; those who tuned in could depend not only on Friday and his cohorts solving every case (and emerging unscathed) but also on the judicial system never failing to convict and sentence the felons appropriately. *Dragnet,* instead, engaged viewers with what seemed to be the accurate, objective depiction of the "truth" of police work through the reenactment of the investigation of what is ostensibly (and usually is truly) an actual case.

Thus the characteristic *Dragnet* scene is not physical action, such as a car chase, but conversation: sometimes the interrogation of either witnesses or suspects, sometimes a discussion among the policemen themselves about how to proceed. It is through such dialogues that the work of investigation, which is more mental than physical, can be best represented; these encounters are linked by stock footage of actual Los Angeles locations. If, as theorists of the medium have suggested, television drama, unlike the cinema, is characterized by the primacy of the sound track (to some degree a legacy of radio), then *Dragnet's* refusal to emphasize action over talk is typically televisual. This seems true enough, but we should add that Webb, who had a good visual sense, frequently animated these rather static scenes with extreme close-ups, filling the small screen with the single human face in a fashion that was quite innovative and often remarked on at the time. As he said, "The close-up is the thing that pays off on the small screen, . . . it has more impact."[13] In this way, the episode's conversational scenes were dramatized, an effect heightened by quick cross-cutting between or among speakers as well as by deftly positioned reaction shots. Dialogue scenes were, of course, also cheaper and quicker to produce than action scenes, especially since Webb, always pressed for time, eschewed complicated rehearsals. Economic considerations, given the very limited budget available, were therefore hardly negligible. But, once again, Webb was also concerned about authenticity. For the radio version of *Dragnet,* he had developed a style of delivery for his own character that he termed a "dramatic monotone." This might be most accurately described as a form of naturalist acting quite opposed to the Method style then in fashion for actors on the stage and silver screen. Relying on the then recently invented teleprompter to speed production, Webb instructed the actors to read their lines for the first time off the screen as the cameras rolled. Actors were not to "get into the part," which Webb claimed would produce a stagy rather than realistic effect. *Dragnet* became famous for its rapid, uninflected dialogue—no more realistic, of course, than the more obvious histrionics and mumblings of Method acting, but studiously undramatic and therefore understood by the show's audiences as more realistic.

From *He Walked by Night* and other noir semi-documentaries, Webb borrowed the device of the opening narration that attested to the show's authenticity. Every week viewers heard an authoritative voice intone: "The story you are about to see is true. Only the names have been changed to protect the innocent." In Werker's film, however, this narrator (who exists outside of and apart from the story world) then also narrates the opening montage of Los Angeles shots. Webb's innovation was to have Friday take over the narration at this point, with the lines "This is the city. Los Angeles, California." Friday thus dominates not only the world of the story, as the main character responsible for solving the case, but the manner of its telling, which is both confessional and commentative (Friday's opening remarks ironically address the anomaly of lawlessness in a city devoted to good citizenship and productive living) and officially reportorial. As narrator, Friday introduces each episode by stating the date and time, the section he is working with (burglary, traffic, et cetera), and the names of his partner and commanding officer, sometimes, more informally, remarking on the weather. As each episode of the story unfolds, Friday, once again in voice-over, details the date, time, and place. Such commentary personalizes the narrative, but, perhaps more important, it offers a continuing stream of marks of authenticity, "reality effects" that in their excessiveness (such indications of date, time, and so forth are not important to the narrative) mark it off as an ostensibly real record ("only the names have been changed . . . "). The concluding formula Webb devised had a similar effect. After the dramatic scenes of the investigation, the opening narrator makes a second appearance, which seems even more official since his comments, which never deviate from the formula, are also printed on an insert shot. Like a legal notice in the paper or a court record, these provide the date and location of the trial. Each episode then closes with something like a mug shot of the malefactors, now convicts, who stand uneasily against a white background as their prison sentences (they are always found guilty) are read aloud. Information about their incarceration then appears below their faces, testifying to the speed and inevitability of justice being done.

Webb, it should come as no surprise, originally hoped to film *Dragnet* in LAPD headquarters. Meeting with the inevitable refusal, he set about reconstructing the building in Disney's Burbank lot, using photographs of City Hall interiors. One story, perhaps apocryphal, is that the set designers found it impossible to buy the same kind of doorknobs as found on the police department office doors. Webb, however, would not be denied. He had plaster casts of the originals made so duplicates could be manufactured. Fearful that his scriptwriters might introduce inauthentic elements into the series, he hired police consultants to catch any errors. More than any police procedural series before or since, *Dragnet* was designed to incorporate those "things characteristic of real life," bringing to the small screen the kind of imitative realism that had hitherto been found only in the cinema, and even there only in the European realist art film and its few domestic remodelings.

But the show was not content merely to show life as it was. With its focus on the institutions of law enforcement rather than on individuals, *Dragnet* proffered a social realism to its viewers, much as Italian neo-realist films had done with their thematic interest in the political and social difficulties of the postwar era. Such texts, theorists Julia Hallam and Margaret Marshment explain, "encourage identification not merely with characters but with the situations and events they experience," and their narratives work toward "conventional patterns of resolution and a restoration of some kind of equilibrium."[14] Perhaps the secret of its incredible popularity was that *Dragnet* not only offered the pleasures of the tranche de vie with an illusionism carefully constructed by the obsessive Webb; it mustered considerable rhetorical force in its support of a just society, policed by dispassionate and dedicated public servants, and served by a judiciary that accorded suitable punishment to criminals, thus preserving the rights and property of the law-abiding. Never focusing on the criminal or dramatizing the crime, *Dragnet* avoided the failed romanticism of the film noir as well as that genre's fascination with the bizarre and perverse. Through its connection to postwar realism, it discovered entertainment value as much in a potent message as in a powerfully attractive sense of authenticity, demonstrating the capacity of the new medium to provide both pleasure and instruction.

Notes

1. Quoted in Michael J. Hayde, *My Name's Friday: The Unauthorized but True Story of* Dragnet *and the Films of Jack Webb* (Nashville, TN: Cumberland House, 2001), 245.

2. Quoted in Hayde, *My Name's Friday,* 46.

3. W. Gerhardie, as quoted in Julia Hallam, with Margaret Marshment, *Realism and the Popular Cinema: Inside Popular Film* (Manchester, England: Manchester University Press, 2000), 5.

4. *Fifties Television: The Industry and the Critics* (Chicago: University of Illinois Press, 199), 1–2. See also Christopher Anderson, *Hollywood TV: The Studio System in the Fifties* (Austin: University of Texas Press, 1994), 1–45.

5. The roman noir, or "black novel," encompasses not only what in the United States is usually referred to as "hard-boiled detective fiction" but also similar writing in related genres such as the thriller that emphasizes urban settings, criminality, and a general rejection of establishment values such as "the American dream." For further discussion see William Marling, *The American Roman Noir: Hammett, Cain, and Chandler* (Athens: University of Georgia Press, 1995), 11–72.

6. For further details see Daniel Moyer and Eugene Alvarez, *Just the Facts, Ma'am:*

The Authorized Biography of Jack Webb (Santa Ana, CA: Seven Locks Press, 2001), 45–53.

7. See Hayde, *My Name's Friday,* 18–21 and Moyer and Alvarez, *Just the Facts, Ma'am,* 56–62.

8. Quoted in Hayde, *My Name's Friday,* 20.

9. Leonard J. Leff and Jerold L. Simmons, *The Dame in the Kimono: Hollywood, Censorship, and the Production Code from the 1920s to the 1960s* (New York: Doubleday, 1990), 141

10. Bosley Crowther, review of *Open City, New York Times,* February 26, 1946.

11. Bosley Crowther, review of *The Bicycle Thief, New York Times,* December 3, 1949.

12. Bosley Crowther, review of *The Men, New York Times,* July 21, 1950.

13. Quoted in Hayde, *My Name's Friday,* 43.

14. Hallam and Marshment, *Realism and Popular Cinema,* 194.

NAKED CITY: THE RELATIVIST TURN IN TV NOIR

Robert E. Fitzgibbons

Film noir's evolution from the silver screen to the television screen was untidy at best; and this is nowhere more evident than in the transition from the feature-length movie *The Naked City* (Jules Dassin, 1948) to the TV show of the same title some ten years later. Although the movie was not the best of the noir genre, it was good and had many of the unmistakable classic noir markings: high-contrast black-and-white photography, stark images, severe camera angles, brutality, (a bit of) suggested sexual promiscuity, mystery, a major touch of evil, and moral absolutes. It was an exciting police story, even if somewhat stylized. But what made the movie especially intriguing for the time was that it was filmed in a semi-documentary style and shot almost entirely on location in New York City. Images of daily life in the city functioned as a backdrop for actors who intermingled with regular citizens, offering an attention-grabbing new milieu that helped *The Naked City* win two Academy Awards.[1] The Oscar night of March 24, 1949, might very well have been the high-water mark for *The Naked City*, had it not been for ABC Television and Stirling Silliphant.

In television's early days, ABC typically trailed far behind both NBC and CBS badly in the prime-time ratings. But by the 1958–1959 season, this had begun to change; and one of the major factors was the introduction of ABC's new series *The Naked City*. The thirty-nine half-hour shows contained many of the features of their noirish 1948 feature-length progenitor, including the semi-documentary style and filming on location in New York City. But there were some significant modifications. Although they were still police stories with an element of mystery, the episodes focused much more on the (presumably) real-life stories of different inhabitants of the city than on the police—conforming to the tagline repeated at the end of each show: "There are eight million stories in the naked city. . . . This has been one of them." Stirling Silliphant wrote most of the scripts of these early shows; they were exceptionally well-done and equally popular. Indeed, contributing significantly to ABC's move toward a position of prominence in prime-time viewing, *The Naked City* won the 1959 Emmy for the best dramatic series of less than one hour. Then the series abruptly ended, not to be seen in the 1959–1960 season.

The Relativist Turn

In 1960–1961, however, it returned with a new title—*Naked City,* having dropped the "The"—and a new hour long format with some *very different* kinds of storylines.[2] Not only had it shed all vestiges of a crime drama, it was no longer even a police story, except incidentally. To be sure, police remained continuing characters and always figured prominently in the script. Yet the dramas—and they were *dramas*—centered primarily on critical events in the lives of various inhabitants of the city. Each episode depicted another of the eight million stories in the naked city. Many of the core noir characteristics of the original feature film were softened, and some completely disappeared. Most notable among the missing was the stark distinction between absolute good and evil. Evil was replaced by psychological and/or sociological malfunction—neither of which was presented as necessarily bad. The central characters were mostly misfits who suffered from varying degrees of psychological and/or sociological deficiencies. They were, in short, abnormal. Yet usually they were sympathetically presented as not *really* abnormal, as not *really* immoral. This shift to the abnormal (that seemingly was not *really* abnormal) introduced a strain of relativism into the previously almost completely absolutist world of prime-time television in general and of noir television in particular.

In "Ooftus Goofus," a strange little supermarket worker, who has been sending bizarre letters to the police, first lowers prices in the store to almost nothing and then threatens to explode a bomb in a fight arena as a way of gaining notoriety.[3] Arnold Platt, in "To Walk Like a Lion," embezzles from his company to pay his mother's medical bills and finally her funeral and grave-site expenses.[4] Since he has spent none of the money on himself, the woman who loves him convinces him to take what he has left and splurge for just one day. After that, she allows, he could surrender to the police. Arnold proceeds to spend the money while leading the police on a merry chase, and, true to his agreement, he turns himself in the next day. In "Take and Put," a formerly well-to-do odd couple throws parties at which their equally odd maid steals jewelry from some of the wealthy guests.[5] Together with the maid, a whiz at the stock market, they pawn the jewelry, invest the money in stocks, after a very short time sell the stocks for a significant profit, reclaim the jewelry from the pawn shop, return each piece to its owner, and retain the remainder of the profit for themselves. In each of these episodes, the main characters consider their own behaviors quite normal. The normal and the abnormal get mixed up with right and wrong, and one is left to question whether any behavior is *really* normal and whether any behavior is *really* moral; perhaps morality and normality are only relative.

In many episodes of *Naked City*, this relativistic message was covert rather than overt, implicit rather than explicit. Presumably normal people caught up in some critically trying circumstances, most of the characters were actually quite abnormal to the typical viewer of the early 1960s. And most of their choices were wrong by conventional moral standards. Yet one was left—indeed almost forced—by the end of many episodes to wonder whether perhaps those choices might not have been right in some way. "Sanity," says Dr. Wirtz in "Which Is Joseph Creeley?" "is a relative term."[6] This conflation of the normal with the abnormal, of the moral with the immoral, and the promotion of relativism permeated *Naked City*.

Relativism of Morality and Normality

It also permeated the relativism of the anthropologist Ruth Benedict, among the first to argue explicitly for the relativism of both normality and morality. In a classic statement of the relativistic position, Benedict maintained:

> No one civilization can possibly utilize in its mores the whole potential range of human behavior. . . . The possibility of organized behavior of every sort, from the fashions of local dress and houses to the dicta of a people's ethics and religion, depends upon a similar selection among the possible behavior traits. In the field of recognized economic obligations or sex tabus this selection is as non-rational and subconscious a process as it is in the field of phonetics. It is a process which goes on in the group for long periods of time and is historically conditioned by innumerable accidents of isolation or of contact of peoples. . . .

> Every society . . . carries its preference farther and farther, integrating itself more and more completely upon its chosen basis, and discarding those types of behavior that are uncongenial. Most of those organizations of personality that seem to us most uncontrovertibly abnormal have been used by different civilizations in the very foundations of their institutional life. Conversely the most valued traits of normal individuals have been looked on in differently organized cultures as aberrant. Normality, in short, within a very wide range, is culturally defined. It is primarily a term for the socially elaborated segment of human behavior in any culture; and abnormality, a term for the segment that that particular civilization does not use. . . .
>
> It is a point that has been made more often in relation to ethics than in relation to psychiatry. We do not any longer make the mistake of deriving the morality of our locality and decade directly from the inevitable constitution of human nature. We do not elevate it to the dignity of a first principle. We recognize that morality differs in every society, and is a convenient term for socially approved habits.[7]

Moral relativism was nothing new when Benedict presented this argument in 1934. As an ethical theory, it has been around at least since the time of the Greek sophist, Protagoras (circa 481–411 B.C.), who "was the first to maintain that there are two sides to every question, opposed to each other, and he even argued in this fashion, being the first to do so. Furthermore he began a work thus: 'Man is the measure of all things, of things that are that they are, and of things that are not that they are not.'"[8]

In 1960—the first year of the third incarnation of *Naked City*—even though most Americans had not heard of Ruth Benedict, moral relativism was gaining a following. World War II was a dimming fifteen-year-old memory, Korea was a fading blip on the radar screen, Vietnam was barely visible, and times were good. By 1962—when Marilyn Monroe sang "Happy Birthday" to President John F. Kennedy—the popularity of moral relativism had grown right along with the popularity of *Naked City*.

The fundamental claim of moral relativism is that all of morality is relative, that is, there is no real right or wrong, no real good or bad, no real ought or ought not to be done or occur. Morality is simply relative to some set of standards, and no one set is superior to, or more true than, another. In the final analysis, according to moral relativism, there are no absolutes when it comes to morality: anything can be moral, and anything can be immoral—it is all relative. Whether an action is moral or immoral depends simply on the standards to which the action or type of action is relative.

In claiming that the truth of a moral proposition, say "m," is relative to a certain set of standards, the relativist means that given a particular set of moral standards (plus possibly some empirical propositions, plus possibly some definitions), one can validly deduce "m." And at the same time, given a different set of moral standards (plus possibly some empirical propositions, plus possibly some definitions), one can validly deduce "not-m."

From a purely logical point of view, this is certainly true. But, at the same time, it would be logically inconsistent to claim that all of the premises in these two arguments are, or could be, true while the arguments are both valid. The relativist solves what would be an insurmountable logical problem by simply stating that when it comes to the standards themselves (which function as premises), they are neither true nor false, that no one set of standards is superior to, or more true than, another—they are just different.

Although it is possible to solve the purely logical problem in this way, there remains a serious ambiguity with regard to what standards the relativist considers relevant for justifying moral propositions. Depending on how the ambiguity is removed, we typically get one or another of the two most popular forms of moral relativism—cultural relativism or individual relativism. As a moral theory, cultural relativism holds that the rightness or wrongness of a person's action depends exclusively on the standards of the actor's culture, while the individual relativist maintains that the rightness or wrongness of a person's action depends exclusively on the standards of the individual actor himself or herself. By far the most popular of these theories has always been cultural relativism.

Cultural Relativism

Today, the primary advocates of cultural relativism are (many but certainly not all) anthropologists, sociologists, social-work theorists, educators, and various government officials. Often under the heading of multiculturalism or cultural pluralism, we are told (or at least led to believe) that no one culture is better or worse than another, that they are just different, and that we have to be accepting of *all* cultural differences. Most important, it is emphasized, we cannot use the moral standards of our culture to judge the behavior of a member of another culture—we must avoid being ethnocentric. Indeed, in some cases, the mere articulation of a moral judgment using one set of cultural standards to judge a member of another cultural group—let alone acting on that articulated judgment—is considered a hate crime and may be criminally prosecutable. According to cultural relativism, if you are going to make moral judgments about a member of a different culture, you must use the moral standards of that person's culture and not those of your own, because morality is relative to the standards of a particular actor's culture.

THE DIFFERENCE ARGUMENT

The two most common arguments in support of cultural relativism are the difference argument and the conceptual argument. The essence of the difference argument is straightforward. People are different. Cultures are different. The moral standards of any one culture are different from those of any other culture. Therefore, no one set of cultural moral standards is superior to, or more true than, another. And because this is true, cultural relativism is true. This is the essential form, or the minimal version, of the difference argument. In this stripped-down version it is not especially convincing; yet dressed up, as it most always is, it can be very persuasive.

Ruth Benedict offers a prototypical example of a dressed-up version of the difference argument. In her essay, she provides fascinating insights into some very different cultures with their differing moral standards and differing judgments of normality and abnormality and of morality and immorality.[9] These include some of the Indian tribes of California and other American Indian tribes, a Siberian culture, the Zulu of South Africa, the ancient Greeks, the inhabitants of an island of northwest Melanesia, and the civilization of the Kwakiutl—one of the Native American tribes of the North Pacific coast of North America. She tells exceptionally engaging stories of these different cultures. One cannot help but to be fascinated by them. And through these stories (which are, in a way, not unlike many of the stories of *Naked City*), she hopes to establish the empirical point that, just as there are eight million stories in the naked city, there are a great number of possible sets of moral standards, that is, rules to govern human behavior, and that "no one civilization can possibly utilize in its mores [moral standards] the whole potential range of human behaviors."[10] The selection of a particular set of moral standards from among all possible sets is a "non-rational and subconscious a process," she claims, "which goes on in the group for long periods of time and is historically conditioned by innumerable accidents."[11] Consequently, just as with the selection of a set of phonetic articulations from among all possible sets, no one set of moral standards is any better than another—they are just different. And because they are different, no one set is superior to, or more true than, another. "Morality differs in every society."[12] Hence, the argument concludes, cultural relativism is true.

As in Benedict's version, *Naked City* often dresses up the difference argument by telling interesting stories of people with different cultural backgrounds and standards. In "The Contract," a young Chinese man is in love with a young Chinese woman. However, the woman's much older Chinese stepfather also loves her. In accordance with their cultural tradition, to resolve the conflict of who may marry the woman, the two men submit the case to a Chinese arbitration committee.[13] "And If Any Are Frozen, Warm Them" follows three elderly Romanians, who in accordance with their traditions seek revenge on an old adversary.[14] In such episodes, the viewer is presented with very different cultural ways of resolving personal disputes, and the message is that the standards of any other culture, although different from the American culture, are certainly as good.

All of the various versions of the difference argument derive their persuasiveness from the anthropological stories they tell; the stories are engaging. To learn about many different cultures is captivating, and it sets the reader up for the (now tired but still nevertheless often compelling) rhetorical question, "Who is to say that my cultural standards are truer than those of the ——?" Fill in the blank with the name of any of the different cultures—Native Americans, Siberians, Zulu, ancient Greeks, Melanesians, Kwakiutl, Chinese, Romanians or whatever. If the psychological setup has worked, the answer will be "no one." This is the essence of the difference argument.

Even though many find this argument (psychologically) compelling, it is nevertheless a very bad argument. Its essence is that because different cultures have differing (indeed, inconsistent) beliefs, those beliefs are equally true. This is quite simply invalid. Different groups of peoples do have and have had different scientific beliefs, but that clearly does not *imply* that they are equally true or that they are in fact true. For instance, some cultures have believed that the sun orbits the earth, while others have believed that it does not. It does not follow from this fact of differing beliefs, however, that they are equally true or that one is as true as another.

To escape this destructive counterargument, one would have to establish that moral beliefs are significantly unlike scientific or mathematical beliefs, which are either absolutely true or false. But it could not employ the difference argument to do this, because for that argument to be successful it would have to presuppose precisely what it attempted to establish. That is, using the difference argument to show that moral beliefs, unlike scientific or mathematical beliefs, are not absolutely true or absolutely false would simply beg the question against those who deny what the moral relativist is affirming.

THE CONCEPTUAL ARGUMENT

This brings us to the second of the common arguments offered in support of cultural relativism, the conceptual argument. Unfortunately for the relativist, this argument too fails, but for a very different reason.

The essence of the conceptual argument is the following. The concept of morality is "X" (or alternatively, the meaning of the word "morality" is "X"). Therefore, cultural relativism is true. Interestingly, in the same essay noted above, Ruth Benedict offers an instance of the conceptual argument for cultural relativism alongside her difference argument.

Benedict ties her conceptual argument for cultural relativism to her argument concerning the meaning of "normality." "Normality," she claims, "is culturally defined."[15]

> [It] is primarily a term for the socially elaborated segment of human behavior in any culture; and abnormality, a term for the segment that that particular civilization does not use. . . .
> The concept of the normal is properly a variant of the concept of the good. It is that which society has approved. A normal action is one which falls well within the limits of expected behavior for a particular society. Its variability among different peoples is essentially a function of the variability of the behavior patterns that different societies have created for themselves, and can never be wholly divorced from a consideration of culturally institutionalized types of behavior.[16]

Now to be precise, Benedict is not correct in her claim that "normality" is culturally *defined*. It is clear from her discussion that she thinks that different cultures all *define* "normal" in exactly the *same* way. Given that common meaning, they *judge* different actions or types of actions to be normal. For instance, she points out how homosexuality was judged normal within many Native American tribes but abnormal in other cultures.

Nevertheless, for Benedict, there is a direct connection between the concept (i.e., the meaning) of the normal and the concept of the good. One is a variant of the other: "We recognize that morality differs in every society, and is a convenient term for socially approved habits. Mankind has always preferred to say, 'It is morally good,' rather than 'It is habitual.' . . . But historically the two phrases are synonymous."[17] That which is normal is good, that which is good is normal, because they are synonymous—both mean socially approved habits. So, if "morality" means socially approved habits, and if socially approved habits vary from culture to culture, then it (presumably) follows that morality varies from culture to culture, that is, cultural relativism is true.

If possible, this argument is even worse than her version of the difference argument.[18] Benedict gives us no *empirical evidence* to justify her claim that "morally good" historically meant habitual; she merely makes a false claim: "Mankind has always preferred to say, 'It is morally good,' rather that 'It is habitual.'" This is not just false; it is outrageously false because it logically presupposes that mankind has always spoken English.

Perhaps she meant that people have always preferred to say, "It is morally good," in their own language rather than "it is habitual" in their own language. But this is not empirically verifiable. Leaving this problem aside, her claim that "mankind has always preferred to say . . ." involves another serious problem. This claim about "mankind" includes prehistoric peoples and ex hypothesi there is no way of scientifically verifying that this is true. Benedict makes a claim that either is obviously false or that is empirically unverifiable. In either case, it is just bad science. Yet these are not the worst errors with the conceptual argument.

The argument's major problem is that it presupposes that a word (or concept) has one and only one true or real meaning, and this presupposition is false. The conceptual argument fails to recognize that in fact most words have several different meanings, that is, most have several true definitions. Moreover, any word may be given any number of true stipulative definitions. Hence, there is no one and only true or real definition or meaning of a word. The *Oxford English Dictionary* lists sixteen different definitions for the noun "morality" and not one of them is "habitual." More important, anyone who has any sort of background in ethics knows that very many more different definitions of "morality" can be found in the scholarly literature. So, to claim, as the conceptual argument must, that there is just one "real" definition or concept of "morality" is simply mistaken.

Problems with Cultural Relativism

I will discuss only three problems with cultural relativism even though there are many that could be specified.

THE FIRST PROBLEM

The first major issue is that the word "culture" is so unclear that for the most part the very statement of the putative position is neither true nor false but simply gibberish.[19] That the ordinary meaning of "culture" is unclear is not surprising; most ordinary meanings are. Consider, for instance, the ordinary meaning of "old man." There are some things (108-year-old men, 97-year-old men) that certainly are old men and there are some other things (10-year-old boys, 23-year-old men) that just as certainly are not old men. Yet there is a range of cases (which includes 57-year-old men and 62-year-old men) wherein it is theoretically impossible to determine whether those things are or are not old men. This is because the ordinary meaning of "old man" contains no definitive criteria that mark off where old men begin and not old men end. Insofar as it is theoretically impossible to determine whether a 57-year-old man is (or is not) an old man, a sentence such as "Henry, who is fifty-seven years old, is an old man" does not express a proposition that is either true or false. Indeed, in the final analysis, it makes no sense. In such a case, it is not possible to engage in serious rational thinking about whether he is an old man and rational argumentation is impossible.

Nevertheless, the fact that "old man" is unclear is not particularly bothersome to us, for generally we do not attempt any serious thinking with the concept. It would be a problem, however, if we did. For instance, if we were to draft a law granting all old men a yearly governmental bonus of ten thousand dollars, then in some cases we would not be able to operate successfully with the ordinary meaning. Should 57-year-old Henry get the bonus, because he is an old man? The problem is obvious. It is theoretically impossible to prove that Henry is (or that he is not) an old man, because we do not even know what the sentence "Henry is an old man" asserts in this case. And we do not know what it asserts because it asserts nothing. When a word with an unclear meaning is used in a sentence to apply to a thing with regard to which it is unclear, the sentence does not express a proposition that is either true or false or that can be argued either for or against. Serious rational thinking requires clear concepts, and the ordinary meaning of "old man" is quite simply not up to the task.

The major problem, then, with the ordinary meaning of "culture" is that it is much too unclear—exponentially more unclear than that of "old man"—to be theoretically useful. For example, the *Merriam-Webster Online Dictionary* (www.m-w.com) identifies the ordinary meaning of "culture" in which we are interested as

> a: the integrated pattern of human knowledge, belief, and behavior that depends upon the capacity for learning and transmitting knowledge to succeeding generations b: the customary beliefs, social forms, and material traits of a racial, religious, or social group; *also*: the characteristic features of everyday existence (as diversions or a way of life) shared by people in a place or time <popular *culture*> <southern *culture*> c: the set of shared attitudes, values, goals, and practices that characterizes an institution or organization <a corporate *culture* focused on the bottom line> d: the set of values, conventions, or social practices associated with a particular field, activity, or societal characteristic <studying the effect of computers on print *culture*> <changing the *culture* of materialism will take time—Peggy O'Mara>

That this meaning is very unclear is obvious. What exactly is a culture? Where does one culture begin and another end? Is there such a thing as the American culture? What about the African American culture? There are no rationally defensible answers to these questions, because the ordinary meaning of "culture" is so extraordinarily unclear. Except for the few instances where the word clearly does apply—as was the case with "old man"—sentences formulated using it do not express propositions that are either true or false and that can be argued either for or against. Consequently, no sound ethical theory can be stated using it. Or, to put it another way, a large part of the very *statement* of cultural relativism is simply gibberish, even though at first glance it may not seem to be.

Theoretically, of course, this problem may be solved by identifying a clear stipulative definition of "culture." But in practice this is not as easy as it may sound.[20] So, until the cultural relativist provides a reasonably clear definition of "culture," the conclusion must be that the very statement of the position is unworkably vague such that we cannot determine just what the position is or even that there is a position.

THE SECOND PROBLEM

The second major problem with cultural relativism is that as ordinarily stated (assuming some reasonably clear meaning of "culture") it is logically inconsistent. According to the most popular versions of the theory, there are no absolutely true, universally applicable moral propositions. Moral truth is relative to culture, and what is moral for a member of one culture is not necessarily moral for a member of another. At the same time, the position maintains that one cannot make cross-cultural moral judgments, to do so would be ethnocentric. To judge the behavior of a member of another culture, you have to use the standards of his or her culture: one cannot use the moral standards of one culture to judge the behavior of a member of another.

At first glance, this latter claim appears to be an empirical one similar to "You cannot run a mile in under eight minutes." However, as an empirical claim the latter is obviously false. "You cannot run a mile in under eight minutes" can be proven false by getting out on the track and actually running a mile in under eight minutes. In general, if someone claims that you cannot do A, you can prove the claim false by simply doing A. Now, "One cannot use the moral standards of one culture to judge the behavior of a member of another culture" as an empirical claim is just as easily proven false by actually doing it. And in fact people do this all the time. Indeed, it is often in response to someone's using his or her culture's moral standards to judge the behavior of a member of a different culture that the relativist says, "You can't do that!" If this were an empirical claim, the appropriate response would be, "Oh yeah, just watch me!" So, if "One cannot use the moral standards of one culture to judge the behavior of a member of another culture" were an empirical claim, the cultural relativist would be saying something factually false because people in fact make such cross-cultural moral judgments all the time. So, either the relativist is ignorant of this fact or the claim is not an empirical one. And surely Ruth Benedict and many other relativists are not ignorant of this fact.

Analysis shows that "One cannot use the moral standards of one culture to judge the behavior of a member of another culture" is actually a disguised *moral* claim, namely, "One *ought not* use the moral standards of one culture to judge the behavior of a member of another culture." This moral proposition is put forward as being both absolutely true and universally applicable, and consequently it is logically inconsistent with the other part of the theory, which states that there are no absolutely true, universally applicable moral propositions. The cultural relativist cannot have it both ways. To save the position, one or another of these claims must go. However, if one is given up, the position that remains is no longer cultural relativism as ordinarily stated.

THE THIRD PROBLEM

The third major trouble with cultural relativism is that, given any meaning of "culture" that even slightly resembles the ordinary meaning, cultural relativism devolves into individual relativism.

To apply cultural relativism in making moral judgments, there is an invariant three-step process.

1. Identify the culture of which the actor is a member.
2. Identify the moral standards of that culture.
3. Use those standards to judge the actor's behavior.

The problem centers on how to establish (1), that is, how to determine cultural membership.

Taking the *Merriam-Webster* definition cited above as the ordinary meaning of "culture," it is clear that sharing certain moral standards is one of the defining characteristics of cultural membership. In a recent review of different studies that themselves had identified many of the diverse definitions of "culture," the authors state that "the review reveals that most authors agree that culture is a very complex term and difficult to define in words. Culture consists of several elements of which some are implicit and others are explicit. Most often these elements are explained by terms such as behaviour, values, norms, and basic assumptions."[21]

Since most (and maybe all) of the various meanings of "culture" that are anything like the ordinary meaning take sharing certain moral standards to be one of the defining characteristics of cultural membership, then to establish (1) above one must first identify the moral standards of the individual. Therefore, the sequence identified above must be modified as follows.

1. Identify the moral standards of the individual.
2. Identify the moral standards of many (possibly all) different cultures.

3. Find (among other things) a match between the standards of the individual and the standards of a culture.
4. Identify the culture of which the actor is a member.
5. Identify the moral standards of that culture.
6. Use those standards to judge the actor's behavior.

Since (1) and (5) will always be the same, there is no point in going through the steps (2) through (5). In other words, steps (2) through (5) are irrelevant in determining the morality of an actor's behavior. In the final analysis, all that is actually relevant are that individual's own moral standards. And this is individual relativism!

Individual Relativism

Individual relativism maintains that the rightness or wrongness of an action depends exclusively on the standards of the actor. The major difference, then, between individual and cultural relativism is that cultural relativism takes the standards of the culture as the only foundation of morality, whereas individual relativism considers cultural standards per se to be irrelevant: only the standards of the individual actor determine the morality of his or her behavior. Each individual has his or her own moral standards, and they are all equally true and appropriate. You cannot judge another person using your own personal standards; you must use that person's standards. Insofar as this is so, the position maintains, there is no "real" right or wrong. Any behavior can be right, and any behavior can be wrong; it is all relative to the individual's standards. We need to respect each person as an individual and recognize that no one set of moral standards is superior to, or more true than, another. Just as any behavior can be moral or immoral, so any behavior can be normal or abnormal. The individual's moral standards define not only what moral behavior is but also what normal behavior is for that person.

As some episodes of *Naked City* promoted cultural relativism, others promoted individual relativism. For instance, in "Memory of a Red Trolley Car" a chemist, Professor Johns, has lived his whole life on the brink, challenging death.[22] Depicted as a person who "feels most alive on the verge of disaster," he accidentally inhales slow-acting toxic fumes but knowingly refuses to seek help. In the episode, Dr. Branson, a psychiatrist, indicates that such behavior is not abnormal nor is it immoral—it is just *that* person's way. Some people are like that; it just depends on the standards (in his terminology "the Gods") one has. According to Dr. Branson,

> We're all primitive in many ways. . . . Imagine a native who makes a pact with the Gods in his life. "You want me to be unhappy and miserable," he says to his Gods. "O.K. I'll be happy to please you. Being miserable will make me happy," he says to his Gods. Now, what if that primitive man suddenly finds all sorts of joy and success coming his way, it would scare the living daylights out of him, wouldn't it? Terrified of defying his Gods, so what does he do? Drives all of the joy and success out of his life. And then—and only then—does he feel happy. Now, if the joy won't go away . . . , well he . . . he . . . might just die of fright. . . . We all have our personal Gods, to whom we pledged ourselves, starting way, way back with the parents we wanted to please. . . . Joy is sinful.

Joy is sinful—immoral—for *that* person but not necessarily for others. It all depends on what Gods—moral standards—one has. Reminiscent of Ruth Benedict's cultural relativism, individual relativism conflates morality and normality in a similar manner.

Individual relativism is a very strange moral theory indeed. Yet it has had its defenders. Consider John Hartland-Swann's argument which begins as if he were advocating cultural relativism but quickly slides into a defense of individual relativism.[23]

> Morality then—despite the sophistications often favoured by moral philosophers . . . —is, I suggest, the term or concept which refers to the keeping or violating of customs considered socially important—important in the mutual relations between man and man and between a man and his community. . . . The moral [is] what is regarded freely or by conditioning, as the socially important as regards conduct and dispositions. . . . At the same time—as earlier arguments have been designed to show—there is nothing which is "intrinsically" or "unconditionally" or "absolutely" moral—or immoral; what is moral, or immoral, depends on the degree of social importance attached to its performance, or avoidance, by some particular community at some particular time and in some particular place. Or, where there is a divergence between individual

and community moral appraisals, what is moral or immoral depends, so far as the individual is concerned, on what *he* regards
as socially important and thus considers ought to be regarded as
socially important by the community, or perhaps by humanity as
a whole. . . . This same thesis explains . . . how it comes about that
both communities and individuals differ, not only about what is
morally justifiable or nonjustifiable, but about what is to be regarded
as a moral issue at all.[24]

It is important to recognize that according to Hartland-Swann, in the final
analysis the morality of an action depends not at all on what the community (culture) regards as socially important but only on what the individual
does. What the individual regards as moral as far as his or her behavior is
concerned *always* trumps anything that other—even all other—members
of "the community" regard as moral.

A key word in Hartland-Swann's account of individual relativism is "regards." For Hartland-Swann what is *in fact* socially important is completely
irrelevant to the morality of an action. All that is relevant is what the actor
regards as socially important. Indeed, not only is it relevant, but it is also
completely determinative. "The moral," as he says above, is "what is regarded
freely or by conditioning, as the socially important as regards conduct and
dispositions." As a relativist in good standing, Hartland-Swann places no
restriction upon what an individual might regard as socially important.
Indeed, to restrict what may be regarded as moral would be inconsistent
with relativism. So, an individual may regard any form of behavior as socially important and in such a case it is moral for him. So, since any form of
behavior may be regarded as socially important by an individual, any form
of behavior may be moral for that individual.

Consider, for example, the case of Professor Johns, who held as one of
his moral standards that he should not act in any way that will bring him joy
or success. According to individual relativism in general, as long as this was
his standard, it was a perfectly legitimate standard for him; and according to
Hartland-Swann's particular version, as long as Professor Johns *regarded* this
form of behavior as being socially important, it was a perfectly legitimate
standard for him. Moreover, this standard, along with any other standards
that he held, determined in part what was actually moral for him—at least
as long as he held it.

Given this position, the relativity of morality may be taken to any extreme. There are no limits on what one may legitimately hold as a moral standard. Hence, there are no limits on what may actually be moral behavior for an individual. This, of course, also holds pari passu for cultural relativism. And this implies some generally unacceptable conclusions. Consider, for instance, what many would think a rather silly moral standard—but a moral standard nevertheless—that someone might hold, for example, that on Tuesdays he should rob and kill anyone he meets. Suppose further that he meets you on a Tuesday and attempts to rob and kill you. Now, if you were a typical person—and trying to be polite—you might say something like, "Hey, this is wrong. You shouldn't do this. Leave me alone." As an individual relativist, he would respond, "You don't understand. I have a deeply held moral conviction that on Tuesdays I should rob and kill anyone I meet; today is Tuesday; and I have just met you." If you too were an individual relativist, logical consistency would demand that you say something like, "Oh, I'm sorry. Who am I to impose my moral standards on you? Here, please go ahead and rob and kill me, you fine upstanding fellow." Now consider the not-so-silly case where an individual has a deeply held moral conviction that he or she should kill all babies who are mentally retarded. Insofar as most of us would find such a standard abhorrent, we would find individual relativism repulsive. Nevertheless, that we are repulsed by the position is not a good reason for thinking that individual relativism is false.

This suggests a common argument type that should be mentioned here. Such an argument is often offered in arguing against not only both forms of relativism but also other ethical theories. The essence of the argument is this.

1. If individual relativism is true, then under certain circumstances it would be moral to ——. (Fill in any horrible action you would like here: rape little children, cut the eyes out of dogs, kill Jews, et cetera.)
2. But surely it is not moral to —— (Fill in the same action as above.)
3. Therefore, individual relativism is false.

Although a common type of counterargument, this is a very bad argument because it commits the fallacy of begging the question. This fallacy occurs if one of the premises in an argument logically presupposes the conclusion. In this argument, (2) logically presupposes (3), because (2) is a moral proposition that is put forward as being absolutely true and (2) can be absolutely true *only if* the conclusion (3) is true, that is, only if individual relativism is false. When arguing against an ethical theory, this fallacy should be avoided.

So then, are there any serious problems with individual relativism or any reasons for thinking that it is false? Well, surely it suffers from essentially the same problem as the second one adduced above against cultural relativism, that is, that it is false because it is logically inconsistent. And the argument here is essentially the same as that offered above. Yet although by itself this is a devastating counterargument against the position as defined, establishing inconsistencies in this way can be a very frustrating way of arguing.

Ordinarily, when such a counterargument is presented against an ethical theory, the theorist simply modifies the position to avoid the particular inconsistency identified. Clearly, this problem is solved and that charge of inconsistency falls by the wayside if a position is inconsistent and one drops one or another of the conflicting claims. However, if such a move is made, to be precise, what remains no longer is the original position, even though the proponent may think that it is. It is in fact a *new* theory with the old name. The history of ethics (not just the history of relativism) is replete with such modifications in the face of identified inconsistencies.

The best way to prove once and for all that any form of moral relativism is false is by showing that any proposition, including any moral proposition, is either absolutely true or absolutely false and not just relatively true or relatively false. To do so would strike at the heart of relativism, for it would show that its essential claim, for example, Hartland-Swann's statement that "there is nothing which is 'intrinsically' or 'unconditionally' or 'absolutely' moral—or immoral," is absolutely false. Such an argument needs to be carefully developed, however, and consequently lies well beyond the scope of this essay.

Notes

1. It won Academy Awards for cinematography (black and white) and film editing, and it was nominated for writing.

2. The series concluded with the 1962–1963 season.

3. Televised December 13, 1961.

4. Televised February 28, 1962.

5. Televised June 21, 1961.

6. Televised November 15, 1961.

7. Ruth Benedict, "Anthropology and the Abnormal," *Journal of General Psychology* 10 (1934): 72–73.

8. In Thomas V. Smith, ed., *Philosophers Speak for Themselves: From Thales to Plato* (Chicago: University of Chicago Press, 1968), 60.

9. For the moment, I will assume some reasonably clear meaning of "culture" and its cognate forms. Later we shall see that this assumption is not all together warranted.

10. Benedict, "Anthropology and the Abnormal," 72.

11. Ibid.

12. Ibid., 73.

13. Televised January 24, 1962.

14. Televised May 9, 1962.

15. Benedict, "Anthropology and the Abnormal," 72.

16. Ibid., 73.

17. Ibid.

18. What this shows, if anything, is that one should not stray too far from one's area of expertise. If you do, you run the great risk of making egregious errors and embarrassing yourself. Benedict was a very good anthropologist but a very bad philosopher.

19. This issue also holds for other words often substituted for "culture," such as "civilization," "a people," "a way of life," et cetera. What I have to say here about "culture" applies pari passu to these.

20. Alfred L. Kroeber and Clyde Kluckhohn, *Culture: A Critical Review of Concepts and Definitions,* Papers of the Peabody Museum of American Archaeology and Ethnology 157, no. 1 (Cambridge: Harvard University Press, 1952), 223. Kroeber and Kluckhohn identified 164 different definitions of "culture," and no one of them is any clearer that the ordinary meaning of "culture." Even if they were all clear, this would still create a major problem for any theorist who wants to do serious intellectual work in the area. Imagine trying to do geometry with over 164 different definitions of "triangle"—not impossible but very confusing.

21. Stefan Groeschl and Liz Doherty, "Conceptualising Culture," *Cross Cultural Management: An International Journal* 7, no. 4 (2000): 14.

22. Televised June 13, 1962.

23. It should be noted that this is a version of the conceptual argument discussed above, although here it is offered in an attempt to justify individual relativism.

24. John Hartland-Swann, *An Analysis of Morals* (1960), reprinted in *Philosophical Ethics: An Introduction to Moral Philosophy,* ed. Tom L. Beauchamp (New York: McGraw-Hill, 1982), 8–10.

JOHN DRAKE IN GREENELAND: NOIR THEMES IN *SECRET AGENT*

Sander Lee

The television series *Secret Agent,* though regarded as mere entertainment by most viewers, contains philosophical themes that raise it above most television shows of its time and connect it with themes found in such noir espionage films as *The Third Man* (Carol Reed, 1949) and *Ministry of Fear* (Fritz Lang, 1944), both of which were based on the work of the British writer Graham Greene.[1]

Known in Britain as *Danger Man, Secret Agent* debuted in September 1960 as a half-hour espionage thriller starring Patrick McGoohan in the role of John Drake, an American agent for NATO who traveled the globe. Each episode began with Drake leaving an unidentified federal building in Washington, lighting a cigarette, and heading toward his car, as the voice-over said:

> Every government has its secret service branch. America its CIA, France Deuxieme Bureau, England MI5. A messy job? Well, that's when they usually call on me. Or someone like me. Oh yes, my name is Drake, John Drake.[2]

The success of this initial series led to a second, hour-long one that ran in the United Kingdom from October 1964 through November 1965. This second series was shown on CBS in the United States under the name *Secret Agent* in 1965 and 1966, attracting a popular following. In the second series, not only was the show lengthened from a half hour to an hour, but Drake was transformed into an Englishman working for a mythical British intelligence service called M9.

Perhaps as a result of their common Catholic backgrounds, Graham Greene and Patrick McGoohan share an interest in exploring the moral dimensions of situations in which good men are confronted with the realization that the world has become a place void of meaning, haphazard, and morally indifferent. In discussing this negative view of the world, Greene says the following in the second volume of his autobiography *Ways of Escape:*

> Some critics have referred to a strange violent "seedy" region of the mind . . . which they call Greeneland, and I have sometimes wondered whether they go round the world blinkered. "This is Indochina," I want to exclaim, "this is Mexico, this is Sierra Leone carefully and accurately described. I have been a newspaper correspondent as well as a novelist. I assure you that the dead child lay in the ditch in just that attitude. In the canal of Phat Diem the bodies stuck out of the water . . ." But I know that argument is useless. They won't believe the world they haven't noticed is like that.[3]

Like Greene's protagonists, John Drake travels the world only to find that he is continually confronted with moral depravity, not only on the part of Britain's enemies (e.g., the Soviets, corrupt foreign governments, international criminals, etcetera.) but also in the actions of his supposedly more virtuous employer, the British government. Repeatedly Drake must confront his own role in perpetuating moral injustice. In some cases he reluctantly goes along with his employer's morally ambiguous dictates (e.g., at the end of the episode "Colony Three"), while on other occasions he directly disobeys the orders of his superiors in order to place the dictates of his own conscience above the demands of professional obedience and patriotism (e.g., in the episode "Whatever Happened to George Foster?").

Why Drake Is Not Bond

Although the literary James Bond appeared in 1953, *Secret Agent* predated the first James Bond film, *Dr. No* (Terence Young, 1962) by two years, and because of his popularity in *Secret Agent,* Patrick McGoohan was originally offered the role. McGoohan's decision to reject the film initially seems puzzling: while of course he had no way of knowing how successful the Bond franchise would become, it is hard to see why a television actor would refuse the chance to star in a major motion picture, especially given that the part appears to be so similar to his TV series role. Playing James Bond in the film might well have brought McGoohan considerably more money and fame for considerably less work.

To understand his decision it is helpful to compare the roles of Bond and Drake to see why McGoohan rejected the former while accepting the latter. James Bond has become an icon, a character whose qualities are emblematic of the societal changes taking place in the 1960s. This was a time when Western culture was becoming much more open about sexuality, when such magazines as *Playboy* became popular with their celebration of male sexual fantasy. Traditional mores were challenged by the so-called sexual revolution and the emergence of the youth counterculture with its acceptance of hedonism as a way of life

Despite their apparent similarities, McGoohan's John Drake has little in common with Bond. Whereas Bond is depicted as a womanizing playboy type who nevertheless courts danger and is willing to kill on command, Drake is presented as a deeply moral character. Apparently at McGoohan's insistence, Drake never kills and does not even carry a gun. When attacked, he fights back but uses only the minimum amount of violence necessary to subdue or escape his enemies. Bond, on the other hand, routinely kills enemy agents in a variety of unusual ways and often with a flip remark.[4] Furthermore, Drake never becomes romantically involved with the women he meets, even when his mission may seem to require it. In "The Colonel's Daughter," Drake uses his supposedly romantic interest in his target's daughter as his cover, yet we never see him do anything that might be interpreted as a romantic advance, so, in the end, Drake can turn her over to the police without having had to exploit her emotional vulnerability.

In some episodes Drake clearly cares for women (e.g., Lisa in "Fair Exchange," Pauline in "Whatever Happened to George Foster"), yet we are given only hints of his feelings for them—he displays no romantic sentiment. In both of these cases, we surmise that Drake has known these women for a long time, yet the true nature of these relationships is kept hidden from us, almost as though it is none of our business. From episodes of both *Secret Agent* and his later series, *The Prisoner,* it is clear that McGoohan is concerned with issues of privacy in a society in which technology has the potential to make even the most intimate scenes public.[5] Thus, while it is hinted that Drake has a private life, and that, unlike Bond, he is not just a spy, that side of Drake's life is simply not open for our voyeuristic enjoyment.

Another suggestion of Drake's private life comes in an offhand comment at the beginning of "Say It with Flowers." Posing as a cabdriver to receive instruction from a superior in British intelligence, Drake suggests that a missing double agent, Hagen, might have simply decided to retire. When his superior responds, "Retire?" in a puzzled voice, it is clear that such a possibility had never occurred to him nor could he take it seriously. No one in the intelligence business is ever allowed to retire voluntarily. It simply is not done. Like members of the Mafia, intelligence agents are either forced out or killed. Drake does not pursue the point, yet we cannot help but wonder if he is thinking of himself, of his desire to be his own person, no longer required to obey the orders of his morally bankrupt employers. While McGoohan has always denied that Number 6 in *The Prisoner* is John Drake, it is not hard to imagine Drake angrily resigning out of moral indignation.

Drake's lifestyle also has very little in common with Bond's. When he drives, Drake's cars are no Aston Martins. This point is illustrated vividly in "Whatever Happened to George Foster?" where Drake follows Certhia Cooper's Rolls-Royce from the London airport in his cheap, boxy Mini (presumably all he can afford on his salary). In this episode wealth and luxury are associated with greed and corruption. Drake is repeatedly offered large bribes to drop his investigation but he never accepts them nor would he consider doing so.

Drake's opponents, unlike most of James Bond's, are quite plausible. In "It's Up to the Lady," he tries to stop a British scientist from defecting to China by way of Albania. In "Colony Three," the training school for spies is clearly located in an Eastern Bloc country, while "The Galloping Major" takes place in a newly independent African nation that seems very real. In "Judgement Day" Drake attempts to outwit Israelis to procure for Britain the services of a former Nazi scientist and war criminal. Drake never saves the world, nor is it always clear that he is in the right and his enemies wrong.

And, of course, there are the gadgets. Every Bond film attempted to outdo its predecessor with ever more outrageous toys and devices—from ejector seats to flying jet packs. John Drake also had his gadgets, but they were realistic and useful, like small wiretapping devices or the electric shaver that is actually a tape recorder. Obviously it was the Bond approach that came to dominate spy thrillers throughout the 1960s and beyond. TV shows such as *The Man from U.N.C.L.E., The Avengers,* and *The Wild Wild West* competed with each other and the Bond films to present the silliest, most nonsensical stories and situations.

By valuing realism and a genuine concern for ethical issues over the morally indifferent pursuit of escapist thrills, the *Secret Agent* series places itself in the tradition of films noirs such as *The Third Man* and *Ministry of Fear,* which also use the setting of the espionage thriller to explore serious philosophical issues.

The Influence of Graham Greene

THE MINISTRY OF FEAR

Graham Greene's novel *The Ministry of Fear* was presented to the public in 1943 as a spy thriller. In 1944 it was released as a film directed by Fritz Lang with Ray Milland starring as Stephen Neale, a Londoner who inadvertently stumbles upon a nest of Nazi spies trying to smuggle important photographs out of England.

The film *Ministry of Fear* unquestionably takes place at the exact time it was made, that is, during the London blitz. The backdrop for the story is a city being destroyed by daily bombing raids, a place in which the geography changes on a daily basis. Neale's mental condition is identified with both his physical surroundings and a more general psychosis affecting everyone. Indeed, he represents the future as a time of bleakness and moral relativism.

Throughout the work, Greene contrasts Neale's current situation with that of the serene and beautiful past of his childhood memories. To Neale, that golden time (England before the onslaught of World War I), represents a period in which life had both order and meaning. Right and wrong were clearly differentiated, and happiness and love were still possible. In the new world, life has lost all meaning and the strongest emotion available is pity, an emotion described in Greene's initial title for the novel as "The Worst Passion of All."[6] Remembering his trial for the euthanasia of his terminally ill wife, Neale "saw reflected in the crowded court the awful expression of pity. . . . He wanted to warn them: don't pity me. Pity is cruel. Pity destroys. Love isn't safe when pity's prowling around."[7]

Neale confronted such a decision in the face of his wife's suffering. Filled with pity, he murdered his wife, an act Greene clearly condemns. As a result of his choice, Neale now lives in a world that mirrors his moral vacuity, a vacuity shared by us all. Neale is a kind of "everyman"; his guilt symbolizes the moral relativism of his age.

Neale's position as prophet of the coming age is reflected in his intuitive use of the correct password at the book's beginning. Visiting the tent of the fortuneteller at a local fete, he quickly responds to her fairly accurate description of his past by demanding, "Don't tell me the past. Tell me the future." Thinking he is a Nazi agent because he has given the correct response, she tells him the proper weight for the prize cake, which contains the vital photographs. It is no accident that Neale is now identified with the Nazis he supposedly opposes.

He too wishes to overcome and forget the past and is willing to ignore his former moral sensibilities to do so. This point is emphasized when Neale meets Willi Hilfe (Carl Esmond), the Austrian refugee who turns out to be Neale's primary Nazi opponent, even though he is the brother of Carla (Marjorie Reynolds), Neale's eventual romantic partner. In the novel Hilfe tells Neale,

> The difference is that these days it really pays to murder, and when a thing pays it becomes respectable. . . . Your old-fashioned murderer killed from fear, from hate—or even from love very seldom for substantial profit. None of these reasons is quite—respectable. But to murder for position—that's different, because when you've gained the position nobody has a right to criticize the means. . . . Think of how many of your statesmen have shaken hands with Hitler.[8]

One of the striking things about *Ministry of Fear* is that on the surface the villains appear to be no worse, and sometimes even more affable, than the heroes. Indeed, Mr. Prentice (Percy Waram), the police detective who helps Rowe, is bad-tempered in comparison with the polite and friendly Hilfe. At the film's end, when Hilfe is unmasked as a Nazi spy, he tells Neale how much he has always liked him. But, unfortunately, he explains, Neale and Carla would not stop involving themselves in his business, so he regretfully attempted to kill them with a bomb.

When Neale demands, "How could you kill your own sister?" Hilfe responds, "You killed your wife." Hilfe is Neale's evil doppelgänger. In Hilfe, Neale is forced to face his greatest fears about who he has become. Neale and Hilfe struggle for the gun and Hilfe manages to knock Neil down. Carla picks up the gun as Hilfe runs out the door saying, "You couldn't shoot your own brother!" But Hilfe is wrong: Carla shoots him through the door, killing him. Thus, like Neale, Carla now has her own guilt to bear. Although the movie has the usual happy ending, with the couple even joking about having a cake at their wedding, one cannot help wondering how genuinely happy they can be. For Greene, moral innocence and goodness can only exist in childhood, adulthood necessarily brings with it immorality and remorse.

THE THIRD MAN

Based on an original screenplay written by Greene and directed by Carol Reed, *The Third Man* begins with a voice-over narration describing life in Vienna during the four-power occupation following World War II. The narrator depicts Vienna as one enormous black market where anything could be bought and sold. The four powers did their best to maintain order, but this was impossible given their inability to speak the language, their unfamiliarity with the terrain, and their distrust of one another. Like London during the blitz, postwar Vienna is a place of bleakness and despair.

The narrator says he has a funny story to tell us, one that illustrates the moral corruption of this place. It seems that there was a naive American, Holly Martins (Joseph Cotten), a writer of cheap pulp westerns who came to Vienna because he was down on his luck and needed a job. A childhood friend, Harry Lime (Orson Welles), sent him a plane ticket and the promise of work. The story turns out not to be very funny and, having done his job, the jocular narrator disappears from the film.

When he arrives, Martins is told that his friend Harry is dead, killed in an automobile accident. At the funeral he meets Major Calloway (Trevor Howard), a British officer who tells him that Harry was a racketeer. The major gets Martins drunk to pump him for information. With an almost childlike innocence, Martins refuses to believe that his friend did anything wrong. Like the hero from one of his westerns, Martins sets out to get to restore his friend's good name. Unfortunately for Martins, it proves impossible to impose his American ideals onto the noir environment of Vienna. Everyone he meets recognizes this and tells him to go home, but he fails to grasp the import of what they are telling him.

For example, Martins is shocked to discover that Harry's girlfriend, Anna Schmidt (Alida Valli), is using false papers to claim Austrian citizenship. He does not realize that he has entered a world in which decent people need forged papers to avoid deportation, a world in which the Russians would claim her and she would be forced to return to her native Czechoslovakia. Major Calloway understands all this and tries to puncture Martins's naiveté. Martins declares that he will only leave Vienna when he has gotten to the bottom of things. Echoing Heidegger, Calloway responds, "Death is at the bottom of all things. Leave death to the professionals."

After a number of futile attempts to clear his friend, Martins is finally convinced by Calloway's overwhelming evidence that Harry was guilty of horrific crimes. Using a medical orderly named Joseph Harbin to steal scarce penicillin for him, Harry had been diluting it and selling it on the black market for huge sums. Because of the dilution, the tainted penicillin is lethal when given to the ill, especially children.

Martins eventually discovers that Harry is still alive and is following him. He chases Harry but loses him in the shadows. Returning with Calloway to the city square, they discover that Harry has escaped by entering a kiosk and going down into the sewers.

Martins tells Harry's associates that he must see him and waits alone beside Vienna's famous Ferris wheel with its enclosed stalls. At last Harry appears and they ride the wheel together. Welles does an extraordinary job of communicating both Harry's allure and the frightening nihilism of his philosophy. Very much like Hilfe in *Ministry of Fear,* Harry is an apostle of the noir ideology, a cheerful rejection of all traditional values, including loyalty toward one's loved ones and friends. Harry is very amusing as he defends his actions by comparing himself to a modern government. "Governments accept that civilians must occasionally be harmed for the sake of their overall goals. I am like one of those governments," he tells Martins. "They have their five-year plans and I have mine."

Martins is horrified to discover that Harry has purchased his own safety in the Russian sector by feeding the Russians information, including that Anna is carrying the forged papers Harry had made for her. He cheerfully betrays Anna and, before Martins tells him that Calloway knows all, he even plans to throw Martins from the Ferris wheel to stop him from revealing his secret. At this point Harry presents Martins with his most chilling justification for his acts. With the door to the stall open in preparation for killing his best friend, he asks Martins to look down at the people below and asks, "Would you really feel any pity if one of those dots stopped moving forever? If I said you could have twenty thousand pounds for every dot that stops, would you really, old man, tell me to keep my money without hesitation? Or would you calculate how many dots you could afford to spare?"

Martins makes no response to Harry's arguments. Like the audience, he intuitively knows that Harry represents all that is evil, but in the noir world, Martins is unable to articulate arguments in response. Harry leaves Martins with this delightful speech: "In Italy for thirty years under the Borgias they had warfare, terror, murder, and bloodshed, but they produced Michelangelo,

Leonardo da Vinci, and the Renaissance. In Switzerland they had brotherly love—they had five hundred years of democracy and peace, and what did that produce? The cuckoo clock."

In the end, Harry himself is betrayed and killed by Martins in a superbly filmed sequence in the sewers, a classic distillation of noir camera angles and shadows. Holloway persuades Martins to betray Harry by first promising to provide new papers for Anna. With a feeling of poetic justice Martins condemns Harry to save Anna, a perfect counterweight to Harry's betrayal of Anna to save himself. But Anna will have none of it. When she discovers Martins's arrangement with Calloway she accuses him of betraying his best friend and tears up her new papers.

Calloway ultimately persuades Martins when, in a hospital, he confronts the young victims of Harry's scheme. And when he comes face to face with Harry cowering in the sewers, he chooses to kill his doppelgänger, becoming most like him in the act of destroying him. The film ends where it began, at Harry Lime's funeral. Just as before, Martins leaves the funeral in Calloway's jeep and watches Anna walking as they pass her on the road. In a last gasp of naive optimism, Martins asks Calloway to drop him off. He waits for Anna to approach him as he leans against a cart. He obviously hopes that Anna will be moved to forgive him for killing Harry and fall into his arms, providing us with the happy ending we would expect from one of his westerns. But *The Third Man* is no western. Without a word, she passes Martins and walks away, leaving him in despair.

Noir Themes in *Secret Agent*

Ministry of Fear and *The Third Man* illustrate the difficulties that confront secular heroes who try to overcome the world's moral indifference through reliance on traditional values and institutions. In both of these tales the protagonists seem to be abandoned by corrupt societies no longer capable of resolving the moral ambiguities that increasingly characterize life during and after the Second World War. In the end each is able to overcome nihilistic adversaries only by becoming complicit in that nihilism through the betrayal and destruction of those for whom they should care most.

Many episodes of *Secret Agent* explore similar issues. In "That's Two of Us Sorry," it appears that a Soviet spy who mysteriously vanished during World War II is responsible for the theft of plans from the briefcase of a scientist named Braithwaite, who works at a Scottish atomic-research lab.

After Braithwaite discovers that the plans are missing, fingerprint testing reveals the spy's prints on the briefcase. Drake's investigation leads him to disrupt the life of a quaint Scottish village whose inhabitants are valiantly struggling to preserve their way of life in the face of modern economic pressures and unwanted governmental interference.

Falsely convinced that the villagers are shielding the Soviet spy, Drake brutally reveals all their secrets including an illegal still and a forbidden romance between a young Scottish woman and a Russian sailor. In the end, he uncovers the identity of the missing spy from World War II. The spy has changed his name to Angus McKinnon, married a local woman, and become a leading member of the community. When his identity is revealed, McKinnon explains to Drake that his spying activities during the war were the result of misguided idealism, and he claims to have done no spying since he moved to the village. Despite his protests of innocence and the pleas of his family and fellow villagers, Drake takes McKinnon into custody.

However, when Drake brings McKinnon face to face with Braithwaite, it turns out that they are friends and McKinnon's prints on the briefcase are entirely innocent. Braithwaite then discovers that the missing papers have been in a drawer in his house all along and that Drake's efforts have been unnecessary. Although, under the circumstances, Drake would like nothing better than to release McKinnon, unfortunately, he has already reported his arrest of the World War II spy who still must face charges. Drake tells McKinnon how sorry he is and McKinnon can only respond, "That's two of us sorry."

This episode presents a common television theme but gives it a noir twist. We are used to watching shows in which the lone representative of the law stands up to a hostile town where it seems everyone is out to get him. Usually in such shows (often westerns) it is clear that the lawman is right and the whole town is wrong; the lawman always gets his man and the town learns a valuable lesson in respect for the law.

So, as we see Drake relentlessly invade the privacy of the town's residents and betray the trust of its most appealing inhabitants (e.g., a kindly tavern owner, an eccentric writer, et cetera), we naturally assume that these characters are really evil and that Drake's actions will be justified in the end. However, exactly the opposite occurs: it is Drake who unknowingly acted the villain and all of the town's accusations against him and the government he represents turn out to be true. In the end Drake realizes this himself, but, by that point, there's nothing he can do but apologize.

In "It's Up to the Lady," Drake is ordered by his superior, Hobbs (Peter

Madden), to use a defector's wife, Paula, to persuade her husband, Charles, to return home. Hobbs promises Drake repeatedly that Charles will not be arrested and that he will no longer even be watched. Drake believes Hobbs, and it is this sincerity that ultimately persuades the couple to return home with him. Throughout the episode, Nikos, the agent for the Albanians, warns Paula and Charles not to trust Drake, that his promises are just lies and that Charles will be arrested the moment he steps foot in England. Drake assures them that Nikos is a paid enemy agent lying to them to win their trust just long enough to get them to Albania, where Charles will be a prisoner. Even after Nikos shows them newspapers trumpeting Charles's defection, Drake reassures them: "The situation has not changed. I've been on to London, and I have their word."

In the end it is Nikos who was telling them the truth. Charles is arrested at the airport the moment he steps foot on British soil. When the arresting officer asks a protesting Drake, "Who are you, sir?" it is clear that Drake has no real governmental authority. Even though he asks them to wait while he telephones, the officers promptly take Charles away. As Paula is blocked from following them, Drake angrily speaks to Hobbs on the phone:

> Drake: Commander Hobbs, what's going on?
> Hobbs: Oh, Drake, well, you've done a good job.
> Drake: The Indians are arresting him!
> Hobbs: Good.
> Drake: But you assured me that they wouldn't. It's the only reason he
>   came back!
> Hobbs: Well, it worked very well then, didn't it?
> Drake: But you gave me your word!
> Hobbs: Did I, Drake?
> Drake: You hypocritical [click of Hobbs hanging up phone].

After hanging up the phone, Drake returns to Paula, now standing alone by the airport gate. As Drake walks towards her, his arm still in a sling from the bullet he took in the course of the mission, Paula stares into his eyes and sees that, like her and her husband, Drake too has been betrayed by an English government morally no better than its enemies. Without a word, she slowly turns and walks away, leaving Drake alone in the shadows with his despair. The look and feel of this ending, like that of *The Third Man,* could not be more noir.

It can be no accident that Drake's superior is named Hobbs. The British philosopher Thomas Hobbes (1588–1687) is perhaps most famous for his claim that in its natural state human life is characterized by "continual fear, and danger of violent death; and the life of man, solitary, poor, nasty, brutish, and short."[9] Life is a war of all against all, and the only possible security comes from a "Leviathan," a powerful government that protects its citizens from the chaos caused by the corruption of human nature. Hobbes's greatest fear is of the "state of nature" (society without strong government) so, like Drake's boss, Hobbes was more than willing to act unethically to ensure the government's power over its citizens even if that means lying and the needless imprisonment of innocent citizens.

In "Colony Three" a mock English village is used to train enemy spies within the borders of some unnamed Eastern Bloc country. The odd juxtaposition of traditional village life with ominous elements of totalitarian moral depravity raises noir concerns. Physically resembling the bombed-out London of the blitz, this ersatz English village in fact makes a mockery of traditional British values, such as fair play and optimism. With its threats of torture and murder coupled with the inevitable lack of privacy, the village represents our worst fears for the future. By the end of the episode Drake has escaped and warned his employers of this attempt to infiltrate and subvert British life. However, this ending suggests that Britain may already have undergone a process of moral subversion when Drake realizes that Hobbs intends to do nothing to rescue the innocent British girl still trapped in the "village." Like Charles in "It's Up to the Lady," the girl is an innocent causality of the war of all against all, a war that will never end. This episode presents us with a village that, despite its charming facade, is explicitly constructed to spy on and manipulate its inhabitants. To this extent, "Colony Three" foreshadows the noir setting of *The Prisoner*.

In "Whatever Happened to George Foster?" Drake realizes almost from the beginning that the British government has entered into a morally dubious pact with a British industrialist who intends to overthrow the democratically elected government of a small nation for purely monetary motives. While his employers are clearly identified as immoral, Drake is able to obtain blackmail material that allows him to prevent the industrialist's scheme. So, in this episode, although Drake may no longer be able to rely on the moral authority of his government, he can still tell right from wrong and bring about a satisfying result through his own efforts even if, like Neale and Martins, he must adapt his döppelganger's immoral tactics to achieve it.

"Judgement Day" removes even that slight hedge against moral chaos while plunging Drake fully into a noir world of ethical ambiguity and impotence. Returning from a mission in a Middle Eastern country, Drake is ordered to pick up a man called Dr. Garriga and bring him to England immediately. Because of problems with the telephone, Drake only receives partial instructions: he knows his mission is vital and dangerous but he does not know why. Like a character in a Beckett play, Drake must do his job without knowing who anyone is or what they want, including himself. Eventually he discovers that Garriga is really a Nazi war criminal who infected and killed innocent civilians to create a vaccine against potential, but currently nonexistent, biological weapons.

Drake's charter pilot is bribed by agents from an outlawed Israeli group that seeks justice for Jewish victims by kidnapping and executing Nazi war criminals. Drake soon comes to realize that his government wants Garriga precisely to put him back to work on his morally dubious research, this time for the British instead of the Nazis.

Drake plays on the consciences of the Israelis to get them to set up a mock tribunal to try Garriga for his crimes. Sounding very much like Harry Lime in *The Third Man* (although admittedly much less charming), Garriga surprises everyone by confessing at once and arguing that the death of a few innocent Jews is a small price to pay for a vaccine against biological weapons. At this point Drake's only defense is to call Garriga a "moral imbecile" and claim that he is not guilty by reason of insanity. Yet, the Israelis point out, such a defense could exculpate all Nazis, indeed all sincere criminals, and destroy any notions we may have of individual moral responsibility. Eventually, one of the Israelis bypasses the tribunal and kills Garriga for the sake of personal revenge for his murdered family. In the end, Drake is asked what he really thinks is the best moral solution to this dilemma. "I don't know," he responds. "Maybe nobody does."

As in *Ministry of Fear* and *The Third Man*, *Secret Agent* takes place in a noir environment in which the old moralities have been jettisoned for the nihilistic hedonism practiced by many, and the nihilistic realpolitik that is its manifestation in governments. Those too naive to realize this (Neale, Martins, and Drake) are destined to be manipulated and exploited by those who do. This nihilism often presents itself in the guise of an affable charm that infects all those who are exposed, implicating them in its amorality.

Thus, like Neale and Martins, Drake could be said to act in Sartrean bad faith. Drake knows with certainty that his British masters often send him on morally dubious missions, yet he continues to work for them Admittedly, when he discovers such immoralities he struggles to correct them, even when this means openly opposing his own government. Yet, how many times has he contributed to the success of missions whose real ends were successfully kept secret from him? Hobbs clearly knows Drake's reliability as an agent is hobbled by his integrity, but he has become expert in turning that liability into an asset, assigning Drake to missions where his apparent sincerity can be used to manipulate those equally naive (like Paula in "It's Up to the Lady").

In the absurd world in which we live, it is seemingly impossible to defeat nihilism. One might be able to occasionally rebel against this meaninglessness and win small limited victories (e.g., "Whatever Happened to George Foster?"), but, in the end, despair too often wins out over hope. For Greene there is an escape through a Kierkegaardian leap to faith, as in his religious novels such as *The Power and the Glory, The Heart of the Matter,* and *The End of the Affair.* However, for those unwilling to make such a leap, or, like Drake, apparently unaware that such a possibility even exists, one can only escape by fantasizing about an unrealizable retirement or embracing the inevitable certainty of death, the destiny that haunts all our lives.

Notes

1. I wish to thank Steven M. Sanders for suggesting the comparison of *Secret Agent* to *The Third Man* and *Ministry of Fear.*

2. Transcribed at Matthew Courtman, "In the Beginning," *The* Danger Man *Website,* September 21, 2003, http://www.mcgoohan.co.uk/.

3. Quoted in Anne T. Salavatore, *Greene and Kierkegaard: The Discourse of Belief* (Tuscaloosa: University of Alabama Press, 1988), 4.

4. For instance, in *Thunderball* (Terence Young, 1965) Bond shoots a man with a spear gun and says, "He got the point," and in *Goldfinger* (Guy Hamilton, 1964) Bond electrocutes a man in a bathtub and declares, "Shocking!"

5. For further discussion of *The Prisoner,* see the essay by Shai Biderman and William Devlin "*The Prisoner* and Self-Imprisonment," in this volume 229–46.

6. Norman Sherry, *The Life of Graham Greene,* Vol. 2: *1939–1955* (New York: Penguin), 146.

7. Graham Greene, *The Ministry of Fear* (New York: Viking, 1945), 234–35.

8. Ibid., 44.

9. Thomas Hobbes, *Leviathan* (1651; New York: Touchstone, 1997), 98.

Action and Integrity in *The Fugitive*

Aeon J. Skoble

The Fugitive aired on ABC from 1963 to 1967 and starred David Janssen in the title role of Dr. Richard Kimble, on the run from the law, wanted for a crime he did not commit. It was classic TV noir, both stylistically and thematically. In terms of the noir aesthetic—the first three seasons were in black and white, and even though the fourth season was in color, for its entire run—the series was filmed with a distinctly noir sensibility: unusual and unsettling camera angles, shots and scenes that emphasized the loneliness and isolation of the protagonist, extensive use of alleyways, warehouses, deserted streets at night, and fleabag hotels, and of course a voice-over narration. Thematically, film noir is often characterized as involving an inversion of values; this is practically guaranteed by the premise of *The Fugitive:* a wrongly accused man trying to capture the real killer while being pursued by law enforcement. This is what makes *The Fugitive* such compelling TV noir. Every week, Richard Kimble is obliged to live an underground existence and is compelled to adopt a wary, if not paranoid, stance toward not only law-enforcement officers but all decent people.

As we see in many flashbacks over the run of the series (and summarized in the opening to every episode), one night, Kimble returns home to see a one-armed man fleeing his house. Inside, he finds his wife, murdered. But the police do not believe his story about a one-armed man, and neither does a jury, which has heard that Kimble and his wife had had a terrible argument that night. Kimble is sentenced to death, but en route to death row, as we hear in the series' voice-over opening, "fate moves its huge hand," and the train is derailed, allowing Kimble to escape. The series chronicles his quest to find the one-armed man, and the simultaneous quest by "the police lieutenant obsessed with" recapturing Kimble, Lieutenant Philip Gerard (Barry Morse). In the pilot, we see a longer montage of backstory and narration, including a scene of Kimble looking out of the window of his train just before it crashes as the narrator (William Conrad) intones "Richard Kimble ponders his fate as he looks at the world for the last time . . . and sees only darkness. But in the darkness, fate moves its huge hand." Over the course of the first season, the opening flashback and narration were trimmed down, and by the second season, had become "*The Fugitive*, a QM Production, starring David Janssen as Dr. Richard Kimble, an innocent victim of blind justice, falsely convicted of the murder of his wife, reprieved by fate when a train wreck freed him en route to the death house; freed him to hide in lonely desperation, to change his identity, to toil at many jobs; freed him to search for a one-armed man he saw leave the scene of the crime; freed him to run before the relentless pursuit of the police lieutenant obsessed with his capture."[1]

Superficially, then, the police are the bad guys, while the good guy is a fugitive from justice; hence the seeming inversion of values. At a deeper level, though, each episode of *The Fugitive* is a self-contained morality play, in which the protagonist's ongoing story intertwines with another tale concerning people he has become involved with: a boy who needs to get to a hospital, a woman with an abusive husband, a man who gets in trouble and needs help, workers oppressed by a sadistic boss.[2] The protagonist of this morality play, Dr. Richard Kimble, frequently finds himself in a dilemma: Can he do the right thing in his interactions with others while at the same time avoiding detection by the authorities? Another way to characterize that dilemma is this: Can he simultaneously maintain his integrity and his safety? Although it sometimes seems to exacerbate the situation, Kimble's integrity turns out to be one of his chief assets. I've argued in previous essays on film noir that the "standard view" of noir as involving moral ambiguity is mistaken, that noir is better understood as demonstrating moral clarity and practical reason.[3] *The Fugitive* is yet another source of examples of this, as Kimble is consistently shown making tough decisions about what (to him) are clearly defined standards of right and wrong, struggling to preserve his integrity (and succeeding), doing the morally right thing without jeopardizing his quest to find his wife's killer and exonerate himself. I will analyze situations or dilemmas from several episodes in terms of the issues at stake, the moral reasoning that goes into Kimble's resolution of them, and the way his integrity plays a key role.

Kimble is a medical doctor—specifically, a pediatrician. This means that it is in his nature to help the sick and injured, and this characteristic manifests itself in a general concern for those in distress. He seems almost constitutionally incapable of the sort of Seinfeldian indifference that would make it easier for him to elude Gerard. Indeed, he sometimes goes out of his way to help others, even in cases where he could have saved himself a lot of trouble by turning a blind eye. For example, in "Bloodline," Kimble helps a dog breeder whose family is planning on fraudulently selling a sick dog and in the process draws the attention of the authorities. In "Angels Travel on Lonely Roads," he helps a troubled nun recover her faith and falls into a classic noir police dragnet. Of course, in many cases, his help is needed because others have tried to help him. For example, in "The End Is But the Beginning," Aimee Rennick (Barbara Barrie) gets shot helping Kimble escape. He feels compelled to help her, partly out of his normal, characteristic sense of duty but also because he is responsible for her injury. He knows that Gerard is nearby and on his way to the scene, but Aimee will die without attention to her gunshot wound. Kimble is still being held at gunpoint, by John Harlan (Andrew Duggan), Aimee's jealous lover, and he has to make the case that he should be allowed to help her: "If I leave, she'll die within a minute. I don't want that on my conscience. . . . I'm not going anywhere." His actions to save Aimee help persuade John to release Kimble, moments before Gerard arrives.

Duty and Motivation

Kimble's explanation to John is a very frank statement of one possible source of motivation for his risking his life to help another (and just to be clear, since he is a fugitive from death row, *every* case where he risks capture by Gerard is an instance of risking his life). In this case, at least, it is not so much that he has a duty to risk his life to save her but that his life would be unbearable if he had to carry the guilt his knowledge of her death would entail. Yet in other cases, Kimble is not himself responsible for the medical problems he feels compelled to solve—for example, in "All the Scared Rabbits," he treats a young girl with meningitis. So it is important to ask: What is duty, first of all, and how does it motivate? What might motivate besides duty?

The nineteenth-century German philosopher Immanuel Kant argues that we can discern moral duties through our faculty of reason.[4] If a rational creature cannot will that the universe be governed by the rule "do X," then X is forbidden, and if a rational creature cannot will that the universe be governed by the rule "avoid doing X," then X is obligatory. (He calls this the "categorical imperative.") Kant says that we ought not to consider the consequences of our actions—including negative consequences for the actor—nor our sentiments, but only whether we are acting out of a rational recognition that what we have deduced is a universal moral obligation. On this view, helping another is one's duty just because it is the right thing to do as commanded by the categorical imperative. This ethical theory might be seen as an illuminating way to understand Kimble, and it is tempting to see a physician's special duty to care for the sick and injured as additional evidence.

But Kimble cannot actually be a thorough-going Kantian, since Kantian theory prohibits lying, which Kimble does in every episode. One might argue that Kimble actually is a Kantian who has no choice but to lie but then feels guilty about it because he knows he has violated the categorical imperative. But rather than try to establish which ethical framework Kimble "really" has, I am trying to show what sort of ethical theory best accounts for what we see, and I do not think the Kantian ethic of strict duty-obeying/rule-following captures it at all, even though it is tempting to characterize him, qua physician, as being "duty-bound to help the sick."

What, then, accounts for his propensity to help others even when this entails risking his life? An alternative explanation to the Kantian one might be character-based motivation: his maintenance of his integrity. As we saw in the case of Aimee Rennick, Kimble has a conscience, and he takes seriously what is on it. In "Scapegoat," Kimble discovers that someone in a town he had passed through some time ago has been convicted of murder, the ostensible victim being Kimble's alias at the time. Since it is obvious that the man is innocent, Kimble returns to clear the man. His rationale here seems to be less a matter of unemotionally acting on Kantian duty theory than of not wanting to live with the knowledge that he could have saved the man but did not. His sense of personal integrity motivates him to do what he sees as the right thing to do. Wishing to preserve one's integrity, wishing to have a clean conscience—these are emotional desires, which, to a Kantian, ought to be irrelevant to decisionmaking. That they are emotions does not preclude there being a cognitive basis for them, however. Aristotle, for example, suggests that there is a cognitive component to emotions. There is an objective right or wrong as to what one's emotional reactions are; this is shown in several episodes. For instance, in "Bloodline," we see Kimble having emotional reactions to animal cruelty. It would be evidence of a vicious character for him not to feel compassion in these cases, just as it is evidence of a virtuous character when he responds with compassion. There are feelings one ought to have, and on this view it is right to want to seek justice.[5] This includes, of course, evading recapture by agents of the law so he can clear his name and bring his wife's real killer to justice. But his sense of personal ethics places boundaries on how he may act in the course of his quest. What sort of person would turn a blind eye to the abuse of a lame dog or a battered wife? Not the sort of person Kimble sees himself as being.

Kimble lies on a regular basis, but other than that he makes a point of being ethical. He rarely steals, and when he does, he repays what he has taken (as he does, to his great peril, in "End of the Line"). He does not take advantage of the emotional vulnerabilities of the many troubled women he encounters who are attracted to him. He will not be complicit in the criminal schemes he often finds himself embroiled in (although he is frequently coerced into playing some kind of role). When he gets a job, he does it with diligence and industry. In short, while his main quest entails both defiance of the law and a good deal of deception, he remains committed to all the other moral principles he held in his previous life. I've argued elsewhere that integrity is best understood as fidelity in action to moral principles one has arrived at through a reasonable process of discovery and reflection.[6] On this view, there is no logical contradiction between Kimble's defiance of the law, on the one hand, and his responsibility and morality, on the other. But much drama hinges on the conflicts and dilemmas that result.

Angels Travel on Lonely Roads

This drama is nowhere more in evidence than in the several occasions in which Kimble actually saves Gerard's life. In "Ill Wind," for instance, Kimble has been captured after one member of the migrant worker community with which he had been living is coerced into revealing Kimble's escape route. But a hurricane forces Gerard and Kimble, handcuffed together, to shelter with the migrant workers, who resent Gerard for bullying them. Their loyalty is to Kimble, whom they see as a benevolent figure. Gerard dozes off, waking up as Kimble is pulling him aside: one of the workers had tried to run him through with a pitchfork and Kimble was saving his life. Gerard is appreciative: "They must be impressed. I suppose even I am." But he is not so appreciative that he would set Kimble free in gratitude. In response to Gerard's remark, Kimble says: "But that doesn't change anything," and from his tone of voice we know he is not really asking. "No," Gerard replies, "it doesn't change anything." Their staccato, hard-boiled dialogue is classic noir both in style as well as substance.

The workers cannot quite understand why Kimble would intercede—as Naomi (Jeanette Nolan) puts it, "It just don't seem right to us, helping him when we know he's agin ya." But for Kimble, letting them stab Gerard would cross a line he is unwilling to cross. Kimble needs to escape from Gerard, to elude him, but he cannot be complicit in murdering him or even be an indifferent spectator when he knows he could have done otherwise and prevented his murder. In "Corner of Hell," Kimble likewise saves Gerard from being murdered by backwoods moonshiners. (In this particular episode, we see the noir inversion of values folded back on itself: here, Gerard cuts a sympathetic figure.) While Gerard's sense of justice requires him to relentlessly pursue Kimble, Kimble's sense of justice requires him to prevent a murder, even the murder of his nemesis.

Ed Robertson suggests a slightly different motivation for Kimble's willingness to protect Gerard, one that goes beyond his sense of moral responsibility: "Despite the personal torment the lieutenant has caused him, Kimble continues to rescue his adversary because he needs him alive. Just as Kimble represents a failure to Gerard, Gerard represents a failure to Kimble because the lieutenant insists that the one-armed man is a fantasy. To keep the moral order straight (as well as to clear his own name), the Fugitive needs Gerard as much as he needs Fred Johnson."[7] I think there is a great deal of insight in this analysis, and it is entirely compatible with the ethical analysis I've been suggesting. Indeed, there is ample evidence from the show to support the idea that Kimble has a strong sense of moral responsibility even regarding Gerard. And indeed, we see on several occasions that Gerard respects Kimble for it, even if he will not allow that respect to prevent him from bringing Kimble to justice. After the pitchfork incident in "Ill Wind," Gerard remarks, "What you did, it didn't surprise me." After Kimble reminds Gerard that he will nevertheless escape if he can, Gerard replies, "That doesn't surprise me either." Gerard views Kimble as a man of integrity, with the one ethical "lapse" of having murdered his wife. He believes that Kimble invented the one-armed man as an alibi, and may now actually believe there is such a man. In Gerard's view, Kimble's subsequent good deeds do not warrant evading punishment.

Of course, we the viewers, like Kimble, know that there really was a one-armed man, Fred Johnson (Bill Raisch), and that Kimble did not kill his wife.

So from Kimble's point of view, and from ours, Gerard seems determined to an unreasonable degree to capture Kimble. But Gerard has ethics also: he is willing to risk losing his captive to enable Kimble to give medical attention to the sick or injured. For instance, in "Ill Wind," one of the children in their hurricane shelter has a bad fever, and Gerard unlocks Kimble's hands so he can tend to her. Also, in the two-part series finale "The Judgment," he grants Kimble a twenty-four-hour reprieve after arresting him and bringing him back to Stafford, so that Kimble can pursue Johnson. (Granted this is a plot necessity to allow the story to come to a conclusion, but it is nevertheless an example of Gerard acting magnanimously.)

The White Knight

One of the most explicit discussions of Kimble's sense of integrity and moral responsibility occurs in "Ill Wind," after the pitchfork incident. Later in the evening, a section of the shelter's roof collapses on top of Gerard. Kimble naturally tends to the serious injury, and when he realizes that Gerard has lost a lot of blood, he announces to the migrant workers that Gerard needs a transfusion, and he asks them to check their worker cards to see whether they have compatible blood types. They find this appeal even more baffling than Kimble's earlier intervention, and they all refuse even to look at their cards. A young woman who has shown herself to be attracted to Kimble, Kate (Bonnie Beecher), engages him in a very revealing dialogue:

> Kate: Don't help him! . . . If that man lives, he'll see you killed, so why
> are you trying so hard to save his life?
> Kimble: For a doctor, every life is worth saving.
> Kate: I guess I'm just too stupid to understand.
> Kimble [slightly annoyed reaction]: No you're not, Kate.

This brief exchange is revealing in several ways. First of all, Kate gives voice to what the viewer might well be thinking. But Kimble's answer gives us some insight into the nature of his integrity: as in "The End Is But the Beginning," he will not give up being the kind of person he is—a healer, one who cares for the sick and injured, a compassionate man—even if that means his recapture. His integrity—his fidelity to himself—requires that he make some effort to save his patient's life, regardless of the fact that the patient wants him dead. The dialogue is also interesting in that Kate tries to dismiss

Kimble's explanation as too abstract, or, engaging in a kind of reverse elitism, too "highfalutin" for simple folk like her (read: nonsense). But Kimble finds this irritating and shows this in his simple, yet effective rebuttal, the point of which is that moral principles about what is good and right are accessible to the human mind, and that Kate would see the truth of Kimble's claim if she would just think about it, unclouded by bias or personal resentments. Many philosophers have argued that this is so. Kant's categorical imperative is a simple test that anyone is capable of applying. Plato describes justice as "a model laid up in heaven, for him who wishes to look upon," suggesting that through contemplation, we can come to know right from wrong.[8] Aristotle, in his *Nicomachean Ethics,* argues that people have natural judgment-making capacities that allow us to discern what is right and good.[9] And Thomas Aquinas argues that the "natural light of reason" lets us differentiate between good and evil.[10] Kate's claim irritates Kimble partly because her suggestion that she (or anyone else) is "too stupid" to understand ethics misses the point that having a moral code is available to everyone, and refusal to think deeply about these matters is a way of abrogating personal responsibility.

Never Stop Running

If Kimble's integrity gets him into trouble at times, it is also (and almost always) an asset. Most obviously, we frequently see other characters coming to trust him and believe in him because of his ethics and integrity. More centrally, though, his integrity is an asset because it is what keeps him a whole person. Notice the etymological similarity between "integrity" and "integrated"—in this context, it is one's character that might be said to be "fully integrated." Plato, for example, describes the just person as having attained a state of inner harmony, harmony with respect to himself. The just person "rules himself. He puts himself in order, is his own friend, and harmonizes the three parts of himself . . . , and from having been many things he becomes entirely one, moderate and harmonious."[11] In this view, the three "parts" of the psyche (namely, reason, emotions, and appetites) are brought together for the sake of one's overall psychological well-being. One way to understand integrity, then, is to see it as involving the pursuit of a kind of psychological wholeness. Though it is agonizing for him to risk capture to save Aimee Rennick's life, it is so obviously (to him) the right thing to do that it is worth the risk. This wholeness helps mitigate the temptation to violate his own principles for the sake of expediency, even in cases where he risks capture.[12] Kimble is thus not only a person others might see as worth saving, he is a person he himself sees as worth saving, and that is partly responsible for his fortitude. His perseverance in pursuit of the one-armed man must have required considerable strength of character—never giving up, never giving in to despair. It would be difficult to continue that way if one were additionally burdened by a guilty conscience or if one had lost all sense of personal value. Although it put his quest—and his life—at risk, his commitment to his real self, to his principles, is also what made it possible for his quest to have a successful resolution. And in the final episode, Kimble does clear his name, and Gerard kills the one-armed man. The finale brings home even for the casual viewer that *The Fugitive* really is classic TV noir: we learn in flashbacks (shot in even more than usually unsettling camera angles) that there had been a witness to the slaying of Helen Kimble, whose testimony might have saved Kimble all the trouble, but whose efforts at redemption help set the stage for a tense climactic chase sequence in an abandoned amusement park. As in the best of classic film noir, Kimble successfully emerges from his dark world. After four years slinking around in alleys and freight yards, in the last scene he walks in the sunlight on a crowded street. Kimble and Gerard shake hands and go their separate ways.

Notes

I am very grateful to Steven M. Sanders for many helpful comments on various drafts of this essay, from inception to completion. I am also indebted to Christeen Clemens for making her video library available to me, enabling me to review key episodes.

1. Transcribed in Ed Robertson, *The Fugitive Recaptured: The Thirtieth Anniversary Companion to a Television Classic* (Los Angeles: Pomegranate Press, 1993). Robertson calls this "the most famous run-on sentence in television history" (78).

2. I am grateful to Chris Sciabarra for suggesting the expression "morality play" as a way to characterize the show, as well as for several other helpful comments.

3. Aeon J. Skoble, "Moral Clarity and Practical Reason in Film Noir," in *The Philosophy of Film Noir*, ed. Mark T. Conard (Lexington: University Press of Kentucky, 2005), 41–49; and "Justice and Moral Corruption in *A Simple Plan*," in *The Philosophy of Neo-Noir*, ed. Mark T. Conard (Lexington: University Press of Kentucky, 2006), 83–91.

4. For example, in Immanuel Kant, *Grounding for the Metaphysics of Morals*, 3rd ed. trans. James W. Ellington (Indianapolis: Hackett, 1993).

5. Again, it is not important whether a Kantian might challenge the contrast I'm drawing between the role of emotion in ethical decisionmaking in virtue ethics and what seems to be Kant's admonition that we look not to our inclinations and passions, since

there is no fact of the matter about whether Kimble is "really" a Kantian. I am interested here in seeing which ethical theory fits *The Fugitive* best. I am grateful to Steven M. Sanders in this and the preceding paragraph for suggesting a different reading of Kant, which prompted greater precision on my part.

6. "Integrity in Woody Allen's *Manhattan,*" in *Woody Allen and Philosophy,* ed. Mark T. Conard and Aeon J. Skoble (Chicago: Open Court, 2004), 24–32

7. Robertson, *The Fugitive Recaptured,* 98.

8. Plato, *Republic,* trans. by G. M. A. Grube (Indianapolis: Hackett, 1974), 592b.

9. Aristotle, *Nicomachean Ethics,* trans. by T. Irwin (Indianapolis: Hackett, 1999).

10. Thomas Aquinas, *Summa Theologiae,* Question 91, in *St. Thomas Aquinas on Politics and Ethics,* trans. by Paul E. Sigmund (New York: Norton, 1988), 46–47.

11. Plato, *Republic,* 443d.

12. I explore this analysis of integrity in greater detail in "Integrity in Woody Allen's *Manhattan,*" 25–28.

Part 2

Existentialism, Nihilism, and the Meaning of Life

NOIR ET BLANC IN COLOR: EXISTENTIALISM AND *MIAMI VICE*

Steven M. Sanders

> Crockett: It's just the waiting, I hate the waiting. I feel like a
> character in a Beckett play.
> Tubbs: Since when do you know Beckett?
> Crockett: Charlie Beckett, down at the corner shoeshine. He
> writes plays on the side.
> —Sonny Crockett and Ricardo Tubbs, *Miami Vice*

The connections between existentialism and TV noir are shown by the way the concepts of alienation, absurdity, existential freedom and choice—expressed with such fluency in novels, short stories, essays, and plays by thinkers associated with the existentialist movement—appear among the central themes of the classics of film noir and their television counterparts.[1] Of course, there are disputes about the nature of existentialism that were not resolved by the existentialists themselves in their own time, and I shall not attempt to settle them here. "Sartre resisted identification with existentialism as an intellectual fashion," writes historian George Cotkin in *Existential America*, "believing that his ideas would be diminished through such commodification." Sartre himself said in 1960, "I do not like to talk about existentialism. To name it and to define it is to wrap it up and tie the knot."[2] Indeed, those who read Sartre's popular exposition of existentialist doctrines, "Existentialism Is a Humanism," in the hope that he was going to untie the string on the package of existentialist thought were quick to discover that he had left them with another knot instead.

Nevertheless, there is sufficient unity in the existentialist movement to permit us to identify its salient themes. Existentialist thought is not limited to the phenomena of alienation, absurdity, dread, and death. It also gives scope to the possibility of creative engagement with existential crises. Sartre's idea that we are condemned to be free gives rise not only to anguish over the weight of taking personal responsibility for ourselves and our actions but also to the exhilarating prospect of attaining authentic existence and rising to a higher level of being. "For human reality," Sartre writes in *Being and Nothingness*, "to be is to choose oneself," thereby expressing an outlook on personal autonomy at odds with that doom-laden determinism so widespread in film noir.[3] As we shall see, the alienated protagonists of TV noir take from existentialism this generalized sense of the contingency of things and the ways in which life can go unpredictably off-course, but they also take a sense of engagement in the name of individual freedom.

The writing of the existentialists combines philosophical abstraction with an immersion in the immediacies of human experience. This endows their work with a novelistic attention to detail that mitigates the vague, metaphysical detachment. Once one has read them, one never feels the same about the ordinariness of life and commonplace things, in much the way that film noir exploits the dark underside of quotidian life. The work of the existentialists, written out of the depths of their (often conflicted) personalities, gives *Miami Vice* philosophical significance when we interpret the program against this background. For the way personality is woven into the fabric of existentialist thought is reflected in the master theme of the show itself. Consider the alienation Sonny Crockett (Don Johnson) must endure as he lives an undercover existence, with its pressures on personal identity and the unresolved conflicts of moral responsibility that arise while he masquerades as a denizen of the criminal demimonde. The undercover cop must negotiate a world of assumed, and therefore precarious, identities and tenuous loyalties, a world where his unmasking is tantamount to his death. Crockett's existential backstory is continuous with that of many of those central characters of film noir who attempt (and often fail) to achieve personal transformation in which their fractured, fragmented identities are rendered whole, their selves unified.

Amphetamine Theatre

Greater Miami is an unexpected setting for a TV noir series. In the early episodes of *Miami Vice*, which are shot in a glossy array of pinks, whites, turquoises, and mint greens, the stylish location photography reflects a warm, sunny, and opulent atmosphere, hardly what one would expect to find in noir. In fact, *Miami Vice*'s use of color is one of the most striking breaks with TV noir of the *Dragnet, Naked City,* and *Fugitive* variety. As Nicholas Christopher observes in connection with color films noirs of the classic period, "It is the noir elements . . . that demand colors: the wild swings in the characters' emotional lives, their intense sexual energy, and the violence rippling all around them."[4] When one combines sophisticated lighting changes with the impact of color, "the possibilities of expression grow exponentially with regard to character delineation and imagery development." Although Christopher is in fact describing the 1958 film *Party Girl* (Nicholas Ray), his account could just as easily apply to *Miami Vice,* especially when he adds that "background colors are used to reveal and open out the characters' inner emotional states, to tint the fault lines of their shifting relationships, and to define the director's intentions rather than simply to ornament the scene of action."[5]

Michael Mann, the executive producer of *Miami Vice,* told an interviewer that his first reaction to seeing Miami was "Wow! What fabulous locations! My second reaction was, 'That can't be Miami.' My third reaction was, 'If that really is Miami, let me see more.'" And the noir significance of his two stars, Don Johnson and Philip Michael Thomas, was not lost on Mann. "We loved the way a dark star and a blonde star played off each other—visually, it's very exciting."[6] *Noir et blanc* in color.

The signal achievement of *Miami Vice* is to have conveyed a noir sensibility despite its representation of metropolitan space as, in the words of the poet Morgen Kapner, an "amphetamine theatre," a highly colored, brightly lit zone of fast-paced activity. In addition to upscale locations such as Key Biscayne, Coral Gables, and Coconut Grove, episodes often included downscale sites like Gino's Wine Garden, the Deuce Bar, and the Gayety, a Miami Beach burlesque theater dating from the 1950s. These low-end venues went against the grain of *Miami Vice*'s deceptively stunning South Florida locales and served to consolidate the image of the debased lives of the drug users, strippers, pimps, prostitutes, con artists, shady lawyers, and corrupt officials with whom the Vice Division dealt.

Numerous episodes of *Miami Vice* are philosophically textured and darkly toned, offering a wealth of interpretive possibilities along existentialist lines. The pervasive traits of the human condition—the absurdity of human existence, the anguish of individual choice, the dreadful weight of radical freedom, the permanent possibility of death that sets a limit to one's aspirations and achievements—are indicative of an existentialist subtext that can be found throughout the five seasons of *Miami Vice*. These traits also reflect the affinity of the series for themes found in film noir from the outset: a concern with the dilemmas and paradoxes of freedom and personal identity; the central issue of troubled pasts; alienation, rootlessness, and angst in the character formation of the protagonist; and the essentially combative nature of human relationships, especially when they involve encounters with the femme fatale. The association of existentialist themes with those found in TV noir is not coincidental, for noir television embodies an outlook on life in which the themes of alienation, absurdity, meaninglessness, and nihilism are foregrounded.[7]

Points on a Compass of Cultural Reference

The criminal adversaries with whom Crockett and Tubbs must contend are largely rootless and self-chosen, lacking an essential tie to tradition, family, or community. But the irony of *Miami Vice* is that this is also the existential profile of Crockett and Tubbs themselves. Consider some of the most pertinent details. Tubbs's brother is shot to death, in flashback, in the series pilot, and it is not until season 5 that Crockett mentions his father, and then only to describe the way the elder Crockett taught the young Sonny how to shoot pool while Hank Williams played on the jukebox. Late in the fifth season, the episode "Jack of All Trades" gives us a comic look at Crockett's larceny-prone cousin, Jack (David Andrews). With these exceptions, the backstories of the two principal characters make scarce mention of parents, grandparents, siblings, aunts or uncles.[8]

In the series pilot, Sonny's estranged wife, Caroline (Belinda Montgomery) tells him, "You get high on the action," and this remark presages the breakup of their marriage. By the fifth episode of season 1, their divorce is final. The remaining 106 episodes depict his and Tubbs's romantic relationships and encounters as a shambles. Between them, they are involved with the daughter of the cocaine dealer responsible for the death of Tubbs's brother ("Return of Calderone"), a gambling addict who is murdered by a racketeer ("One-Eyed Jack"), a femme fatale who murders her accountant boyfriend ("The Great McCarthy"), a rogue cop ("Rites of Passage," "Prodigal Son"), a femme fatale with a homicidal boyfriend ("Definitely Miami"), a flight attendant who overdoses on the cocaine she has smuggled into the country ("Yankee Dollar"), a French Interpol agent who is in reality an assassin for a sinister organization ("French Twist"), a drug-addicted physician ("Theresa"), the proprietor of an escort service/prostitution ring ("By Hooker by Crook"), the wife of a drug kingpin ("To Have and to Hold"). These dysfunctional relationships and romances are not entirely coincidental. Crockett and Tubbs are unmoored from social structures that would provide them with access to anyone but prostitutes, drug addicts, and assorted hustlers and players. Nevertheless, Crockett, for one, comes to realize that he must take personal responsibility for some of his poor choices and prolonged adolescence in which, as his wife had told him, "You get high on the action."

None of the principal characters seems to have much interaction in the world of ideas, art, or culture generally. Even Castillo's familiarity with the cultures of Southeast Asia and China and Tubbs's ability to pass, very briefly, as an art collector, do not go against this general point.[9] In one episode, Larry Zito (John Diehl) is shown reading a paperback copy of *Miami Blues*, by pulp-noir cult figure Charles Willeford, and Gina is shown at the beach with a copy of Robert Bolt's play *A Man for All Seasons*. Stan Switek (Michael Talbott) is a devoted Elvis fan, and Switek and Zito are shown enjoying cartoons on television in numerous episodes.[10] Sonny has a prized collection of Buddy Holly LPs and his musical tastes run to Waylon Jennings, Jimmy Buffett, and Dicky Betts, rather than jazz, pop, rock, or classical, judging from the selection of tapes on board the *St. Vitus Dance*. Both Crockett and Tubbs are aware of the theater of the absurd playwright Samuel Beckett, per the exchange in the episode "Definitely Miami" (from which I have taken my epigraph). Bolt, Buddy, Buffett, Beckett, Betts: these points on a compass of cultural reference demarcate a highly circumscribed region. Our culturally undernourished protagonists are alienated from a dimension of thought and emotion that might have grounded them in a sense of the self that in the present instance seems lost. The principals' complacency and lack of cultural awareness abets the impoverishment of their relationships and affairs. Their neglected or diminished exposure to art, literature, and philosophy deprives them of sources of enrichment and, in the end, fulfillment in life. In a very real sense, Crockett's existential crisis is in part a reflection of the cultural vacuum from which he has sprung.

Life Lessons and Death Sentences

An episode from season 1, bearing the title of Jean-Paul Sartre's play *No Exit*, registers an early encounter with existentialist themes and gives some indication of the philosophical orientation of later episodes. Bruce Willis is Tony Amato, an international arms merchant trying to sell a shipment of stolen stinger missiles to undercover vice detective Ricardo Tubbs. This draws the attention of the FBI, as Crockett and Tubbs discover when the bureau threatens to take over their operation. Once the detectives convince the Feds that they have already placed listening devices throughout Amato's house and installed taps on his phones, the two law enforcement agencies agree to join forces in a common cause.

Vice intercepts a call from Tony's wife, Rita, as she sets up a meeting with a hit man to arrange to have Tony killed. She feels trapped in an abusive and demoralizing marriage and needs to find a way out. Her plight is dramatically illustrated when Tony, enraged, pushes her fully clothed into their swimming pool because he thinks she's inappropriately dressed for a party that calls for formal wear. He is mistaken, of course, but nothing stands in the way of his getting what he wants. Rita's repeated pleas for a divorce are met by Tony's declaration: "That will *never happen!*" Her attempt to hire a lawyer has already led to an assault on the lawyer's wife, and Tony threatens to do the same to their child. "And he would do it," Rita affirms to Crockett who, posing as the hit man, keeps the appointment. After identifying himself as a police officer, Crockett asks for Rita's cooperation in buying some time as he and Tubbs work with the FBI to set up a sting operation that, Crockett promises Rita, will put Tony away for good and Rita out of harm's way. Nothing must appear out of the ordinary, he tells her, while he and the Feds set things up.

Although the sting is a success and Tony is arrested, the pervasive apprehension running through "No Exit" culminates in a memorable closing scene on the steps of the Dade County Courthouse where officials from yet another federal agency intervene with a court order mandating Tony's release. At that moment, Castillo, Crockett, and Tubbs learn that Amato is on the end of a conduit that supplies certain factions with arms and that he operates with the consent of the federal government. "I got the *juice*," Tony boasts just as Rita arrives to witness Tony's release. "You're letting him *go?*" she asks, incredulously, as we cut to three reaction shots: first, Tony's startled expression as Rita points a gun at him at point-blank range; then Rita, desperate and determined to go through with the shooting; and finally Crockett as he lunges at Rita, his look of anguish caught in freeze-frame as his cry of "No!" and the sound of the gunshot reverberate on the soundtrack and close out the episode.

What is so clearly in evidence here is Sartre's grim view that human relationships are essentially conflict-laden struggles for control. This is not just a highly contingent and variable feature of many affairs, relationships, and marriages, according to Sartre. Rather, it stems from the very structure of that consciousness in terms of which we inevitably relate to others. The oppositional forces of what Sartre terms being-in-itself and being-for-itself give rise to an inherent conflict in human relationships. Given that conscious, self-aware beings, or *êtres-pour-soi* (beings-for-themselves), are bound to see others as *êtres-en-soi* (beings-in-themselves), to be manipulated and controlled, or to become beings-in-themselves for control by the other, the only possibilities in human relationships are sadism, masochism, or indifference. "From these structures there is no exit," writes the philosopher Arthur C. Danto, echoing Sartre's most famous phrase—"hell is other people"—"and the dividing line between hell and ordinary daily life is not there to be drawn; other people are hell in and out of any specific inferno."[11]

Existential Errors

The "No Exit" episode of *Miami Vice* can be seen as an application of not only Sartre's depressingly negative account of human relationships but also his familiar formula: recognize life's absurdity, accept responsibility for who you are and what you do, and then take action. On closer examination, however, the Sartrean notion of action has some not altogether harmless implications. For one thing, there is the slippery slope from the fervor of revolt to the endorsement of violent action as an existential blow against oppression. This makes Sartre's position all the more applicable to Rita, who, we are led to believe, has no exit from her oppressive and degrading marriage and must end it by taking Tony's life. As Sartre's notorious introduction to Frantz Fanon's *The Wretched of the Earth* makes plain, a bullet in the body of an oppressor is a Sartrean-sanctioned blow for freedom. "Killing a European is killing two birds with one stone," he writes, "eliminating in one go oppressor and oppressed: leaving one man dead and the other man free."[12] In contrast with the moderation of his fellow existentialist Albert Camus, "Sartre made a fetish of violence," in the words of the philosopher Ronald Aronson, "deeming it necessary for human liberation and social change without calculating its costs."[13]

It may be no accident that Sartre wrote a biography of the writer and criminal Jean Genet. In his rejection of middle-class lifestyles and values, the thief and sexual transgressor Genet exemplified the Sartrean hero. But the association between Sartrean existentialism and violence runs deeper, as a glance at historian George Cotkin's discussion of novelist and essayist Norman Mailer's existential hipster will confirm. This "rebel psychopath who acknowledges and lives under the sign of death" is described by Mailer as beating in the brains of a fifty-year-old candy-store keeper and is said by Mailer to have "courage of a sort . . . for one murders not only a weak fifty-year-old man but an institution as well, one violates private property, one enters into a new relationship with the police and introduces a dangerous element into one's life. The hoodlum is therefore daring the unknown, and so no matter how brutal the act, is not altogether cowardly."[14] Elsewhere, Mailer writes that "a murderer in the moment of his murder could feel a sense of beauty and perfection as complete as the transport of the saint." The theme of the liberating power of murder is never far from Mailer's fiction, as in *The Deer Park* and *The American Dream*.[15]

Hazel E. Barnes, who translated Sartre's *Being and Nothingness* and who is perhaps Sartre's best known American acolyte, called Mailer's account "nihilistic fulfillment" and claimed that such ideas were "contrary to that of any writer associated with existentialism."[16] But Barnes is forgetful and far too kind, as the example of Sartre's introduction to Fanon's book confirms. There is also the German existentialist Martin Heidegger's enthusiastic support of the Third Reich and the French existentialist Simone de Beauvoir's defense of the Marquis de Sade, from whom the term "sadism" comes, titled *Must We Burn Sade?* Beauvoir writes: "Sade's merit lies not only in his having proclaimed aloud what everyone admits with shame to himself, but in the fact that he did not simply resign himself. He chose cruelty rather than indifference."[17] But note the fallacy of false alternatives, as if Sade's only options were cruelty and indifference. Note also that Sade left victims in his wake, a fact that must not be ignored in an assessment of his "merit."

In exposing these applications of the thought of some existentialist philosophers, I am employing the methodological principle that philosophical beliefs can be undermined by our responses to their consequences. The idea here is that existentialist beliefs have normative implications or consequences that people may find impossible to accept. When that happens, the belief has to be modified so that it no longer carries the unacceptable implication, or it must be abandoned. Ironically, this is itself the underlying rationale of the existentialists' own view that one cannot (or should not) isolate morality from conduct. Of course, our responses themselves are open to modification, revision, and rejection. For example, one who believes, as Sartre apparently did, that the Soviet Union was a necessary bulwark against U.S. imperialism and capitalism may be able to modify his or her response to Stalin's totalitarian practices so that he or she no longer finds them unacceptable. Nevertheless, one's beliefs should accommodate as many of one's responses as possible, a goal that may be impossible to achieve, given the implications of existentialist beliefs.[18]

This problem with Sartre's existentialism as a guide to commitment and action is not the only difficulty with his approach: there is also a weakness in his account of authenticity. It would be one thing for Sartre to maintain that the authentic self is the autonomous self and to characterize autonomy in terms of those values and commitments that are freely chosen by the well-informed individual who is open to criticism about them. But Sartre is far too influenced by the European romanticism of Kierkegaard and Heidegger to be altogether content with this way of thinking about authenticity. When Sartre speaks of the choice of life-constituting principles by which the individual guides his or her conduct, he leaves little room for the self-reflection that comes with choosing in a way that is free, well-informed, and responsive to criticism. Authenticity for Sartre remains an amorphous and largely nonrational response to the various demands a person must face in the often arduous task of living.

Miami Masquerade

We learn the extent of Crockett's difficulties reconciling his true self with his undercover identity, Sonny Burnett, in an early episode from the first season, "Heart of Darkness."[19] Arthur Lawson (Ed O'Neill), an undercover FBI agent, has infiltrated the operation of a Miami porn dealer, Sam Kovics (Paul Hecht). Lawson has succeeded in penetrating the small, tight-knit outfit because he identifies so completely with his undercover persona, Artie Rollins, that he becomes indispensable to Kovics's criminal activities. He stops filing reports with the bureau and moves out of the apartment in which they had set him up and takes up residence in a luxury waterfront condo. This leads some in the bureau to suspect that Lawson may have gone over to the other side and provides the basis for the otherwise somber episode's running joke: the FBI agents checking up on Lawson are named Doyle and Russo, the surnames of the Gene Hackman and Roy Scheider characters in *The French Connection* (William Friedkin, 1971).

Lawson also breaks off contact with his wife. In the scene at a fancy restaurant where Crockett and Tubbs, posing as out-of-town porn-theater owners, break bread with Kovics, an attractive blond is at Lawson's side. He has indeed put his mundane married life on hold to embrace an existence of money, sex, and crime. The putative reason for this dramatic change, the one he gives Crockett and Tubbs when he discovers that they are vice cops, is his compelling undercover mission: "I'm on an investigation here! If I make a strategic decision to cut corners, to throw the book away, it's my decision, 'cause it's me out here and nobody else." But we begin to suspect that Lawson likes the life he has begun to live and that his extreme measures and undercover intrigues are attempts to create meaning in his life, a realization he confesses when, near the end of the episode, he tells the vice detectives: "I don't know if I can go back to my wife and that life. It's like I've been riding an adrenaline high, all that money and all those women. And after a while, all of the things that went before, it got like a . . . it's like a . . . I don't know."

The changes Lawson is undergoing and the way he now feels about his wife and *that life* can be explained by reference to his realization of existential freedom: Lawson has come to accept that he is condemned to be free and must take responsibility for his choices. This realization, in turn, is a source of anxiety. He seems unprepared to either wholly accept or totally reject the drives and desires he has kept suppressed as Arthur Lawson but expresses through the persona of Artie Rollins. In part, this is a reflection of the typical noir notion of the far-reaching effects of the past: the conventional norms of bourgeois morality by which Lawson has defined himself and guided his life are difficult to simply abandon, sustained as they are by the forces of habit and convention, even as they break up when he recognizes the dreadful freedom of existential choice.

There is, in fact, more than one such existential recognition going on in "Heart of Darkness," since Crockett's understanding of what the conflicted undercover agent is going through is based on a profound identification with him. His identification is a reflection of his own ambivalent attitude toward the masquerade that he, Crockett, must play out as Sonny Burnett. Crockett sees not only Artie but also himself, and he understands and empathizes with the estranged agent's anxiety, since he, too, is at war with himself.

A midnight drug deal between the vice detectives and Kovics goes awry, and the vice detectives' covers are blown. Kovics (who is unaware that he is an undercover agent) orders Artie to kill the pair, but instead Artie comes to their rescue and then proceeds to execute Kovics and his bodyguard. Motivated by a flawed commitment to the ideals of law enforcement, Lawson, the typical noir protagonist, knows that he is compromised beyond redemption. His masquerade, his casting off of the bourgeois life of the law enforcement officer and his embrace of a fantasy life, in fact has been a flight from authenticity. As he is taken into custody for debriefing, an overlapping sound track, George Benson's "This Masquerade," extends into the next scene, inside the Blue Dolphin Lounge, where Crockett and Tubbs are having a drink and trying to decompress after the evening's harrowing events. The ensuing dialogue complements the theme of the soundtrack lyrics: the need to perpetually choose one's identity and the risk of being trapped inside the roles dictated by one's multiple masquerades, which reflects the moral ambiguity of the noir universe.

> Crockett: You know those mirrors at amusement parks, the ones that warp everything out of whack? I feel like I've been staring at myself in one for the past three days.
> Tubbs: It's not a reflection of you, Sonny. It's the job. I don't see how you've been doing it as long as you've been doing it.
> Crockett: Neither do I. You gotta be a little nuts.

While at the bar, the pair is informed that during a break from his three-hour debriefing, Lawson called his wife, then went into the men's room, where he hung himself. And so the episode ends as the haunting lyric of "This Masquerade" makes its ironic commentary on the overwhelming of the tormented FBI agent by his own masquerade. "Heart of Darkness" is thus an existentialist morality play about the challenge of living authentically and the costs of the failure to do so.

An "I" Exam Is Existential

Another similarity between existentialist fiction and film noir is indicated by a shared narrative strategy. By 1947, Sartre was advocating a literature without the omniscient narration of "all-knowing witnesses" or those who had "a privileged point of view."[20] This approach has its counterpart in one of film noir's most venerable devices, the voice-over narration, particularly in what Andrew Spicer calls its confessional mode.[21] In connection with this narrative device, Spicer observes, "flashbacks can undermine the apparent

objectivity of the images as they can question the reliability of the narrator"—Sartre's all-knowing witness with his privileged point of view—"whose
flashbacks try to make sense of a past that is rendered as strange, threatening, and unfinished." In *Sunset Boulevard* (Billy Wilder, 1950), for example,
which features a flashback voice-over narration by a character who is already
dead, "although the protagonist appears to be in control of the retelling of
the story, it is really the past events that are still controlling him, which
he would love to alter if he could."[22] But in this respect, classic film noir's
idea of the fatalism that afflicts the noir protagonist reflects a significant
dissimilarity to both existentialism and TV noir.[23] The repudiation of classic film noir's determinism is one of the distinguishing characteristics of
both existentialist thought and TV noir. Consider the dedication of Fox
Mulder and Dana Scully (*The X-Files*), the resolve of Jack Bauer (*24*), the
perseverance of Richard Kimble to establish his innocence (*The Fugitive*),
the crusading (and clearly obsessive) anticrime campaign of Mike Torello
(*Crime Story*), and, as we shall see, Sonny Crockett's commitment to sur-
mount his existential crisis. Everywhere in TV noir we find protagonists
who struggle to create meaning in an absurd world out of the resources of
their own freedom.

A dramatization of the ideas of existential crisis and recognition and the
invocation of existential choice focuses on Crockett late in the series. Several
episodes, beginning with "Mirror Image," the last episode of season 4, and
continuing in season 5 with "Hostile Takeover," "Redemption in Blood," and
"Bad Timing," dramatize the subjective experience of Crockett's commitment to raise himself from the depraved and degraded state into which he
has fallen once he has taken on the persona of Sonny Burnett. They depict
the way Crockett handles the problem of a self in crisis and the depth of his
conviction to work his way through it.

Crockett's existential crisis can be characterized more fully against the
backdrop of a family of problems bearing on matters of personal identity.
When philosophers address these problems, they are typically concerned
with one or more of the following questions: What is it to be a person, as
opposed to a nonperson? What are the criteria of personhood? What is
it to be the same person over time? But there is a more informal sense of
the problem of personal identity where our concern is with the conflicts a
person experiences as he or she attempts to come to terms with who he or
she is. In this sense, the conflicts Crockett undergoes in the episodes under
discussion have a crisis dimension to them.

Two Existentialist Approaches

Numerous approaches to existential crisis, recognition, and choice can be found among existentialist thinkers, each giving intellectual heft and nuance to the task of achieving (or reclaiming) personal identity. For the sake of comparison, I shall briefly contrast Kierkegaard's religious existentialist approach with Sartre's atheistic existentialism before I discuss the latter at greater length and apply it to Crockett's existential crisis in *Miami Vice*.

Kierkegaard and Sartre know how difficult it is to attain genuine self-knowledge, despite being acute diagnosticians of their own personal infirmities. With their focus on perspective and interpretation, they teach us that it is no easy matter to attain self-knowledge and an understanding of one's own purposes in life. Kierkegaard, with his emphasis on a nonrational leap of faith, and Sartre, with his fundamental decisions of principle that are not themselves rationally grounded, can be interpreted as showing the difficulty (if not the impossibility) of providing an acceptable account of rational agency.[24]

The first approach is embodied in Kierkegaard's idea of a redemptive leap of faith. Kierkegaard distinguishes among the aesthetic, the ethical, and the religious modes of life. Because his complex and wide-ranging views resist brief summary, it must suffice to say that the first represents the life of delight in the senses and the second the life of duty. The distinctive character of the third, religious, mode of life is its affirmation of a dimension of living under the aspect of faith, where the individual must make a radical leap, a commitment to an infinite and absolute God who transcends reason and human understanding, a being "objectively uncertain and in the last analysis paradoxical."[25] According to Kierkegaard, the ascendancy from one mode of existence to a higher one is accomplished by individual choice, and he rejects the Hegelian suggestion that these distinct stages on life's way succeed one another in a logically or dialectically necessary fashion.[26]

In several of his plays and novels, Sartre presents us with an existential hero who confronts meaninglessness and death without succumbing to bad faith. In Sartre's atheistic existentialism, meaning or purpose in life is a product of the individual's free choices rather than a divine plan (or anything else with religious grounding). In this connection, Sartre contrasts authentic with inauthentic living and claims, as we have seen, that to be is to choose oneself. His remarks in *Being and Nothingness* and elsewhere suggest despair and relativism to some, but while Sartre has been reviled (or hailed) on these grounds, he says he sees things differently. Sartre wants to establish that existentialism "is a doctrine of action, and it is only by self-deception, by confusing their own despair with ours that Christians can describe us as without hope."[27] But against this and similar passages, we must weigh his assertions that man "cannot find anything to depend upon whether within or outside himself," and that life begins "on the far side of despair."[28]

Both Kierkegaard and Sartre recognize a distinction between higher and lower stages or modes of living and see the transition from the latter to the former as a way to deal with existential crisis. In this respect, they imply, perhaps not altogether consistently, that certain ways of life are objectively higher than others. This presupposes an objective standard whose truth the individual does not invent but discovers. Both thinkers know that such a standard cannot be derived from our conventional preferences or existing social structures, for we use evaluative concepts to criticize these. Kierkegaard himself was a relentless opponent of the religious practices of his day that passed for Christianity, and Sartre, ever the critic of middle-class lifestyles and values, attacked America for what he took to be its "technological determinism," capitalist profit-making, and "numbing mass culture."[29] Sartre's repudiation of bourgeois outlooks and lifestyles in the name of authenticity are to a considerable extent motivated by myths of absolute freedom and self-invention—which he later came to reject in the name of Marxist collectivist tales that led him, as I have already noted, to endorse violence as a means to an end. Existentialism, at least Sartre's version of it, seems committed to the view that there is nothing intrinsically valuable about the core principles of Western culture—such as liberty, equality, freedom of speech and belief—and that there are no grounds for thinking that the preference for these over alternative conflicting ones is rationally justified.

For both thinkers, diagnosis is followed by prescription. The crises that occur in the lives of individuals make the transition to a new form of life necessary. But since the higher form of life embodied in living authentically in either Kierkegaard's or Sartre's sense is chosen by the individual, the means of resolving existential crises and achieving authenticity are interpretable only on an individual basis.[30] Indeed, for Sartre, as for Kierkegaard before him, the commitment to a way of life is something we must do for ourselves, an individual action that has no objective justification.

Out of Whose Past?

Film noir protagonists are notoriously reticent, evasive, or opaque about their pasts. In the most extreme cases, the protagonist speaks to us from death in voice-over narration, as in *Sunset Boulevard,* or faces its imminent prospect, as in *D.O.A.* (Rudolph Maté, 1950) The events revealed to us in flashback have already taken place, and there is neither room nor need for the exercise of agency. In other instances—most notoriously *Out of the Past* (Jacques Tourneur, 1947)—whatever the exercise of agency, there is still the sense of the long arm of the past reaching into the present. As numerous noir films from the classic tradition illustrate, failure to engage with the past and the instruction it offers can break apart the unity of the person that is essential to personal identity and moral agency. TV noir in general and *Miami Vice* in particular break with film noir's fatalist tradition without denying that the past plays a significant role in the formation of the protagonist's character and his present conflicts.

Miami Vice begins in medias res, and by starting in the middle of things *Miami Vice*'s narrative commences in crisis, when Crockett is already burdened by angst from his past, and arcs toward resolution. By his own account, Crockett is insufficiently supportive when his police academy buddy, Mike Orgel, comes to grief because he cannot withstand the career-ending stigma to which his coming out of the closet consigns him. Orgel volunteers for a suicide mission and is killed by a shotgun blast to the chest. Crockett's former partner, Scott Wheeler (Bill Smitrovich), an FBI agent as the first season begins, is exposed as a source of insider information for Calderone, the very drug dealer responsible for killing Tubbs's brother and a target of Crockett and Tubbs's investigation. Crockett's next partner, Eddie Rivera (Jimmy Smits), is killed by a car bomb explosion in what was supposed to be a routine drug buy. Crockett is separated from his wife, Caroline, and has begun an abortive affair with a coworker, Gina Calabrese (Saundra Santiago), which will blow up in his face. All this is part of Sonny's history and his burden of grief.

By the time we reach the end of season 4, Crockett's unassimilated grief for the death of his new wife, Caitlin Davies (Sheena Easton), and his disposition to suppress it, provides the motivation for his ill-starred undercover mission to host a mob summit during which he sustains a severe head injury that causes amnesia and symptoms of dissociative identity disorder.[31] He comes to believe that he *is* his undercover persona, Sonny Burnett, and, as

Burnett, he goes to work for Miguel Manolo, a Columbian crime boss in Fort Lauderdale. Crockett's transformation into Burnett is so thorough and convincing that he becomes an active and trusted participant in the Manolo criminal enterprise.

Thus traumatized, Crockett appears on the scene in season 5 bearing the psychological wounds of the extant damage. But Crockett-as-Burnett is hardly a unified self. He begins increasingly to revisit the narrative of his own past, shown in a series of flashbacks. Although Crockett is driven by his need to reclaim his identity, he is thwarted by Burnett's nihilism, as shown in the criminal acts, including murder, he commits on a regular basis. But as Burnett, he pays a price far worse than suffering the anxieties of nightmares and recurring flashbacks to his former identity as Crockett: he undergoes an inexorable decline into feelings of helplessness, hopelessness, and guilt. For Kierkegaard, this condition prompts the leap of faith and the hope of salvation. But this is no way out for Crockett because a redemptive leap of faith into the salvational embrace of religion is impossible in the resolutely secular world of *Miami Vice*.

In "Bad Timing," the final installment of this multi-episode exploration of his crisis, Crockett submits to psychological counseling and voices aloud the question that Tubbs, Castillo, and Switek have themselves no doubt been thinking about him: "What kind of a person *am* I?" Early in the episode, Crockett has his first session with the police therapist, where he talks about the stresses and confusions of undercover work in which he is alienated from himself because he is always playing a role and masquerading as someone else. This gives the scene a self-reflexive character because there is a sense in which Don Johnson, the actor who portrays the character Sonny Crockett, is in a similar position with respect to his character as his character, Sonny Crockett, is with respect to Sonny Burnett. It is Don Johnson, after all, who must masquerade as the character Sonny Crockett to ground the masquerade Sonny Crockett suffers from and complains about. When the philosopher Richard A. Gilmore relates a parallel scene in Woody Allen's *Crimes and Misdemeanors* (1989), he invokes Arthur C. Danto's analysis of an artwork as a transformation of the commonplace to explain the self-reflexivity of the film.[32] But I do not want to try to apply Danto's analysis to the case we have here. Instead, I use Sartre's idea of existential recognition to explain Crockett's way of dealing with his existential crisis.

As Crockett confronts the alienation that follows from his need to en-act a series of masquerades over the course of his career on the vice squad, he achieves a moment of existential recognition that reaffirms his identity and, not coincidentally, facilitates the restoration of narrative continuity required for completion of the series. Using the threadlike images of his past as a guide, Crockett traces back his history to the Vice Division, where he shows up one day to confront his past. *Miami Vice* thus can be seen as developing the existentialist theme of the possibility of authenticity in a world of self-deception, which Sartre explored in his play *Dirty Hands*. In this respect, Crockett is like the Sartrean authentic man. As it is worked out in the episode "Redemption in Blood," he puts himself in a life-threatening situation that pits him against a wily and ruthless adversary, Cliff King (Matt Frewer), who has taken over the drug operation that Crockett-as-Burnett once controlled. Knowing that King has entered an alliance with a renegade Mexican military officer to import drugs into the United States, Crockett masquerades as Burnett as he sets out to regain control of the operation and trap King, a man who has already orchestrated several attempts on his life. The choice Sonny makes to enter such an extreme situation is, for the existential protagonist, the resolution of his crisis. In choosing to take such dangerous action, Sonny affirms his authenticity and in the process reclaims his identity. In Sartrean terms, Sonny confronts the anxiety of the dangerous assignment he undertakes, and out of the existential expression of his freedom, he emerges as his authentic self—something, we may recall, that Arthur Lawson, in "Heart of Darkness," was unable to do.

New Hope for the Living

Miami Vice comes to a redemptive ending in the series finale, "Free Fall," when Crockett and Tubbs recognize the limits of their ability to alter political events that have forced their hands. They toss away their badges in a gesture of repudiation and disgust reminiscent of Gary Cooper's sheriff in *High Noon* (Fred Zinnemann, 1952). Of course, the link between drug trafficking and corporate interests already had been disclosed in the second-season two-part episode, "Prodigal Son." In that story, Crockett and Tubbs learn from a New York City banking executive that he and his colleagues in the financial community are not going to let the South American governments default on their massive loans, even if that means ignoring their cocaine exporting activities. But in "Free Fall," we witness a new attitude toward concentrated state power, for the episode seems to confirm the conspiracy among the U.S. government, a Latin American dictator, and the drug cartels. The message seems clear: an imperial, militaristic, corporatist America, determined to entrench its empire. "There's only two things that count," the high official of an unnamed U.S. federal agency tells Crockett and Tubbs at the episode's end, "American interests and anything that's counter to 'em." Thus, conspiracy and hegemony are identified as the real engines of U.S. policy.

As Crockett and Tubbs grasp the scope of the government's complicity, they understand the dimensions of a corruption they cannot combat. This, too, is a moment of existential recognition, but one that by no means involves a passive acceptance of life's limits, accompanied by disillusion and defeat. It is not, in the words of Alain Silver and Elizabeth Ward, the "resignation to being annihilated by a relentless, deterministic abstraction."[33] As Robert Porfirio writes, "the precipitous slide of existentialism toward nihilism is only halted by its heavy emphasis on man's freedom," and we have seen in connection with the thought of Kierkegaard, Camus, and Sartre that existentialism can accommodate a variety of actions and reactive attitudes toward the human condition, including leaps of faith, rebellion, heroism, and scorn.[34] In a striking display of narrative closure, *Miami Vice* turns back on itself with the same dialogue between Crockett and Tubbs that ended the series pilot. Crockett asks: "Ever consider a career in Southern law enforcement?" Tubbs replies: "Maybe . . . may*be*." The final aerial shot is a dramatic expression of their lives, as Crockett and Tubbs drive south, leaving behind five years as partners in the Vice Division with few satisfactions, and head toward an unknown future that their existential choices will help create.

Notes

I want to thank Aeon J. Skoble for reading and commenting on earlier drafts and for our numerous conversations about *Miami Vice*. I am also grateful to Christeen Clemens for her helpful comments on earlier drafts.

1. For a seminal essay on film noir and existentialism, see Robert G. Porfirio, "No Way Out: Existential Motifs in the *Film Noir*" (1976), reprinted in *Film Noir Reader*, ed. Alain Silver and James Ursini (New York: Limelight, 1996), 77–93.

2. George Cotkin, *Existential America* (Johns Hopkins University Press, 2003), 6; Jean-Paul Sartre, *Search for a Method*, trans. Hazel E. Barnes (New York: Vintage Books, 1968), xxxiii.

3. Jean-Paul Sartre, *Being and Nothingness: An Essay on Phenomenological Ontology*, trans. Hazel E. Barnes (New York: Washington Square Press, 1966), 538.

4. Nicholas Christopher, *Somewhere in the Night: Film Noir and the American City* (New York: Free Press, 1997), 227.

5. Ibid., 227–28.

6. T. D. Allman, *Miami: City of the Future* (New York: Atlantic Monthly Press, 1987), 97.

7. For an early and important discussion of film noir and *Miami Vice,* see Jeremy G. Butler, "*Miami Vice:* The Legacy of *Film Noir*" (1985), reprinted in Silver and Ursini, *Film Noir Reader,* 289–305.

8. In this, of course, *Miami Vice* is no exception, since, until fairly recently, it was rather typical for families to enter into the proceedings primarily as objects of ridicule and foils for the principal characters' antics. Some crucial exceptions to this include *The X-Files, Millennium,* and *The Sopranos.*

9. Tubbs's conversation with Brenda in "Nobody Lives Forever" indicates some knowledge of architecture ("Now Crockett, he doesn't know the difference between Bauhaus and outhouse"). Nevertheless, he gets it wrong when he tells her he "likes the art deco buildings they're putting up in South Miami." In 1985 art deco hotels were being *renovated* in South Beach, a place both literally and existentially miles away from the city of South Miami. My thanks to Aeon J. Skoble for reminding me of Tubbs's interest in art and Castillo's knowledge of Southeast Asia.

10. See "Everglades," "Return of Calderone, Part 1," and "Made For Each Other," to name only three. In true reductive fashion, males are shown as adolescent, incompetent, criminal, or idiotic. Female principals, on the other hand, are rarely depicted as scheming, superficial, ruthless, or dumb.

11. Arthur C. Danto, *Jean-Paul Sartre* (New York: Viking, 1975), 109. Danto offers a view of Sartre very different in tone and emphasis from the one provided here, describing his life as "a paradigm of commitment and courage as well as of creativity, full of positions taken and fine causes promoted and hideous ones opposed, an articulated and sometimes futile conscience and moral witness against the outrageous twentieth-century history" (ix). The famous phrase is from Sartre's play *No Exit* (*Huis clos,* 1947).

12. Jean-Paul Sartre, preface to *The Wretched of the Earth,* by Frantz Fanon, trans. Richard Philcox (New York: Grove, 1963), lv.

13. Ronald Aronson, *Camus and Sartre* (Chicago: University of Chicago Press, 2004), 224. Camus condemned the use of revolutionary violence in the Algerian war of independence from France, a position Cotkin describes, oxymoronically, as "extreme moderation" (*Existential America,* 233).

14. Cotkin, *Existential America,* 192. The passage is from Norman Mailer, "The White Negro," quoted on page 197.

15. Norman Mailer, *Existential Errands* (New York: Little, Brown, 1972), 210.

16. Hazel E. Barnes, *An Existentialist Ethics* (Chicago: University of Chicago Press, 1978), 194; quoted in Cotkin, *Existential America,* 197.

17. This passage from Beauvoir's essay *Must We Burn Sade?* is taken from Stanley Kauffmann, "Excessive Freedom," *New Republic* (May 20, 1992): 22.

18. Jonathan Glover provides a succinct discussion of the scope and limits of moral

argument in *Causing Death and Saving Lives* (New York: Penguin Books, 1977), chapter 2. For Sartre's Stalinist beliefs, see Cotkin, *Existential America,* chapter 6.

19. I provide a postmodernist interpretation of this episode in "Sunshine Noir: Postmodernism and *Miami Vice,*" *The Philosophy of Neo-Noir,* ed. Mark T. Conard (Lexington: University Press of Kentucky, 2007), 190–92. Several additional passages from this essay appear, in paraphrased form, in the present essay.

20. Jean-Paul Sartre, *What Is Literature?* trans. Bernard Frechtman, quoted in James Naremore, *More Than Night: Film Noir and Its Contexts* (Berkeley: University of California Press, 1998), 24.

21. Andrew Spicer, *Film Noir* (Harlow, England: Pearson Education, 2002), 75ff.

22. Ibid., 76.

23. I defend this point in "Film Noir and the Meaning of Life," in Mark T. Conard, ed., *The Philosophy of Film Noir* (Lexington: University Press of Kentucky, 2006), esp. 97–98.

24. My Aristotelian-Kantian approach to this issue is indebted to Jonathan A. Jacobs, who develops an account of rational self-mastery that attempts to accommodate the existentialist emphasis on interpretation and perspective. See his *Virtue and Self-Knowledge* (Englewood Cliffs, NJ: Prentice-Hall, 1989).

25. Patrick Gardiner, *Kierkegaard: A Very Short Introduction* (New York: Oxford University Press, 1992), 66–68.

26. Ibid., 52.

27. Jean-Paul Sartre, "Existentialism Is a Humanism," in *Existentialism from Dostoevsky to Sartre,* ed. Walter Kaufmann (New York: New American Library, 1975), 369.

28. Sartre quotes from, respectively, "Existentialism Is a Humanism," 353; *Being and Nothingness,* 538; and *The Flies,* trans. Stuart Gilbert (New York: Knopf, 1962).

29. Cotkin, *Existential America,* 114. According to Cotkin, "within a few years of the introduction of existentialism in America, most New York intellectuals had cooled toward existentialism in general and strongly dismissed Sartre and Beauvoir in particular" (110).

30. Gardiner raises a similar difficulty for Kierkegaard's view in *Kierkegaard,* 55.

31. See Jacobs's discussion of the emotion of sadness, *Virtue and Self-Knowledge,* 37. Of course, Jacobs is speaking generally; he is not addressing the dramatization of this phenomenon in *Miami Vice.*

32. Richard A. Gilmore, *Doing Philosophy at the Movies* (Albany: State University of New York Press, 2005), 87–88.

33. Alain Silver and Elizabeth Ward, eds., *Film Noir: An Encyclopedic Reference to the American Style,* 3rd ed. (Woodstock, NY: Overlook, 1992), 4.

34. Porfirio, "No Way Out," 87. I discuss existentialist reactive attitudes to the human condition in "Film Noir and the Meaning of Life," esp. 101–3.

24 AND THE EXISTENTIAL MAN OF REVOLT

Jennifer L. McMahon

One does not have to watch Fox's hit series *24* for very long to see the noir elements in it. The focus on crime (namely terrorism), the stunning amount of violence; the cynical air of many of *24*'s lead characters; the presence of several femmes fatales, and the stoic resolve of the show's protagonist, Jack Bauer (Kiefer Sutherland) are all suggestive of the noir style. I shall argue specifically that in addition to fitting the profile of the noir protagonist, Jack Bauer is also an example of Albert Camus' existential hero, the man of revolt.

Before turning my attention to Jack Bauer, however, it is first important to establish that *24* is an example of the noir style. For some, *24* may seem more obviously an example of the action genre than of TV noir. Certainly, it bears action trademarks. The plot moves at a blistering pace. Action sequences command a substantial portion of each episode. And of course, the show capitalizes on its audience's interest in violent spectacle: explosions are frequent and sizeable, car chases are commonplace, danger is always imminent, and weapons are ubiquitous and consistently employed. While *24* has action to spare, however, it counts as a TV noir series because it is rendered in the noir style.

24 and Noir

While most people are familiar with instances of film noir, it is unlikely that many would be able to offer a succinct definition of it. I shall use the term noir here to refer not only to the classical period (generally recognized as beginning in 1941 with John Huston's *The Maltese Falcon* and ending in 1958 with Orson Welles's *Touch of Evil*), but also to a contemporary style that is inspired by that period and exemplifies prominent features of it.

One of the most notable features of noir is its focus on crime. As Jason Holt remarks in his essay "A Darker Shade: Realism in Neo-Noir," the term noir refers "essentially (among other things) to a type of crime film."[1] As Holt rightly notes, works rendered in the noir style place a central focus on crime. In particular, they emphasize violent crime and moral corruption. Moreover, these works also tend to focus on individuals who are either enmeshed in, or involved in the detection of, crime. *24* clearly exhibits this sort of focus. Centered on the agents and activities of the Counter Terrorism Unit (CTU), it concerns itself principally with threats to national security. Since first airing in 2001, *24* has placed an unwavering emphasis on violent crime. The criminal plots on which it has focused have ranged from plans for political assassination to biological warfare. CTU agents have sought enemies varying from religious zealots from foreign lands to corrupt members of our own government. While *24* manifests other elemental features of noir, it clearly exhibits the focus on crime that is characteristic of this style.

Another feature characteristic of noir is a certain cynical air. As its name suggests, central to noir is its invocation of a dark mood. Indeed, noir is frequently noted as displaying an "existential attitude toward life" insofar as it generally inspires a "mood of pessimism, loneliness, dread, and despair."[2] Certainly, "bleakly existential" themes are present throughout the corpus of classical noir films and are emblematic of contemporary works characterized as neo-noir.[3] While the fact that the good guy always seems to win in *24* does ultimately inspire optimism, it does not eliminate the program's cynical tone. Like classical works of noir, *24* is "expressly dark and laden with conflict."[4] Essential to its cynicism is the fact that the conflict upon which the show focuses never receives any true resolution. As I shall discuss in detail later, the characters in *24* fight against an invincible enemy: terrorism. Though the end of each season brings viewers the satisfaction that comes from the eradication of the immediate terrorist threat, *24* never creates the impression that a unilateral victory has been achieved. Rather, it fosters the sense that the peace and security achieved are tenuous and that new and greater dangers are lurking. In addition, *24* attends quite explicitly to the sober themes of "meaningless existence" and "moral ambiguity" commonly addressed in noir.[5] The menace of meaninglessness (e.g., the threat of a loss of order and purpose) is evident both in dangers like the decimation of multiple urban centers through nuclear means (season 4) and, more subtly, in situations where prominent characters struggle with the loss of loved ones to senseless violence (e.g., both Jack Bauer and Tony Almeida (Carlos Barnard) lose their wives and are brought to crisis by their losses). The theme of moral ambiguity is demonstrated in a variety of ways, including the focus on corruption and, more obviously, through *24*'s explicit consideration of the ethics of torture.

Certain formal elements are as central to noir as a focus on crime and a cynical tone. Indeed, "noir is a genre identified by a variety of stylistic conventions: unsettling or otherwise odd camera angles, the dramatic use of shadow and light, hard-boiled dialogue, settings that emphasize isolation and loneliness."[6] *24* exhibits all these stylistic conventions of noir. Like classical noir, it employs techniques such as skewed camera angles, rough edits, and its signature split screen (accompanied by temporal countdown) to further an overriding sense of urgency, even "disorientation."[7] Likewise, though not rendered in black and white, dramatic contrast of light and shadow are frequently utilized, most obviously in the grim depiction of setting in *24*. For example, a sense of darkness and desolation pervades the scene at the headquarters of CTU. With the exception of the offices depicted on *CSI* (whose agents are frequently left to conduct their investigations by flash-light), there are very few television offices with such a dark, uninviting, even sterile interior. Obviously, rendering the setting in such a manner furthers the impression of danger to the extent that CTU, the symbolic haven of the forces of good, is itself imbued with darkness. Likewise, the dialogue of *24* mimics the hard-boiled dialogue of classic film noir and detective fiction; conversations are unembellished and focus on the immediate. Moreover, the central innovation of *24*, namely that it is presented in real time, fur-thers not only the program's dramatic tension but also its realism. As Holt discusses, gritty realism is also a principal, but often overlooked, formal feature of noir.

The presence of certain character types is a final feature elemental to noir and evident in *24*. The femme fatale and a particular sort of protagonist are characteristic of noir. Contributing to the air of cynicism elemental to noir is the presence of the femme fatale; Holt states that she is "one of the mainstays and most salient icons" of noir.[8] As the term indicates, the femme fatale not only dupes and manipulates the protagonist (and others), she also causes his (and classically her own) downfall. In *24*, viewers are witness to two prominent examples of a femme fatale: Nina Myers (Sarah Clarke) and Sherry Palmer (Penny Johnson Jerald).

Though Nina's role as a femme fatale is not made evident until the end of the first season (a fact that magnifies her role to the extent that she dupes the audience), she is an obvious example of a malevolent female who "beguile[s]" and manipulates others to further the achievement of her own selfish ends.[9] Though she does not ultimately cause the downfall of *24*'s protagonist, Jack Bauer, she robs him of something as precious to him as his own life, his wife, Teri (Leslie Hope).

Less surprising to audiences is the discovery that Sherry Palmer is a femme fatale. Portrayed unsympathetically from the start, the revelation of Sherry's illicit activities does not come as much of a surprise to viewers. Nonetheless, her actions arouse indignation to the extent that she seeks to sabotage not only her husband but also the presidency. Whereas the diabolical women of neo-noirs often "escape justice," in classic fashion neither Nina nor Sherry does.[10] Instead, their sinister plots are foiled, and both pay for them with their lives.

Jack Bauer: Noir Protagonist

Most significant for present purposes is the fact that Jack Bauer fits the profile of the noir hero. Characteristic of noir is the presence of a strong male protagonist, a hardened but sympathetic figure who struggles, sometimes unsuccessfully, against violence and corruption. Conventionally a detective or an individual otherwise involved in the investigation of crime, the classic noir protagonist tends to be an intense but emotionally guarded individual whose integrity is put to the test by circumstance. Typically, this figure is plagued not only by external threats but also by internal demons and his redemption—if it is to be achieved—requires the overcoming of both. Stereotypically, the noir hero enters into a relationship with a femme fatale whose influence either causes his downfall or, in the very, least frustrates his success. Classic examples of the noir hero include Bogart's Philip Marlowe and Sam Spade; more contemporary ones are William Hurt's Ned Racine (*Body Heat,* Lawrence Kasdan, 1981) and Michael Douglas's Nick Curran (*Basic Instinct,* Paul Verhoeven, 1992).

Though unquestionably an action hero, *24*'s Jack Bauer also exemplifies many of the traits of the noir protagonist. As such, he is an action hero rendered in the noir style. As the lead agent in CTU, Jack displays an unwavering focus on violent crime. A modern rendition of the hard-boiled private detective, Jack, in his whole being, is devoted to the detection and prevention of crime. Armed with classic wits and modern technology, he ventures into the dark and baleful world of terrorists and arms dealers in an effort to foil plots aimed at the destruction of national security.

Also consistent with the profile of the noir protagonist, Jack's exposure to criminality has hardened him and engendered a cynical outlook. Though his fierce devotion to family and deep attachment to romantic interests like Audrey Raines (Kim Raver) make it clear to viewers that Jack is a man of strong feeling, he normally keeps that side of his character hidden. Instead, he is typically aloof, cool, detached. Interestingly, rather than compromise the viewer's appreciation of Jack, his detached demeanor augments it. It furthers the audience's sympathy for him because the emotional reserve that Jack displays seems not natural to him but, instead, an attitude necessitated by his professional (and personal) commitments. Jack is an extraordinarily committed individual. His thoroughgoing commitment to the maintenance of law and order motivates his professional activities and demands great personal sacrifice, such as the degree of intimacy he can achieve with people. To the extent that emotional attachments could interfere with Jack's ability to function professionally, he consciously maintains a certain distance from others. Though he seems to long for connection, insofar as his life is in constant jeopardy, he often discourages others from developing attachments to him, in an effort to protect them from the losses that a relationship with him might bring. Thus, like many of the classic noir protagonists, Jack is portrayed as a loner who suffers from, rather than seeks, isolation.

Another noir protagonist feature Jack displays is his involvement with a femme fatale. Though her malevolent nature is not revealed until the end of the first season, a central element in the first three seasons of 24 is Jack's relationship with coworker and former lover Nina Meyers. Initially, viewers are encouraged to sympathize with her because Jack rejects a relationship with her in favor of reconciliation with his estranged wife, Teri. However, as the first season progresses, greater suspicion is cast on Nina's character. These doubts are confirmed in the season finale, when Nina is not only identified as the mole in CTU, she also kills several people, including Jack's wife. Subsequent seasons reveal her to be even more malign and diabolical. Indeed, Nina becomes Jack's nemesis, not just taking his wife, but brokering the nation's security itself.

Last, like most noir heroes, Jack Bauer battles external threats and internal demons. This is shown most obviously in the third season as Jack fights both an arms-dealing organization and his own heroin addiction. Born of vulnerability in the wake of his wife's death and professional necessity (that is, in order to develop a successful cover with the arms dealers), Jack's addiction proves a serious obstacle to his success in the third season. Indeed, the external threats he confronts actually help him conquer his addiction by providing him with a clear purpose. In the greater scheme of things, Jack's addiction is significant because it humanizes this typically superhuman hero, making it easier for audiences to identify and sympathize with him. Moreover, it both contributes to the noir character of the series (by showing the most inviolable character to be susceptible to corruption) and magnifies the success of the hero (to the extent that he conquers both external and internal evil).

Ultimately, Jack Bauer exemplifies the traits traditionally associated with the noir protagonist. Like the femmes fatales of the series, Jack fits the classic noir hero model more than the neo-noir one. Whereas the protagonists of neo-noir are as (or more) likely to succumb to corruption and meet violent ends as emerge victorious, the Production Code that dominated the classic period of noir encouraged more optimistic outcomes. Though protagonists sometimes paid with their lives, evil was typically punished and good (in some form) conventionally prevailed. Thus far, and in keeping with the conventions that influence the action genre, justice prevails in *24*. Though it is constantly imperiled, it is protected by the implacable Jack Bauer, a noir-style hero who seems incapable of failure.

Camus' "Man of Revolt"

Having demonstrated that *24* is representative of the noir style and that *24*'s lead character, Jack Bauer, shares notable features with the stereotypical noir protagonist, to determine whether Jack also fits the description of Camus' existential hero, it is now necessary to offer some background on Camus' "man of revolt." To discern the qualities of Camus' figure, one must first understand his theory of the absurd, because absurdity is what Camus' existential hero revolts against.

Like most existentialists, Camus maintains that existence is absurd. More correctly, he contends that humans perceive existence as being absurd. To say that existence is absurd is to say that it lacks any underlying order or purpose. Rather than proclaim that the world is absolutely devoid of reason and purpose, Camus simply says he does not observe them. He states, "This world in itself is not reasonable, that is all that can be said." What Camus says is certain is "[the human] appetite for the absolute . . . and the impossibility of reducing this world to a rational and reasonable principle."[11]

Given that one cannot know for certain whether existence is absurd, Camus contends that absurdity is not properly a state of affairs but a "feeling." He describes it as the feeling of profound discomfort and "dissatisfaction" that results from our inability to know whether the world has any essential order or meaning. As he explains, "the absurd is born of the confrontation between the human need [for order and meaning] and the unreasonable silence of the world." The feeling of absurdity springs from "that divorce between the mind that desires and the world that disappoints." It is the product of a relation that results when one combines a rational agent with rational hopes and "an appetite for clarity" with a world that fails to fulfill that agent's expectations. Because the world is only perceived as being absurd by virtue of its failure to meet the human standard of reason, Camus states, "the absurd depends as much upon man as on the world. . . . The world in itself is [simply] not reasonable . . . what is absurd is the confrontation of this irrational and the wild longing for clarity whose call echoes in the human heart."[12] In short, the feeling of absurdity arises when one becomes conscious that neither existence generally, nor any part of it, has the inherent order or meaning one would like it to have.

According to Camus, various things compel the feeling of absurdity. In his essay "An Absurd Reasoning," he cites awareness of one's mortality, the "primitive hostility" of nature, the "mechanical [repetition of] life," and the strangeness of individuals as common catalysts for the feeling. Regardless of the cause, the feeling of absurdity erupts when "one day the 'why' arises and . . . awakens consciousness . . . [of] the absurd." Though Camus believes everyone is vulnerable to the appearance of absurdity, he acknowledges that not everyone experiences this unsettling and unwanted affect. While he contends that the feeling of absurdity can strike "at any street corner," he admits that few become fully conscious of it and that most who do find a way to escape it. Though most may elude it, Camus believes that once one has experienced the feeling of absurdity, one is changed forever. When one experiences the feeling, "the universe [is] suddenly divested of illusions and lights, [and one] feels alien, a stranger." Indeed, formal awareness of absurdity evokes such powerful feelings of anxiety and estrangement that, Camus claims, "there is a direct connection between this feeling and a longing for death." Indeed, the focus of his essay "An Absurd Reasoning" is to determine "the relationship between the absurd and suicide, [and] the exact degree to which suicide is a solution to the absurd."[13]

According to Camus, there are three possible responses to the absurd: actual suicide, "philosophical suicide," and revolt. While he concedes that suicide is a solution to the absurd, he is emphatic that it is not the ideal response. Absurdity is the product of a relation. As such, Camus likens it to an equation. To have absurdity, one needs both a rational agent and a world that fails to conform to the expectations of that individual. As he explains, actual suicide and philosophical suicide succeed in "solving" the problem of absurdity by removing one of the necessary terms of the equation; these solutions are not satisfactory, though because they come at too great a cost to the individual. Actual suicide eradicates absurdity, but the rational agent pays for this solution with her life. Philosophical suicide's solution is not as extreme, but it is also undesirable because it eradicates absurdity by denying the irrationality of the world, the rationality of the agent, or some combination of the two. Whether one believes that there is an order to the universe or takes a religious leap of faith, Camus asserts that dishonesty is central to all instances of philosophical suicide. It requires a forfeiture of reason, specifically the singular opportunity that it affords humans to critically observe, reflect upon, and become conscious of, existence. As such, Camus contends philosophical suicide demands a "sacrifice of the intellect" and a "masking [of] the evidence." To the extent that most people refuse to accept the evidence of absurdity, Camus contends that most people have committed philosophical suicide. While he admits that "the point is to live" and prefers philosophical to actual suicide, he finds the former lamentable because it precludes our capacity for lucid consciousness, a defining feature of our humanity.[14]

Ultimately, Camus recommends revolt as a response to absurdity. Unlike actual and philosophical suicides, which eradicate absurdity through the annihilation of the individual or the "negation of [her] reason," revolt is the one response to absurdity that preserves the rational agent and her awareness of the absurd. Where Camus sees both actual and philosophical suicide as forms of submission to the absurd, revolt challenges it by "preserv[ing] the very thing that crushes." Revolt asks me not only to acknowledge absurdity lucidly and unflinchingly, but also to "struggle" against it by making meaning in the face of meaninglessness. The individual who epitomizes revolt, who Camus calls the man of revolt, lives in a state of "permanent revolution." Rather than buy a reprieve from the anguish that absurdity elicits by paying with his life or his reason, the man of revolt preserves his being, his dignity, and his intellectual "integrity" by remaining "on that dizzying crest" that is lucid awareness of absurdity. As Camus indicates, the man of revolt accepts "a crushing fate without resignation." He not only persists, he lives "to the maximum, . . . solely with what he knows . . . without appeal."[15]

There are several traits characteristic of, indeed essential to, the man of revolt. The two principal qualities are lucidity and courage. Above all, the man of revolt is characterized by lucid awareness of existence, specifically its apparent absurdity. Consciousness that existence lacks any discernable order and purpose is a prerequisite for the man of revolt. Indeed, Camus states, "a constantly conscious soul is the ideal."[16] Unlike the person who is either ignorant or in denial of absurdity, the man of revolt "knows the whole extent of his wretched condition."[17] Moreover, he accepts it "without weakness."[18] This strength is the second characteristic of Camus' existential hero. To revolt, one must not only realize absurdity but also courageously confront and actively resist it. Camus' man of revolt displays this stalwart strength. He accepts the futility of life and his own "obscurity" stoically, "without consolation."[19] For Camus, the man of revolt is simultaneously a "tragic" figure and a "hero."[20] He is tragic because of his insight, heroic because he defies the disorder that surrounds him. He embodies a stoic and "solitary courage."[21] He is a "determined soul who restores the "majesty" to his life by refusing to be overthrown by the absurd.[22]

Though they might seem at odds with each other, estrangement and social concern are also characteristic of the man of revolt. There are two main causes for the alienation that affects the man of revolt. The first comes from his lucidity. Despite his "insistence upon familiarity, and [his] appetite for clarity" the man of revolt knows that the world does not comply with his demand for reason. As Camus explains, while "a world that can be explained even with bad reasons is still a familiar world," absurdity divests the world of its reason and its familiarity. It makes man "a stranger," an "exile."[23] The second cause for estrangement lies in the fact that the man of revolt embraces truths the majority of people resist. To the extent that honesty is the defining feature of the man of revolt and most people are in denial about the nature of the human condition, the man of revolt becomes the herald of truths no one wants to hear. As such, he often ends up a "social outsider." Though he is frequently estranged from others, compassion is nonetheless characteristic of the man of revolt. Precisely because of the knowledge he possesses, he appreciates the "value of human life" and the fact that humans are all "in the same boat."[24] Because of the awareness he possesses, the man of revolt displays not only a general "concern for the lives of others," he actively works for their betterment.[25] Thus, the portrait Camus paints of his man of revolt is of a resolute, proud, and highly principled figure, one whose strength and commitment are unmatched and whose insight breeds both a sense of solidarity with others and obligation to them.

Jack Bauer: Existential Hero

Having enumerated the features of Camus' man of revolt, it should already be clear that there are striking similarities between *24*'s Jack Bauer and Camus' existential hero. Indeed, Jack displays all of the characteristics discussed. Most notably, he exhibits the principal traits of the man of revolt, namely lucidity and courage.

Whether it is natural to him or an ability born of experience, *24*'s Jack Bauer displays remarkable insight. He is astute. He displays real acumen. Where those who surround him frequently misread individuals and situations, he evidences an uncanny ability to read both people and circumstances. Arguably, Jack's capacity to read particular individuals and situations is engendered by his general skepticism, namely his refusal to trust appearances, his loyalty to the evidence, and his reluctance to regard anyone as above reproach. For example, until late in the fifth season, few, save Jack, are willing to suspect President Charles Logan (Gregory Itzin) of any serious impropriety. Though it is difficult for Jack to harbor suspicion of Logan because he holds the office Jack both admires and serves, Jack senses that Logan is not only generally unfit but also corrupt. When evidence of Logan's unscrupulous arms dealings and involvement in former president Palmer's assassination is brought to light, Jack's suspicions are confirmed. Nonetheless, his superiors resist taking a sitting president into custody, and Jack must proceed without their support. As this example shows, Jack Bauer bears similarity to Camus' man of revolt in that he displays true intellectual integrity. Like Camus' existential hero, Jack "maintain[s] and defend[s] any truths that [he] discovers" regardless of their palatability.[26] Like Camus, Jack recognizes that "seeking what is true is not seeking what is desirable."[27] He commands viewers' esteem with his intelligence and unflinching honesty.

In addition to lucidity, Jack displays phenomenal courage. In the mere five days of his life to which viewers have been witness, he has risked that life countless times. Virtually every episode showcases Jack risking life and limb to preserve the safety and lives of others. Two powerful examples of Jack's bravery in season 5 are when he risks exposure to deadly nerve gas in order to save the lives of his compatriots at CTU and when he rushes into a volatile fire at a natural gas company to capture a terrorist. Though viewers certainly admire Jack for his wits, he captures their hearts even more successfully through his astonishing bravery and unwavering commitment to protect the public and defend cherished national ideals (e.g., democracy, the presidency). While critics are correct to note that Jack's bravery and dedication at times push the envelope of plausibility, it is precisely because Jack rises to every imaginable challenge that he epitomizes the ideal of absolute courage under fire.

Just as *24*'s Jack Bauer embodies the principal traits of the man of revolt, he also displays the secondary qualities of Camus' existential hero. Clearly, he displays engagement. It is hard to imagine someone more engaged than Jack Bauer. He clearly illustrates the existential maxim that nothing is achieved save through action. Moreover, analogous to Camus' man of revolt Jack's engagement is born of his awareness that the state of the world is determined not by some antecedent design but by the actions of individuals.

Jack also displays real passion. He feels powerfully for people, for his principles, and for life. Thus, like the man of revolt, he "lives intensely," doing everything to the maximum and living every day like it was his last.[28] Again, this intense passion is an outcome in large part of Jack's awareness of his personal situation (e.g., the extreme risk of his occupation and his expendability) and the human condition generally (e.g., the brevity and fragility of life).

Finally, like both the existential hero and the noir protagonist, Jack displays both estrangement from and concern for others. Though he works side by side with CTU and other government agents and is generally esteemed by them, Jack stands apart. While he has strong friendships and displays fierce loyalties, Jack is a loner. His detachment from others is primarily a function of his character. Specifically, his recognition of the dangers implicit in his profession and his awareness of the tasks and sacrifices it might require lead him to be emotionally reserved. Just as Camus' man of revolt is described as displaying "stoical detachment," Jack Bauer is likewise stoic in his reserve.[29] While he has deep attachments (the most prominent being to his daughter, Kim), Jack is anything but effusive in the articulation of his sentiments. Rather than a consequence of some sort of emotional inadequacy, it is Jack's commitment to preserve and defend that forces him to sacrifice a certain intimacy with others. Not only is he aware that allowing individuals to get close to him puts them at risk (not only of losing him but also of being a target for his enemies), he also knows that he cannot let personal feelings preclude his ability to do what needs to be done. Thus, to protect those he cares about, and to ensure he can do his job, Jack consciously disassociates from others. Jack's estrangement is made evident in a variety of ways. From subtle techniques (e.g., his difficulty making eye contact during intimate moments) to more obvious signs of isolation (e.g., his exile at the end of season 4), Jack's distance from others and the motives behind it elicit both viewers' sympathy and respect and in doing so further the audience's appreciation of his character.

Having demonstrated that Jack Bauer displays various traits of the existential hero, it is necessary to show that he also fulfills the defining task of the man of revolt, namely that he combats absurdity. After all, while it may be easy for readers to see that Jack exemplifies characteristics like "lucidity" and "courage," it may be more difficult for them to recognize how he could be said to be revolting against the absurd. Admittedly, it is not immediately obvious that Jack is waging war on absurdity; for most people, absurdity seems both an abstract and elusive philosophical concept. Though his targets are often elusive, the threats Jack seeks to vanquish are concrete, as opposed to conceptual. Alongside his colleagues at CTU, his mission is to thwart the activities of, and capture or kill, terrorists who threaten national security.

While the enemies Jack faces are designed to represent plausible threats to national security, they also are symbolic of the absurd, in two main ways. First, some threats illustrate the absurd by virtue of their target. The clearest example of this is the perennial threat of assassination to David Palmer (the realization of which opens season 5). Second only to Jack Bauer, David Palmer (Dennis Haysbert) embodies strength, integrity, and valor. Throughout the series, particularly during his tenure as president, he is representative of order and security. He is the figurative bastion of meaning and purpose for the nation. By virtue of what David Palmer represents, the threat (or success) of his assassination symbolizes the threat or actual loss of order and meaning. As characters like Mike Novick (Jude Cicolella) express subsequent to the apparent death of the president in season 4, a nation without a strong presidential figure is a nation adrift, a nation whose security, purpose, and identity are compromised.

The second way the threats presented on *24* embody the absurd is through their scale: in each successive season the dangers have magnified in scale. While the threat in the first season was limited to a presidential candidate, subsequent seasons have terrorists seizing control of hundreds of people and gaining control of biological, chemical, and nuclear weapons capable of annihilating millions. Indeed, while Jack is officially charged with protecting the national interest, because of the scale of the threats he combats, he has in fact become a guardian of global security. The extreme scale of the threats shown in recent seasons allows them to function as representatives of absurdity. Because of their scope, namely the breadth and magnitude of the dangers presented, threats like the release of weapons-grade nerve gas in multiple major metropolitan areas in the United States (season 5) symbolize the absurd. Though none of the terrorist plots on *24* have ever achieved its desired end, if it did, not only would millions of lives be lost, life as we know it would be lost as well. To the extent that the success of any of these threats would bring catastrophic loss of life, extensive damage to the nation's infrastructure, and serious social and political unrest, they effectively symbolize the danger posed by the absurd. They do so to the extent that their fulfillment would compromise (or eradicate) the order and meaning we enjoy. The terrorists' achievement of intermediate aims (a device consistently used on *24* to create a sense of urgency and suspense) provides a disquieting glimpse of what would result if their agenda were fulfilled. For example, the chaos and panic subsequent to the release of a biological contagion in the building (season 4) and the violence and lawlessness in Los Angeles after President Logan's declaration of martial law (season 5) illustrate—on a small scale—what would follow if the goals of the terrorists were achieved. Clearly, then, Jack's battle is a symbolic fight against the absurd. While the threats of terrorism and absurdity are themselves unvanquishable, insofar as Jack Bauer stands ready to face any challenge, he represents the first line of defense against both.

Because of the traits he exhibits and the activities in which he is engaged, *24*'s Jack Bauer can be called not only a noir hero but an existential one. The kinship between Jack Bauer and the man of revolt is made complete when one notes that Camus describes his existential hero as a "conqueror."[30] Ultimately, Camus describes the man of revolt as a warrior because he must actively combat absurdity, namely in the form of violence and lawlessness. Camus uses the analogy of war and describes his existential hero as "militant" in order to emphasize the threat posed by the absurd and the means required to confront it.[31] Camus recognizes that to establish order and security, the man of revolt needs strength and discipline and, like a soldier, must sometimes utilize violent methods. Though Camus abhors violence, he admits that it may be necessary for the man of revolt to employ violence in establish peace and justice. What distinguishes the violence used by the man of revolt is that its goal is the "establishment of non-violence" and the achievement of "freedom for each and justice for all."[32] Clearly, Jack Bauer not only figuratively battles absurdity, he is literally an agent of the law. While he is empowered to use—and often employs—extreme means, like Camus' man of revolt, he derives no satisfaction from the exercise of force. Instead, he sees it as a necessary evil justified by the extreme threats to which he responds. Jack is indeed an example of the conqueror Camus describes. Though the commonplace notion of a conqueror is suggestive of an individual whose exploits are geared as much toward personal gain as anything else, Camus' conqueror humbly battles absurdity for the benefit of all. Stoically overcoming every challenge with which he is presented, at great personal risk and without any interest in renown, Jack Bauer embodies Camus' notion of an existential hero. To the extent that he confronts and diffuses threats that embody the absurd, he puts up the sort of resistance to absurdity that defines the man of revolt.

Notes

Many thanks to Steven M. Sanders and Aeon J. Skoble for their insightful comments on earlier drafts of this essay.

1. Jason Holt, "A Darker Shade: Realism in Neo-Noir," in *The Philosophy of Film Noir*, ed. Mark T. Conard (Lexington: University of Kentucky Press, 2006), 24.

2. Robert Portofiro, "No Way Out: Existential Motifs in the Film Noir" (1976), reprinted in *Film Noir Reader*, ed. Alain Silver and James Ursini (New York: Limelight, 1996), 80; Mark T. Conard, "Nietzsche and the Meaning and Definition of Noir," in Conard, *The Philosophy of Film Noir*, 12.

3. Holt, "A Darker Shade," 24.

4. Steven M. Sanders, "Film Noir and the Meaning of Life," in Conard, *The Philosophy of Film Noir*, 103.

5. Ibid., 91, 92.

6. Aeon J. Skoble, "Moral Clarity and Practical Reason in Film Noir," in Conard, *The Philosophy of Film Noir*, 41.

7. Conard, "Nietzsche and the Meaning and Definition of Noir," 19.

8. Holt, "A Darker Shade," 27.

9. Ibid., 27.

10. Ibid., 28.

11. Albert Camus, "An Absurd Reasoning," in *The Myth of Sisyphus and Other Essays* (New York: Vintage Books, 1955), 16, 38.

12. Ibid., 5, 23, 21, 37, 13, 16.

13. Ibid., 11, 10, 9, 5.

14. Ibid., 31, 28, 37, 48.

15. Ibid., 31, 23, 40, 37, 46, 39.

16. Ibid., 47.

17. Albert Camus, "The Myth of Sisyphus," in *The Myth of Sisyphus and Other Essays,* 90.

18. Albert Camus, "An Absurd Man" in *The Myth of Sisyphus and Other Essays,* 68.

19. Camus, "An Absurd Reasoning," 30, 44.

20. Camus, "The Myth of Sisyphus," 89, 89.

21. Camus, "An Absurd Man," 53.

22. Camus, "An Absurd Reasoning," 31, 40.

23. Ibid., 13, 5.

24. John Cruikshank, *Albert Camus and the Literature of Revolt* (Oxford: Oxford University Press, 1959), 155, 94; Albert Camus, *The Plague* (New York: Vintage Books, 1948), 180.

25. Cruikshank, *Albert Camus and the Literature of Revolt,* 107.

26. Ibid., 61.

27. Camus, "An Absurd Reasoning," 31.

28. Cruikshank, *Albert Camus and the Literature of Revolt,* 70

29. Ibid., 24.

30. Camus, "An Absurd Man," 64.

31. Cruikshank, *Albert Camus and the Literature of Revolt,* 83.

32. Ibid., 114, 130.

CARNIVÀLE KNOWLEDGE: GIVE ME THAT OLD-TIME NOIR RELIGION

Eric Bronson

In the first season of HBO's *Carnivàle,* a vagabond, not quite as dirty as the others, sits around a campfire, largely keeping to himself. As the liquor gets passed around, and stories told, the runaway Methodist minister loosens up enough to speak. What has brought him so low, he is asked. Did he lose his girlfriend? His job? After taking a hearty swig, Brother Justin despairingly replies, "I lost my God."

In many ways, Brother Justin's response is vintage noir. As has been well documented, film noir first rose to popularity in the 1940s and '50s, at a time when Europe and America experienced real crises of faith. The wanton destruction of World War II, the unfathomable inhumanity behind the Holocaust, and the ensuing bankruptcy of moral will spurred necessary revolutions in philosophy and art. Traditional Faustian battle lines of good and evil were blurred; real acts of heroism were hard to come by. Instead, a moral malaise seemed to infect everyone, from the highest reaches of academe to the most vibrant churches of Christendom. In philosophy's new field of existentialism, Camus' *Plague,* and Sartre's *Nausea* describe the human condition in stark and morose terms. It is perhaps the logical conclusion to Germany's prewar pessimism, a time in the nineteenth century when philosophers like Arthur Schopenhauer and Friedrich Nietzsche explained our world as inherently meaningless, aesthetically pallid, and morally weak. Where once religion had filled such gaping voids, now there appeared to be nothing. With our traditional markers blown apart, we were left to our "human, all too human" failings to help us through the night. And if our faith in God were not yet dead, as Nietzsche predicted, Martin Heidegger famously wrote in 1938 that such a spiritual quagmire would at least be the impetus for the gods to flee.

Film noir, then, builds its themes and characters from these existentialist worldviews. As Steven M. Sanders writes: "Noir themes and moods include despair, paranoia, and nihilism; an atmosphere of claustrophobic entrapment; a nightmarish sense of loneliness and alienation; a purposelessness fostered in part by feelings of estrangement from one's own past even as one seems driven to a compulsive confrontation with that past. Film noir presents us with moral ambiguity, shifting identities, and impending doom."[1] In 2003, *Carnivàle* first hit the airwaves and invoked all of the above classic noir themes. The two-year series followed a fictional traveling carnival troupe as they meandered through the American Midwest of the dust-bowl 1930s. Though classic noir uses harrowing cityscapes to highlight the suffocating loneliness, *Carnivàle*'s use of drab and dreary landscapes created a similar effect. "I think it's about alienation," *Carnivàle*'s writer, director, and executive producer Daniel Knauf explains, "what it's like to be alienated from the rest of the species."[2] Two separate story lines emerged in the series and had only begun to come together by its abrupt end. On the one side was the aforementioned Brother Justin (Clancy Brown), the old-time preacher who was failing in his attempt to bring the Christian God to his largely Godless community. On the other side were the carnies: Samson (Michael J. Anderson), the dwarfish manager who takes his orders from the invisible management behind the curtain, Sofie (Clea Duvall), the fortuneteller constantly tortured by her mother's telepathic nagging; her admirer, Jonesy (Tim DeKay); and Ben (Nick Stahl), the lead character with mysterious powers, most of which are unknown to him and only vaguely known to others. Ben is somewhat unwillingly picked up by the carnies; given odd jobs; and left to make his way in the small community of snake handlers, magicians, quacks, and geeks. The most intriguing aspect of the critically acclaimed show, however, is that many of the noir themes are explored within a distinctly religious framework. As Brother Justin battles with his identity, he invokes traditional biblical themes in his sermons and his struggles. Knauf himself tells the story of good clashing with evil along the more traditional lines of his heroes J. R. R. Tolkien and Charles Dickens, two writers who incorporated religious themes in their writings.

So what is going on here? Is there really such a thing as religious noir? There is, of course, and even though the unbelievers get all the artistic credit, some of the most disturbing, thought-provoking, even frightening noir stories are told through the prism of Judeo-Christian ideas. As noir, though, it cannot be the plastic, smiley, Ned Flanders brand of suburban American religion. When Brother Justin whips his congregation into a rousing rendition of "Give Me That Old Time Religion," he uses the Sunday service to invoke the despair and alienation, the loneliness and exile of the fire-branding, gut-wrenching Old Testament prophets. Any noirish struggle between good and evil must involve some kind of repudiation of the typical prewar smug satisfaction with God's world. But that kind of painful rejection does not need to be blasphemous. From St. Augustine's *Confessions* to St. John's *Dark Night of the Soul,* we are reminded that violently clawing against God's will can summon a kind of spiritual grace. When Brother Justin faces his own inner demons and devils, he reinforces old-time religious fervor, while at the same time invoking distinctly modern existential ideals. *Carnivàle* has its roots in a long-standing religious noir tradition, one that includes film and literary noir and dates back to the existentialist philosophies of Fyodor Dostoyevsky and Søren Kierkegaard.

Carnivàle and Religious Film Noir

One example of a noir protagonist struggling with religious conceptions of good and evil is Robert Mitchum's haunting portrayal of Reverend Harry Powell in Charles Laughton's *Night of the Hunter* (1955). In truth, there is not much struggle going on—he is pure evil. From the outset, before we ever meet Reverend Powell, we are reminded that the Book of Matthew cautions us, "Beware of *false* prophets, which come to you in *sheep's* clothing, but *inwardly* they are ravening *wolves*" (7:15). We soon realize that the "Reverend" is only really interested in God when his Lord shows him where to find the next unsuspecting widow with the hidden loot. He has the word "Love" tattooed on the knuckles of one of his hands, "Hate" on the other. Powell is quick to show eager onlookers the "story of life." Clasping his hands together is a deathlike grip, he explains, "These fingers, dear hearts, is always a-warring and a-tugging, one against the other." He then calls out the struggle like a horse race, with Love eventually winning out by a nose. Christian love does in the end win out, but only thanks to the humility of old Mrs. Cooper (Lillian Gish), who takes Powell's newly adopted children into her orphanage. In one of the more frightening scenes of film noir, the Reverend sits on a stump outside the window, while Mrs. Cooper sits inside in her rocking chair, a loaded rifle in her lap. Both patiently await the coming of the night, singing Reverend Powell's favorite gospel hymn, Elisha

Hoffman's "Leaning on the Everlasting Arms." Hate is overcome when Mrs. Cooper shoots Powell in the leg and calls the police. "It's a hard world for little things," she sighs, her work, for the time being, finished.

In *Night of the Hunter*, like in all good film noir, comfort is hard to find. The children, John and Pearl Harper, had been on the run from Powell after their father was hung by the state, their mother murdered by the Reverend, and their only other ally too drunk to help in their time of need. By the time Mrs. Cooper finds them sleeping on the river, John (Billy Chapin) is understandably suspicious. Only the story of Moses touches his trust; for the Old Testament Moses, like all good noir characters, is alone, a stranger in a strange land, a frail and damaged protector of the poor, thrown unwillingly into heroism and forever denied entrance into the promised land.

Four years before Mitchum's frightening portrayal, director Robert Bresson brought noir fans a more nuanced priest from the French countryside. In his richly layered *Diary of a Country Priest (Journal d'un curé de campagne),* Bresson uses the more common noir technique of voice-over to convey the tragic downfall of a kind and gentle priest of Ambricourt (Claude Laydu). Bresson's young priest (adapted liberally from Catholic writer Georges Bernanos's novel) is disliked almost immediately as he sets up shop in his new parish. Ignored by the adults and ridiculed by the children, the nameless priest can do little to create a meaningful Christian community. The best he can hope for, as the more practical priest of Torcy explains, is to "make order all day long," knowing full well "that the night will blow away yesterday's work."

Unlike Reverend Powell, however, Bresson's priest is not so easy to figure. Like most film noir characters of the time, he suffers insomnia, drinks too much (locals gossip that he was born pickled in alcohol), suffers a nameless pain in the "pit of the stomach," and walks through the drizzly, indifferent land moody and taciturn. Long before *Carnivàle's* Brother Justin suffered his own crisis of faith, the French priest sounds the existentialist's mantra, "God has left me, of this I'm sure."

His physical body slowly breaking down, his firmest beliefs wearing thin, a life without God can bring him no easy peace. He cannot take mindless pleasure in the hedonistic lifestyle of the young partygoers at the dancehall across from his flat. "I needed prayer like I needed air in my lungs," he writes in his diary. There is a riveting scene at the doctor's office, where his ailing health is confirmed. The doctor quickly challenges him on spiritual matters, finally commenting, "You'd never get through the day if you dwelt on such thoughts." The doctor is relentless, arguing the many benefits of denying God's world once and for all. "We're at war," he says confidently. "Face up to it." The priest notes how the doctor's confidence is false, speaking as he does in "a tone that gives away a deeply wounded soul." True enough, the doctor cannot finally face up to a world without meaning, and, like Ivan endorses in Dostoyevsky's *The Brothers Karamazov,* the doctor commits suicide, another symbolic victim of the postwar meaninglessness that hovers over so much of Europe.

The priest refuses to take that way out, however. And though he understands himself to be "the prisoner of holy agony," he will continue to do God's work on earth. In another moving scene, he converts the Countess (played by Rachel Bérendt) on the night before her death. She had lived without hope after the death of her son, but in a spirited debate, the priest shows her reasons for rediscovering her Christian faith. She thanks him profusely for saving her soul, affirming life in a lifeless village. This conversion is the priest's undoing, as the locals suspect impropriety and force him out. In many ways, they are right. His brand of Catholicism, if not improper, is certainly unorthodox. He offers more questions than answers; the religion he promises brings more pain than peace. Even the kindly priest of Torcy believes that though he may be touched by God's hand, he is not quite cut out for the demanding job of the priesthood. In the final scene, the sickly defrocked priest calls on an old friend from the seminary who has also left the priesthood. As his friend correctly diagnoses, "We've got rotten blood in our veins."

But Bresson, a Catholic, does not mean for us to sympathize so easily with the unreligious characters in the movie. The country priest may have shed the easy, ordered lifestyle of the Catholic Church, but he has not lost his religion, and he dies with a dignity the others lacked. While the structured, hierarchical version of religion may be dead, as many existentialists believed, the religious spirit still has life. Above all, it is the old-time religion of the early prophets that is at the heart of the struggle of the most penetrating religious noir.

In *Carnivàle,* Brother Justin also must learn that the battle lines between good and evil are not so clear, and negotiating one's way is not so easy. Early in the first season, his world is clearly defined: the raucous brothel at Chin's is bad, a cool glass of lemonade from his pious sister, Iris, is good. But like the film noir religious figures before him, the fire-and-brimstone preacher soon learns the lessons of Job. Doing good comes at a hard price. Before long, his church and orphanage, built on the ashes of Chin's, is burnt to the ground, the orphans killed. Cast out, Brother Justin suffers the usual existential crisis. How can one live when the world he has long trusted is completely overturned? That is what he sets out to answer around the campfire with the hobos and later among his fellow patients inside a psychiatric ward. Throughout his journey, we learn of his troubled childhood and how his sister's loyalty rid them of his father's tyranny. By the end of season one, we learn something else about his sister, Iris: it was she who burned down the church in a warped attempt to extend Brother Justin's Christian reach.

His powers growing, the runaway preacher returns home to spread the word via radio and rebuild his old-time church. But now we know it will no longer be the easy religion of his past. Between duties to his sister, responsibility to his Christian God, and the burden of his freedom to choose between bad and worse ways of existence, Brother Justin is hardly a man to be envied. His old mentor, Reverend Norman Balthus, suspects that other powers are at work and suggests an exorcism. Skeptical, Brother Justin uses his vision to reveal his teacher's greatest evil. The move backfires when it is discovered that Norman's worst sin was saving Brother Justin's life when he and Iris were children. How can this be such an evil? "There is a demon within you," Norman logically concludes. But Brother Justin knows better. "There is no demon in me. The demon is me."

As in the story of Job, God's love comes with some terrible considerations, questions that give religious noir its distinctly existentialist flavor.

Graham Greene's Whiskey Priest

As Graham Greene writes: "It would be enough to scare us—God's love. It set fire to a bush in the desert, didn't it, and smashed open graves and set the dead walking in the dark. Oh, a man like me would run a mile to get away if he felt that love around."[3] Powerful words, especially when one has warmed to the speaker, the last hard-drinking priest in a fictional Mexican region, the night before he is shot by the state for attempting to administer last rites to an unrepentant American bank robber. It is classic Graham Greene, and it is why he has always been so troubling for the religious minded. As Pope Paul allegedly told Greene privately, "Some parts of all your books will always offend some Catholics."[4]

Greene's status in the film noir community is beyond dispute, since he wrote the screenplay for *The Third Man* (Carol Reed, 1949), a vehicle for

Orson Welles's captivating portrayal of the sympathetic villain Harry Lime. But it is Greene's "Catholic novels" that have earned him the most respect in the literary world. In those works (*The Heart of the Matter, Brighton Rock, The Power and the Glory, The End of the Affair*), Greene presents a view of Catholicism in particular, and religion more generally, that is fearsome, dangerous, and lonely. Love and hate are interminably mixed in Greene's novels. As one of his spiteful lovers asks, "If we had not been taught how to interpret the story of the Passion, would we have been able to say from their actions alone whether it was the jealous Judas or the cowardly Peter who loved Christ?"[5]

But it is the famous "whiskey priest" in *The Power and the Glory* who best exemplifies the noir struggle against a seemingly absent God. Loosely based on real events in Tabasco, Mexico, at a time when Catholic priests were executed or forced to marry, Greene presents us with the last priest on the run. A drunk and a coward, and though he cannot live up to his image of the Catholic saints, he still longs for the depths of God's love. Reading a flyleaf on a Bible, he finds only superficial guides for the pious reader: passages from the Psalms and the like for those in trouble, poor, needing sleep, already prosperous, et cetera. The priest is disgusted, quickly dismissing "its ugly type and over-simple explanations."[6] There was no real fear or depth of feeling, no passionate calls to a potentially indifferent God. Such "piety" was soulless and, unfortunately, all too common. "God might forgive cowardice and passion," the fugitive priest reasons, "but was it possible to forgive the habit of piety?"[7]

The priest has sinned over and over. He has fathered a child and is at least indirectly responsible for more than a few deaths as he eludes capture, aimlessly performing rituals for a fee. "He was aware of his own desperate inadequacy," and that makes him all the more receptive to rare moments of true Christian spirituality.[8] Once, in an Indian graveyard, he sees giant crosses haphazardly marking graves. It is noteworthy that these are not the markings of the structured Church. The disorderly crosses "had nothing in common with the tidy vestments of the Mass and the elaborately worked out symbols of the liturgy. It was like a short cut to the dark and magical heart of the faith—to the night when the graves opened and the dead walked."[9] For Greene, Catholicism still has power, but it must be found in something other than the easy answers of the traditional party line.

In *Carnivàle,* Brother Justin is not the only religious figure to choose the spirit over the letter of the law. The carnies have their own code of pagan religion. In the same episode where Brother Justin has his crisis of faith (season 1, episode 6), the carnival is camped in Babylon, a town filled with dead souls. On the night the carnival opens its gates, one of its exotic dancers is found defiled and killed. Nobody knows who in Babylon killed her, but that is no matter. "Carnival justice" dictates that one person gets taken, according to ancient custom. They find the one man left still in Babylon, and after circling around him three times with a wagon (saved for this purpose only), they allow the condemned to choose a number, between one and six. The accused (and as it turns out, the killer, too) chooses three. He then learns that he will be the victim of a game of Russian Roulette, one bullet and three shots fired. After three empty shots, he is spared. Immediately, the carnies demand to have him killed anyway. Forget the rituals, they shout. After all, he already confessed. But Samson will not stand for mob justice. The letter of the law is clear. "We got a code here," he explains. "We break the code, we got nothing left." The carnies leave disappointed, and the grieving family members face a second wound, knowing their daughter's killer will go unpunished. However, Samson, like Greene's whiskey priest, believes that even longstanding religious codes must, on rare occasions, be broken. When all is quiet, he slips back into town, again confronts the confessed killer, and this time shoots him dead. It is an especially hard fate to die in Babylon: the souls can never leave. If one dies "over the hill" where there is nothing, one can rest in peace. But in Babylon, the restless souls are confined forever.

This inability to escape is a recurring fate in *Carnivàle* and a theme to which postwar existentialists returned often. "We are condemned to life," Jean-Paul Sartre famously observed. Stumpy, the father of the murdered dancer, decides to leave the carnies once and for all. His other daughter, Libby, goes with him, hoping to strike it rich in Hollywood. And with them goes the world-weary Sofie, finally seeing her chance to be free of her mother. But their plans are predictably thwarted, and they, like their noir predecessors, are condemned to play out their empty and meaningless lives. Ben also tries to escape his fate, hoping to accomplish his rebellion by suicide. But he too is not permitted peace. "It doesn't work that way," he is told, his hand stayed.

Greene's whiskey priest also understands that there are greater forces at work, from which it is impossible to escape. *The Power and the Glory* opens with the priest prepared to board the last boat out of town. A local dentist, Mr. Tench, persuades him that the boat will be late, and they head back to his home to drink the priest's brandy. The dentist soon gives him all he needs to know of the town's history. "It was always an awful place. Lonely. My God. . . . And now I can't get out. One day I will."[10] He will not, of course, and neither will the priest. They are bound to their small sins and petty hopes, but unlike the other "pious" characters, the priest, at least, is consumed by such existential angst.

Depicting these struggles puts Greene not only firmly in the noir tradition but in a larger religious subgroup of real life holy people who believe the quest to find God is not one for the weak of spirit. Catholic saints like St. Francis and St. Theresa of Avila wracked body and soul in their yearning for something more. Jewish mystics like Rabbi Nachman of Bratslav favored going out into the forest at midnight to tremble with God. The Muslim poet Jalaluddin Rumi compares our quest for God to a dog howling for his master. All have one important thing in common—the belief that the most religious experiences must take place outside of organized religion and are usually met not with peace but with crushing isolation and abandonment.

Brother Justin's "Fear and Trembling"

The fathers of Christian existentialist philosophy are Fyodor Dostoyevsky and Søren Kierkegaard, and the best noir owes debts to both nineteenth-century thinkers. Robert Bresson was an avid reader of Dostoyevsky and based his movie *Pickpocket* (1959) on *Crime and Punishment*. Greene also is frequently compared to Dostoyevsky. John Updike agreed with the comparison, calling Dostoyevsky "another problematic believer."[11]

Updike would be the first to admit that while Greene exhibits some important similarities, Dostoyevsky is still in a class unto himself. His enduring masterpiece, *The Brothers Karamazov* still stands as one of the finest explorations into tortured Christian spirituality. Once again, we see a sharp resistance to easy answers. In the lead-up to the famous story "The Grand Inquisitor," Ivan, a philosopher, challenges his religious brother, Alyosha, on Christian faith. With all the horrors in the world, the needless sufferings and cruel deaths that Ivan rehashes in gory detail, how can one still be so complacent in one's belief? One would never pay to see such a macabre show, Ivan challenges. "It isn't God I don't accept, Alyosha, it's just his ticket that I most respectfully return to him."[12]

Alyosha is horrified by his brother's "mutiny" and quickly explains his errors. But soon Alyosha goes through his own existential crisis of faith. After his mentor, Father Zosima, passes away there is talk of whether the good priest was a saint. He seemed as close to a perfect being as one could imagine; goodness and love exuded from his soul. For Zosima, the definition of hell was "the suffering of no longer being able to love."[13] As the people pay their respects, however, a horrible thing happens. Father Zosima begins to smell terribly, putrefying much faster than what is considered natural. Doubt begins to set in, and even Alyosha begins to harbor his own mutinies. Why the sudden change in Alyosha's religious sensibilities? "Is all this really just because your old fellow's gone and stunk the place out?" his friend asks. "Did you really seriously believe that he'd start pulling off miracles?"[14] Not long after, Alyosha has a mystical experience and fully feels God's message. In Father Zosima's lifetime, he performed not miracles but simple acts of kindness. Like fictional noir priests to come, Alyosha leaves his order behind so he can do God's work and "abide in the world."[15]

Kierkegaard is another important influence on the noir tradition. It makes sense that Greene would begin his first autobiography with an epigraph from the Danish philosopher, since Kierkegaard's anxious struggle to find religious truths closely parallels his own. In *Fear and Trembling,* Kierkegaard famously examines Abraham's intended sacrifice of Isaac. The biblical story, as Kierkegaard interprets it, shows us that faith in God is irrational and therefore impossible. It is the impossibility of religious faith that causes the fear and trembling, which for Kierkegaard is what makes the religious life so noble. He writes, "One became great by expecting the possible, another by expecting the eternal; but he who expected the impossible became the greatest of all. Everyone shall be remembered, but everyone was great wholly in proportion to the magnitude of that with which he *struggled.*"[16] Such struggle is what separates the casual believer from the person of faith. As he writes in an earlier draft, "Distress, pain, anxiety—this is the verification, but it is also the saving factor that will discourage people from beginning rashly."[17]

In *Carnivàle,* Brother Justin also invokes the Kierkegaardian struggle to reveal the pain of faith. In the ruins of his burnt out church he sits alone, reciting passages from Genesis, chapter 22—the sacrifice of Isaac. "But you spared Isaac," Brother Justin reminds God. "Why not my children? I know you have your reasons. Please . . . tell me your plan. Help me understand how their deaths serve your will." There is no response, of course, and the crushing prospect of an absent God sends him out into the world, in search of answers to the plight of existential man.

Back at the carnival, it is equally hard to decipher management's will.

In the first season, no one gets a view of management. The most we see is a partially drawn curtain, a spooky voice, and the occasional burning embers from what appears to be a cigarette. Jonesy sneaks into management's trailer when Samson is out and finds nothing. It has all been lies, fairy tales. "There ain't no management," he concludes. "There never was." In the spirit of Dostoyevsky and Kierkegaard, Samson gives Jonesy cold comfort. It all comes down to trust. Samson knows management, and he also understands that management is sadistic, bringing people to Babylon and playing them like chess pieces.

Like Dostoyevsky's Ivan Karamazov, Samson feels the needless suffering that management causes. But like Kierkegaard's Abraham, he will not lose faith. As Brother Justin asks, "Who has more faith in God than those who have borne witness to his fury?" Understanding the cruelty of the world and the impossibility of faith, one should believe, not because belief will be rewarded, but because the ensuing struggle makes life worth living.

The struggle in the religious noir tradition brings no clear paths, no easy answers. If God has temporarily abandoned us, we must rely on our own resources. *Carnivàle*'s Daniel Knauf does not shy away from presentations of existential freedom inside a more traditional religious framework. "Any theory that has anything to do with determinism is probably false," he explains. "And I don't want to ruin anybody's day, but free will is absolutely critical to our storytelling here. Everybody makes choices. Nobody's destiny is spelled out."[18] Throughout the religious noir canon, we see the old existentialist idea of freedom and hope in a seemingly meaningless and hopeless world. Humans *can* make a difference, especially when God seems to avert his eyes. In *Night of the Hunter,* good deeds save the day. In *Diary of a Country Priest,* it is faith that keeps one from madness and suicide. For Graham Greene, even the most uncommitted believer has moments of spirituality. He has the adulterous Sarah Miles tell her rationalist friend, "I believe in nothing . . . except now and then." And "the odd thing is that those are the moments of hope."[19] And these are the messages of hope interspersed throughout *Carnivàle.*

Though the show was cancelled after two seasons, its small but committed fan base flooded HBO with angry emails and set up websites to save the show. Why the attachment to religious noir? It is no secret to *Carnivàle*'s radio DJ, Tommy Dolan (Robert Knepper). "It's the story of a preacher who tried to bring hope to the hopeless, tried to lift up the downtrodden, tried to bring light to those lost in the darkness." Brother Justin represents the modern-day religious existentialist, a noir priest "out there somewhere, walking alone, looking for a sign from God that his work was not in vain." It is a theme that resonates now as much as it did in postwar Europe. We still struggle alone with our faith. And many of us still wait for an answer to DJ Dolan's most pressing question: "Where are you Brother Justin? Where are you?"

Notes

Thanks to Jon Weidenbaum for introducing me to *Carnivàle* and Steven M. Sanders for first pointing me to Graham Greene.

1. Steven M. Sanders, "Film Noir and the Meaning of Life," in *The Philosophy of Film Noir,* ed. Mark T. Conard (Lexington: University Press of Kentucky, 2006), 92.

2. Interview with Daniel Knauf, "The Making of a Magnificent Delusion," http://www.hbo.com/carnivale/behind/daniel_knauf.shtml

3. Graham Greene, *The Power and the Glory* (New York: Penguin, 1990), 200.

4. Greene recounts this line in his autobiography, *A Sort of Life* (New York: Simon & Schuster, 1971), 79.

5. Graham Greene, *The End of the Affair* (New York: Penguin, 1979), 27.

6. Greene, *The Power and the Glory,* 165.

7. Ibid., 169.

8. Ibid., 82.

9. Ibid., 154.

10. Ibid., 15.

11. John Updike, introduction to *The Power and the Glory,* viii.

12. Fyodor Dostoyevsky, *The Brothers Karamazov,* trans. David McDuff (London: Penguin, 1993), 282.

13. Ibid., 371.

14. Ibid., 392.

15. Ibid., 418.

16. Søren Kierkegaard, *Fear and Trembling,* trans. Howard V. Hong and Edna H. Hong (Princeton, NJ: Princeton University Press, 1983), 16.

17. Ibid., 251.

18. Beth Blighton, "Daniel Knauf Interview, Part 2" *Carnivale Interviews,* http://carnivaleinterviews.blogspot.com/2004_03_01_carnivaleinterviews_archive.html.

19. Greene, *The End of the Affair,* 83.

THE SOPRANOS, FILM NOIR, AND NIHILISM

Kevin L. Stoehr

Nihilism and Film Noir

The immensely popular and award-winning HBO series *The Sopranos* is rooted in a nihilistic vision that reflects a general moral decline in contemporary American culture.[1] Nihilism is most generally defined as the belief in nothing at all, the conviction that nothing matters, not even oneself. It is an overall attitude toward the value of life, one evidenced by the words and actions of many of the characters in the series but most especially by those of its morally ambiguous protagonist, Tony Soprano (James Gandolfini). Such a bleak worldview fuels the style and content of most episodes and also echoes the dark atmosphere and themes of film noir and neo-noir classics. These earlier films have had a heavy influence on the aesthetic and thematic framework of David Chase's series, making his episodic creation a primary example of TV noir.

Chase has given us the child of Martin Scorsese's *Goodfellas* (1990), the grandchild of Francis Ford Coppola's *Godfather* saga, and the descendant of those film noir classics that trail back to the earliest crime dramas. Tony Soprano reveals his passion for film noir classics when he is shown enjoying screenings of *Public Enemy* (William Wellman, 1931) and *White Heat* (Raoul Walsh, 1949). His mafia colleagues, especially Paulie Walnuts (Tony Sirico) and Big Pussy (Vincent Pastore), conjure images of neo-noir movies by frequently comparing their experiences to those of characters in the *Godfather* trilogy. Photographs of traditional film noir actors Humphrey Bogart and Edward G. Robinson, captured in gangster pose, flash briefly across the screen in the very first episode of the series, during a killing by Tony's nephew Christopher Moltisanti (Michael Imperioli).

Tony's character is morally ambiguous, like many film noir antiheroes, because he still clings to certain conventional values, despite his frequent failure to live up to them and despite his tendency to reject them when dilemmas arise. Nihilism often results from the disintegration of faith in traditional values, and Tony eventually comes to see his world collapsing all around him. He is the example of an individual who struggles at times to be good but whose basic lack of conviction in his own intrinsic goodness becomes a chief obstacle in this endeavor.

From the very beginning of the series, Tony is presented to us as an individual who does not view himself as fitting neatly into the contours of the world around him. The lives of the main characters in most works of film noir are saturated by the nihilistic condition of alienation, a sense of not-belonging or incompleteness that is often occasioned by the collapse of a stable value system. Such a condition is articulated crudely but clearly by Uncle Junior (Dominic Chianese) in season 4: "Each of us is alone in the fuckin' universe" ("Pie-O-My"). Characters in film noir and neo-noir typically express this feeling of solitary dislocation that results from an underlying relativism concerning ethical truths and values. There are no universal standards or absolute truths in their lives, other than the principle that they must survive in a world gone wrong.

Film noir is typically (though certainly not universally) anchored in a nihilistic—that is, values-negating and life-denying—vision that has cast its shadow on modern Western culture since the nineteenth century, and most especially during, between, and after the two world wars of the last century.[2] Film noir tends to express the psychological, moral, and existential consequences of the collapse of the conventional rules and values of society.[3] These consequences are especially pronounced when primal, irrational instincts have exploded through the repressive facades of civilized life and overwhelmed our feeble trust in some traditional, human-created order. The emergence of such instincts typically drowns any hope of future salvation or redemption. Film noir tends to revel in the shadowy alleys of a passive or pathological nihilism that, as the German philosopher Friedrich Nietzsche (1844–1900) defines it, results in lost opportunities for attaining authenticity, creative individuality, and genuine self-knowledge.[4]

Nihilism involves experiences of negativity, contingency, estrangement, despair, dread, and hopelessness. These experiences are expressed in crystallized form by one of the more famous quotations from Nietzsche, taken from his epic fable and morality tale *Thus Spoke Zarathustra*: "God is dead."

This statement refers directly to the decline of Christianity in particular and organized religion in general. But for Nietzsche and his character Zarathustra, such a decline is occasioned by a general loss of faith, not only in the existence of some transcendent deity but in the value of life itself.

Nihilism also signals the loss of unity and wholeness on both personal and collective levels of existence. A nihilistic attitude often results from personal fragmentation in one's everyday life, a fragmentation that is reflected by the idea of perspectivism, the belief that all knowledge and experience results from our subjective and personal viewpoints, without any overarching pattern or structure that allows us to order these viewpoints in a definitive way. This leads to a subsequent rejection of our belief in objective, universal truths and our conviction in values that are intrinsic or valid in themselves, apart from merely subjective interests and preferences.

God and Gary Cooper Are Dead

Tony Soprano's belief that he inhabits a world of collapsing values is a major theme of the series. The ways he attempts to deal with such a world at first waver between life affirmation and life negation. But as the series progresses, Tony becomes more and more of a nihilist in the most negative and life-denying sense of that term. He is as much a victim of his own psychological weaknesses as he is a man who has been thrown into fated circumstances that weaken him. He is a mob boss whose power has eroded and whose authority has become increasingly fragile. But after a certain point, self-redemption is no longer even his personal goal, and therapy becomes nothing more than a charade. Tony's decreasing sense of the value of life in general has a debilitating effect on his family as well as violent consequences for those who dare get in his way.

Episode 1 ("The Pilot") of season 1 begins with Tony Soprano waiting to meet Dr. Jennifer Melfi (Lorraine Bracco) for his first session of psychotherapy. Tony is the embodiment of underworld machismo. He has summoned the courage to attend these sessions in order to combat the severe panic attacks that have led to his collapse on several prior occasions. Tony is soon established as a man of power, someone whose profession requires control and the ability to manipulate others. He interprets his malady as merely one of physical infirmity, and Tony is highly reluctant even to concede this degree of weakness. He is not willing to go beyond this admission to the further conclusion that his panic attacks may also be a symptom of emotional, psychological, and even spiritual instability. His position as a mob boss demands self-mastery: he can hardly master others without first governing himself. But to retain control and authority, Tony must first submit to his therapist.

The very context of Tony's therapy, a framing device that initiates the series and projects it forward, is significant in that it pronounces the goal of personal wholeness as well as the idea of narrative unity. Via the therapy sessions, Tony can narrate his life to Melfi as well as to the viewer. He uses his therapy as a way of bringing together the fragments of his otherwise disjointed existence. While the events and elements of the series cohere because of their dramatic connections, they are also integrated to a substantial degree because they eventually come to play a role in Tony's narrative, one that depicts his overall psychological and moral state of being.

The therapy session serves as a matrix of emerging narrative order because it provides an occasion for reflection and self-reflection. Tony's ailments and complaints indicate that the different aspects of his life have become compartmentalized and disconnected from one another. So the need for balance and order and stability is articulated most clearly in these sessions that summon him to recognize and act on such a need. If nihilism of a passive or pathological kind is our growing loss of faith in some greater purpose or meaning that integrates the various elements of our lives, some of which are unconscious, then Tony's ongoing therapy represents his struggle to combat such nihilism. If anything, *The Sopranos* is a show about its main character's quest for self-knowledge against a backdrop of moral confusion and despair.

As Tony waits to see Dr. Melfi, he gazes with perplexity at the intimidating statue of a nude goddesslike female, whose fierce, threatening stare pierces the waiting room. At a symbolic or subconscious level, this authoritative figure typically represents motherhood, the matrix (from the Latin *mater,* referring to the maternal) of fertility, generation, and emerging natural order. Indeed, we quickly discover in this episode that Tony has more than a slight problem with his mother, an intimidating woman with a fierce stare of her own. The mother figure, summoning primal energies of the psyche, is no longer associated strictly with nurture and nature. The maternal symbol of the matrix of birth and growth has become transformed for Tony into an icon of threatening power, as shown by both this statue and his own mother, Livia Soprano (Nancy Marchand). And as we learn by the end of season 1, Livia has conspired to terminate her own son's life for vengeful reasons.

This inversion of the archetypal image of birth, nature, comfort, and stability becomes a fitting departure point for a series that will hover persistently around this problematic mother-son relationship as well as around such nihilistic themes as death, rejection, despair, and dread.

Tony tells Melfi that he is back at work and, after describing his profession as "waste management consultant," begins to make a series of points about why he may be suffering from undue levels of stress. His very choice of a professional label, one that disguises his life as a gangster, is revealing in its indication of a life of immorality or even amorality. Tony is slowly coming to see himself as a manager of the moral wasteland that surrounds him. His brief speculation about the possible origins of his panic attacks becomes a monologue on the ills of society at large and how they have affected him. What he has not yet come to recognize is the spiritual wasteland that lurks within him.

Tony tells Melfi from the outset that he is plagued by feelings of decline and loss: "It's good to start from the ground up. I came in at the end. The best is over." His therapist responds: "Many Americans, I think, feel that way." We are already placed within the framework of American cultural commentary, and this commentary indicates a decline in social values and a nostalgia for better days. Tony explains to Melfi that his own father had it much better, that his generation had its firm standards and reasons for pride. "What do we got?" Tony asks pointedly ("The Pilot").

Tony then talks about this decline in traditional values and standards, even though he refers strictly to mob values and standards. Indeed, while nihilism typically involves the rejection or diminishment of traditional and conventional values, the decline of old-fashioned mafia values is doubly nihilistic, in the sense that the mob, with its own internal values and codes, is based on a complete rejection of conventional law and order. Tony complains to Melfi that contemporary mob members have no values: "Guys today have no room for the penal experience, so everybody turns government witness." Tony then laments the loss of the stoic hero of yesteryear: "Whatever happened to Gary Cooper—the strong silent type? That was an American. He wasn't in touch with his feelings—he just did what he had to do" ("The Pilot"). America today is pampered and therefore weak, according to Tony.

Tony often views himself as one of the last of the heroic types, one who at least *attempts* to embody old-style values and standards. He tries to base his life on the virtues of loyalty, respect, and honor—which are supposed to govern both his criminal and conventional life. But he recognizes that these virtues are decaying, in both spheres of his life. He has neither religious faith nor trust in the law to govern his decisions and actions. In addition, the usual supports of family and friendship have become increasingly frag-ile. Tony's family life is more than complicated, due to his own immoral choices, and he soon discovers that his professional colleagues may really be mob informants. His execution of Big Pussy in the final episode of season 2 ("Funhouse") demonstrates the truth of what he is saying as well as the severity of this loss of trust.

Tony's depression about the decline of mob values is reemphasized in episode 2 of season 1 ("46 Long"), which begins with an atypical pre-credits prologue. Tony and his comrades-in-arms are playing cards and listening to a television interview with an expert who describes the contemporary decline of the mob, discussing the failure of present-day mobsters to adhere to the old-fashioned rules of honor and secrecy. The gangsters of today, ac-cording to the interviewee, rat out each other and engage in drug trafficking, activities that were taboo for older mobsters. Tony concurs with the expert: "The shoe fits."

"It's All a Big Nothing"

Nihilism's life-negating orientation is evident in season 2 as well. Here, An-thony Jr. (Robert Iler) becomes acquainted with the teachings of existential-ism through his new high school English teacher. On the eve of his Catholic confirmation, A.J infuriates his parents by spouting nihilistic paraphrases of ideas from Nietzsche ("Nitch," as A.J. calls him) and Albert Camus. His recent homework assignment is Camus' *The Stranger,* a novel that deals with a nihilist who no longer cares about anything after the death of his mother and whose utter amorality is demonstrated by his random murder of an Algerian man on a sun-scorched beach ("D-Girl").

In the same episode, A.J. damages his mother's car in a careless acci-dent, and she (Carmela, played by Edie Falco) warns him that he is lucky that he did not kill his fellow passengers. A.J. replies indifferently: "Death just shows the ultimate absurdity of life." When his mother, horrified, then pleads for God to forgive him for his callousness, he replies: "There is no God." His parents are dumbfounded by his sudden rebellion. The youngster then poses the ultimate existentialist question about the very meaning and significance of his life: "Why were we born?" Though Tony shares Carmela's shock at A.J.'s sudden atheism, he echoes his son's general sentiment later in the series, in season 4, when he responds to the tragedy of 9/11, along with other problems on his mind: "My wife prays to God. What kind of God does this shit?" ("The Strong Silent Type")

Nihilism, as we have already seen, is the rejection of any ultimate or overarching purpose in life. While discussing his problems with his bed-ridden grandmother, Livia, A.J. once again ponders the overall purpose of life. Livia, the ruthless matriarch of the series, expresses her own deeply nihilistic view of human existence, concluding with: "It's all a big nothing. What makes you think you're so special?" ("D-Girl") Livia's statement of utter negativity is echoed by a line from the rap song "World Destruction" by Afrika Bambaata and Johnny Lydon, used in the first episode of season 4: "This is a world destruction, your life ain't nothing" ("For All Debts Public and Private").

While we might wonder whether A.J. is mature enough to question his own partially developed value system in a serious manner, there are clear hints that he may be echoing his father's loss of faith in some unifying purpose or objective moral structure. Or perhaps Tony never had any real faith in the first place; maybe he is finally reaping the psychological and moral consequences of his internalized nihilism. When Tony shares with Melfi his concern about A.J.'s recent expressions of doubt and disbelief, she tells him: "Anthony Jr. may have stumbled onto existentialism." Melfi then explains the gist of this twentieth-century philosophical movement, including its questioning of the possibility of life having a meaning when absolute values and truths have been vanquished. Tony replies: "I think the kid's onto something" ("D-Girl").

A.J.'s initial tendency toward nihilistic despair, in fact, deepens as the series progresses. Tony even pronounces doom for his own son at the end of season 3. A.J. collapses from an anxiety attack, echoing Tony's own earlier attacks. Tony later remarks to Melfi, in a burst of nihilistic fatalism, that his son possesses the same old "putrid, rotten, fuckin' Soprano gene" ("Army of One"). Tony implies here that his life, like A.J.'s, is the product of indifferent, impersonal forces (i.e., his own biology and ancestry) from which he cannot escape. A.J. falls to the floor of his home while modeling the cadet's uniform that he is expected to wear to military school, the institution where Tony now wants to send his son in order to cultivate some self-discipline. The very fact that Tony and Carmela need to resort to a military school says something about their failure in parenting according to firmly respected values. Nihilism as a loss of faith in conventional, traditional values begins at home, one could say, and grows from the inside out. A.J. and Meadow already know about their father's criminality, and they increasingly recognize their mother's acquiescence in this lifestyle for the sake of her material comfort.

Things get worse as the series progresses when it comes to A.J.'s own brand of life-denial. At the beginning of season 5, Carmela must contend with his general attitude of laziness and icy indifference, once she has demanded that Tony move out of the house because of his ongoing adulteries. And in the final episode of season 6, Carmela announces her belief that A.J. has little self-esteem or hope for the future. She confesses to Tony after they learn that A.J. has been fired from his job at Blockbuster: "He's got his dead, nihilistic streak. It chills me to the bone" ("Cold Stones").

Tony's frequent sense of the meaninglessness and nothingness of it all becomes most clearly occasioned through his fear of death, of his own not-being. His fear of death is especially evident in the pilot episode, when he recounts his first collapse and, while undergoing tests, tells Carmela: "We had some good times, had some good years." This dread is also apparent a few episodes later when Tony obsesses about his good friend Jackie Aprile (Michael Rispoli), who is dying of cancer. The episode begins with a symbol of death and dying, at least in Tony's mind: he is disturbed by a painting that hangs in Melfi's waiting room, which depicts a red barn surrounded by peaceful trees. He thinks that the artwork is a psychological test that the therapist has slyly imposed upon her waiting patient. He refers to the rotting trees in the painting, emblems of death, while Melfi finds it intriguing that there is not one detail of the artwork that suggests that the trees are decaying or dead. She realizes that Tony has dying on the brain ("Denial, Anger, Acceptance").

Death is, of course, a recurring theme in the series, and not merely in the form of murder or the threat thereof. For example, the title of the second episode of season 2 is "Do Not Resuscitate." Later in the same season ("House Arrest"), the illness of Uncle Junior (Dominic Chianese) forces the elderly gangster to admit bleakly that all paths in life lead ultimately to the cemetery. Also in that episode, Tony expresses his ultimate sense of the overall meaninglessness of existence when he proclaims to Melfi (after discoursing on the indifference that he felt after watching the film *Seven*): "What's the point? . . . You go to Italy, you lift some weights, you watch a movie. It's all a series of distractions till you die" ("House Arrest"). And in season 3, Tony's general response to learning of Uncle Junior's cancer is simple and bleak: "A lot of death" ("Another Toothpick"). In *The Sopranos* many things are consistently in danger of coming to an end, mainly lives and relationships.

Animals and Animosity

In the pilot episode, Tony reveals to Melfi that he has become obsessed with a family of ducks that have taken refuge in his backyard and that regularly use his swimming pool. Tony is amused by these visitations of wild creatures to his suburban enclave, especially by the ducklings that are learning to fly. He even wades into the pool to feed the ducks while still attired in his bathrobe and begins to study a detailed book on birds. The ducks bring him a welcome sense of serenity amid the panic attacks and general ennui that have emerged in his life.

Melfi suggests at one point that the ducks form a family and that they are therefore an emblem of family life, of a close-knit and unified community. Tony immediately likes this interpretation and believes that he has discovered the core of his problem: he is afraid of somehow losing his family and his corresponding sense of being-at-home-in-the-world. But this is too easy, as Melfi and the viewer no doubt surmise. Tony is, one might suspect, drawn rather to the flight of the ducks and calls for his family to watch as the ducklings begin to take wing. The flight symbolizes, perhaps, the realization of a natural and instinctual ability to elevate oneself beyond certain limitations and to enjoy the freedom of untrammeled movement.

This ability to transcend, to overcome prior limitations, implies self-transformation, a change of condition occasioned by one's own potential and willpower. The ducklings lift themselves finally, from static serenity and dependency, to independent flight. Correspondingly, Tony craves not so much stasis and security as a motion upward to a higher plane of existence. He sometimes reveals, through these therapy sessions, his own instinctual desire to transcend his current station in life and to seek flight from his occasional state of nihilistic self-estrangement. But, ultimately, his feet appear mired in cement.

Tony's obsession with the ducks in season 1 is echoed in season 4 by his passion for a racehorse named "Pie-O-My," an animal owned by the villainous Ralph (Joe Pantoliano). While the ducks may symbolize his desire for self-overcoming, the horse confirms that, at a more basic level, Tony has a fondness for animals, an affection that seems to transcend his affinity for his fellow human beings (other than for his immediate family). Tony is something of a misanthrope, much like his mother, and it is his love of animals that seems to compensate a bit for this lack of emotional connection with other members of his species. As do the many references to food in The Sopranos, the presence of animals in occasional episodes carries symbolic significance.

In a touching scene in season 4, Tony must rush to the stables on a cold and rainy night to pay the veterinarian when Pie-O-My needs medical attention and Ralph refuses to make the payment. Tony stays for a while with the horse, caressing the animal lovingly while the rain pours down outside of the open doorway. They are soon joined by the horse's stable-mate, a goat who comes to check on things while also seeking shelter from the storm. This cozy manger scene is almost surreal in that The Sopranos gives us a world that rarely provides glimpses of the natural world beyond steel and concrete. But this is also a scene that reveals a stark contrast to Tony's usual acts of aggression, cruelty, and ruthless self-interest. Here we see Tony as sympathetic, caring, nurturing, even maternal to some degree, exhibiting qualities he could not find in his own mother ("Pie-O-My").

It is not surprising, in fact, that one of Tony's most graphically violent acts against another human being is motivated by his revenge for Pie-O-My's unnecessary death. His killing of Ralph in season 4 is due chiefly to Tony's suspicions that Ralph had arranged for the death of the racehorse in order to cash in on the life insurance policy for the animal. Tony's wrath is primal and unconditional, and though he often wanted to see Ralph out of the way for various reasons, it took the killing of an animal to occasion that repressed hatred and vengeance ("Whoever Did This"). While Tony had previously given Ralph a lashing due to the latter's brutal killing of Bada Bing dancer Tracee in season 3 ("University"), that did not culminate in Ralph's demise. Tony's henchmen intervened to cut short the beating, mainly out of concern that the commotion might be noticed by customers of the striptease joint, possibly drawing the further attention of the police. But no further punishment for Tracee's gruesome death was doled out. She is forgotten, and Tony promotes Ralph to mafia captain a few episodes later. On the other hand, with the death of Pie-O-My in mind, Tony unleashes his fury against Ralph, no holds barred. And his affection for animals is further confirmed when he becomes highly disturbed, in season 4, when he hears that Christopher accidentally killed Adriana's dog while strung out on drugs ("The Strong Silent Type").

By revealing Tony's compassion for his fellow creatures—even if not for his fellow human beings—a contrast is drawn that makes all the more telling Tony's frequent expressions of an overall indifference toward the value of human life. When he does exhibit a lust for life, it is most often in negative and aggressive terms: reckless adultery and unadulterated violence. But there are those rare moments of quiet epiphany, as in the stable scene during the rainstorm, in which Tony reveals signs of being a more humane person. These are instances in which an appreciation for life does shine through an otherwise darkened sky.

We might also think here of the final scene of season 1, in which Tony and Carmela and the kids take shelter in Artie Bucco's restaurant in the middle of a downpour. Over a warm and peaceful dinner Tony toasts to his family and declares to A.J. and Meadow: "You two'll have your own families someday soon. And if you're lucky you'll remember the little moments, like this, that were good" ("I Dream of Jeannie Cusamano"). A similar tone is struck in the final sequence in the last episode of season 3, when Uncle Junior serenades the reception party after Jackie Jr.'s funeral. Unfortunately, this scene is disrupted by an angry Meadow, who gets drunk and storms out, calling all of the supposedly fake sentimentality a bunch of "bullshit." Yet Junior's song, an echo of the old days, does bring warmth and tears to several listeners ("Army of One").

The ducks and the racehorse bring out a kinder and gentler side of Tony's personality, demonstrated only rarely, but most especially when connecting with the sheer innocence of the nonhuman animal world. Yet, when viewed from a different perspective, the animal world also becomes symbolic of Tony's darker and more nihilistic side, which emerges victorious all too often. The series sometimes makes symbolic reference to Tony himself as a kind of animal or beast in a very negative sense, and not merely in terms of his brutish physical appearance or primitive manners. Think, for example, of the obvious parallels between Tony and the bear that prowls through his backyard, scaring Carmela and A.J., at the beginning of season 5 ("Two Tonys"). Not to mention the fact that the pilot episode, pregnant with sig-nification in its role of establishing major characters and themes, concludes with a Nick Lowe song that includes an intriguing line of prayer: "God help the beast in me." In this light, Tony feels affection for animals because of their instinctual warmth and loyalty and community, but he also may see an unconscious mirroring of the potential for his own animalistic aggression. Unfortunately, Tony's way of dealing with his animal nature leads him in many cases to uncivilized, often savage, ways of dealing with things.

The Sad Clown

Tony's character is complex, in the sense that his personality appears at times saturated by an attitude of nihilism while at other times he struggles actively to overcome such a life-negating stance. As the series progresses, Tony's struggle to conquer his own moral weakness and inner emptiness becomes more intensified. And yet we begin to realize that his is not a success story in trying to rise above these defects, despite his participation in analysis. The transformation of Tony's character could be viewed as increasingly similar to the typical moral decay of those dislocated protagonists in film noir and neo-noir. Since he finds no hope of renewed faith in traditional and conventional values, and since he is actually involved in undermining them, Tony clings more than ever to the past, fears the future, continues to suffer anxiety and self-alienation, and often views himself as a hapless victim of fate—much like the antiheroes who populate the shadowy world of film noir and neo-noir.

Tony must face himself and his inner demons and attempt to gain a sobering picture of where he really stands. The compassion, honesty, and authenticity that are required for personal transformation and self-transcendence do not come easily to him. He must wrestle with his stoic facade and, in breaking down his emotional fortress bit by bit, learn to externalize those inner emotions that have been repressed and compartmentalized for so long in the macho, heroic world of the gangster. He has become saturated by the duplicity of his underworld life, and he has, in turn, buried his own emotional core beneath lies and machismo. He has transmuted a life of deceit into one of self-deception. In the sporadic moments when Tony does choose to reflect on his existence and dig deeper to discover his genuine self, he faces emptiness. So he sometimes feels forced to continue with old habits as a subterfuge. He surrenders too easily to his most elemental desires and instincts. And this leads sometimes to an extreme degree of self-loathing, a self-hatred that is most usually projected outward in the form of violence against others.

As the series progresses into season 3, for example, Tony articulates his belief that his therapy sessions have been working and that he is a happier man, even though he has recently intensified his tendencies toward adultery and murder. At this point, his quarrels with Carmela, according to Tony, have begun to subside and the couple seems more serene, even as he carries on a torrid affair with a disturbed patient of Melfi, named Gloria (Annabella

Sciorra), a woman whose personality is all too similar to that of his mother. He even attempts to offer Melfi extra money for the apparent benefits of the sessions. While the external villains in Tony's life change from season to season (Livia, Uncle Junior, Ritchie, Ralphie, the Russians, the New York mafia), the internal villain in his life remains ever-present: his inability to take account of his own moral decline, even while he obsesses about the weaknesses of others.

At the start of season 4, Tony reports to Melfi: "Things are good. Especially with Carmela" ("All Debts Public and Private"). Yet, later in that season, Tony beats Assemblyman Zellman for having slept with one of his old flames, Irina ("Watching Too Much Television"). He subsequently has an affair with Valentina, after she has ended her relationship with Ralph ("Mergers and Acquisitions"). He then murders Ralph out of revenge for the death of Pie-O-My, and we can guess that the vicious energy Tony unleashes in this killing has some very deep roots in his own fractured psyche ("Whoever Did This"). Not long after killing Ralph, Tony resumes contact with Svetlana, Irina's cousin and his mother's former caretaker. In this same episode, he describes himself to Melfi as a "sad clown" who has to carry on a "brave front," recalling his use of the very same self-descriptive metaphor in the first episode of the series ("The Strong Silent Type").

It is not surprising that Tony confesses to Melfi at this point that he has lost hope for any redemption or self-improvement. His life seems to be a roller-coaster ride that nonetheless always winds up at the bottom, back where he started. Tony states here, in reference to the evolution of his marriage with Carmela: "We never seemed to get anywhere. Kinda like this therapy." He concludes in the same episode that he is still "a miserable prick. I've said that since day one" ("Calling All Cars"). He refuses to continue with analysis. And by the final episode of the fourth season, Tony's increasingly evident weakness in needing to satisfy his animal instincts (particularly his libido) results in the worst of all possible consequences: Carmela demands a divorce and throws him out of their house once Irina phones her and confesses to having an affair with Tony ("Whitecaps").

The depth of Tony's moral decline is reemphasized at the beginning of season 5 when he approaches Dr. Melfi again, but not to return to therapy. Rather, he wants to have sex with her. Melfi, of course, refuses ("Two Tonys"). Toward the end of that season, Tony resents his sister Janice's recent success with her anger management classes. He destroys an otherwise happy Sunday dinner by repeatedly teasing her (Aida Turturro) about her past failures as a mother, knowing that this will drive her over the edge. Janice ruins her brief track record by attacking Tony with a fork ("Cold Cuts"). In the next episode, Tony is haunted by a lengthy and detailed dream in which his old high school coach continually criticizes him for his "unpreparedness," signaling a streak of pessimistic self-doubt ("The Test Dream").

Tony's moral ambiguity persists, however, despite these signs of a clear downward trajectory. Without attempts at saving himself and his family, Tony's downfall would not be as dramatic. The very next episode marks his reconciliation with Carmela and his pledge that his "midlife crisis problems" will no longer interfere with her happiness. At dinner with his wife and son, Tony makes a toast: "To the people I love. Nothing else matters" ("Long Term Parking"). This reunion follows upon Tony and Carmela's having spent a night together again several episodes before ("Marco Polo"). And in season 6, as yet another example that Tony emerges time and again from his own abyss (only to fall back into the darkness and emptiness), after having been hospitalized for a serious injury, he admits to a fellow patient that he is beginning to believe he is connected to something bigger in life ("The Fleshy Part of the Thigh").

But, at the end of the day, Tony remains morally ambiguous at best and nihilistic at worst. In season 6, he asks Dr. Melfi for a "mercy fuck," and, when she asks about his thoughts on having been recently shot and almost killed by a confused Uncle Junior, he declares: "Gloom is your business and business is good" ("Mr. and Mrs. John Sacrimoni Request"). Later in the same season, Tony replies to his therapist with typical sarcasm and pessimism when she asks if he is bored: "I told you my feelings, every day is a gift. . . . It's just—does it have to be a pair of socks?" ("The Ride")

The viewer is sometimes torn between hope for Tony's moral redemption and a rather sadistic enjoyment of his continued ruthlessness. He is a protagonist whom viewers cheer when he confronts the villainy of others (as in his face-to-faces with Ritchie and Ralphie and Johnny Sack), yet he appears as a pitiful specimen of moral weakness when confronting the villainy in his own heart. This is the enticing tension that motivates the entire show. Furthermore, over the course of the series it becomes apparent that therapy has actually permitted Tony to think that the release of his primal instincts, even when leading to acts of deception or adultery or murder, is a sign of psychological power. Tony comes to accept and to rationalize his very worst instincts, ignoring the better angels of his nature, that part of his psyche that has sought assistance and has felt occasional remorse for acts of wrongdoing. So, rather than taking flight and overcoming his past self, he sinks further into degeneracy.

This is precisely the dark irony of the series. It is through the ongoing process of his therapy that Tony learns to become *more* self-deceptive and immoral, because he has become, paradoxically, more open to his ruthless and brutal instincts. Tony feigns success at self-renewal by pretending to know himself better, but he is still trapped in many ways by the negative influences of his childhood and by his nostalgia for the golden days. He has learned, at least for a while, to appropriate his own past in a way that fuels his lust, greed, and violence. He becomes energized, paradoxically, by his own inauthenticity and negativity; he learns to revel in his own resentment, self-loathing, and life-negation—like mother, like son.

Throughout the series, Tony consistently fails in his attempts at self-mastery and self-overcoming. He succumbs to the whims of his inner weaknesses and outer fate, much like the antiheroes of film noir and neo-noir. If he had been consistently unaware of his moral failings due to sheer ignorance or irrationality, then we could fault him at most for being little more than an instinctual animal, wreaking havoc whenever his appetites are aroused. But with a growing recognition of his need for therapy and self-reflection, Tony shows himself to be far worse than a savage animal. He self-consciously neglects his moral character and its required cultivation, with an awareness of the conventional importance of values as well as the traditional difference between right and wrong. Tony substitutes psychology for ethics to suit his own selfish and self-deceptive purposes. Consequently, he continues to feel lost amid the moral wasteland. He can at best accept this bleak reality in a silent and stoic manner, like "the strong silent type" whom he reveres. He comes to feel a sense of accomplishment only in the fact that he has managed to survive in a broken world.

Notes

1. This essay is a substantially revised and updated version of two of my previously published writings: "'It's All a Big Nothing': The Nihilistic Vision of *The Sopranos*" (in *The Sopranos and Philosophy: I Kill Therefore I Am,* ed. Richard Greene and Peter Vernezze, [Chicago: Open Court, 2004], 37–47) and a chapter, "The Nihilistic Vision of Film Noir and *The Sopranos*," from my book *Nihilism in Film and Television* ([Jefferson, NC: Mc-Farland, 2006], 27–54). These prior writings focused primarily on the first two seasons of the series while making the same general argument as the current essay, which refers to

six seasons. I thank the editors at Open Court Publishing and McFarland for their kind permission in allowing me to incorporate some of the material from those works.

2. My general description here follows the standard analysis of film noir as rooted in a nihilistic worldview and centered upon the moral ambiguity of the protagonist, though some scholars disagree. For example, see the essay in this volume by Aeon J. Skoble, as well as an earlier essay in which he gives a moral-realist interpretation of film noir: "Moral Clarity and Practical Reason in Film Noir," in *The Philosophy of Film Noir*, ed. Mark T. Conard (Lexington: University Press of Kentucky, 2006), 41–48.

3. For my general understanding of film noir I have benefited from a study of such articles and books as Paul Schrader, "Notes on Film Noir," in *Perspectives on Film Noir*, ed. R. Barton Palmer (New York: G. K. Hall, 1996; first published in 1972 in *Film Comment* by Film Comment Publishing); Bruce Crowther, *Film Noir: Reflections in a Dark Mirror* (New York: Continuum, 1989); Robert G. Porfirio, "No Way Out: Existential Motifs in the Film Noir," in Palmer, *Perspectives on Film Noir;* Raymond Borde and Étienne Chaumeton, "Towards a Definition of *Film Noir*," trans. Alain Silver, in *Film Noir Reader*, ed. Alain Silver and James Ursini (New York: Limelight, 1996, first published in 1955 in *Panorama du Film Noir Américain* by Les Éditions de Minuit).

4. Nietzsche's references to nihilism may be found throughout his collected works, but see most especially "Book One: European Nihilism" of *The Will to Power*, trans. Walter Kaufmann and R. J. Hollingdale (New York: Vintage Books, 1968). Nietzsche does make a distinction between "passive" or "pathological" nihilism, a basic attitude of life-negation, and "active" or "healthy" nihilism, an attitude that rejects traditional values but that also affirms one's own life and individuality. In this essay I refer primarily to the former meaning.

Part 3

CRIME SCENE INVESTIGATION AND THE LOGIC OF DETECTION

CSI AND THE ART OF FORENSIC DETECTION

Deborah Knight and George McKnight

We analyze *CSI* as an example of TV noir, but before turning to the series, it is worth asking: Just what sorts of narratives count as noir, and why? We find examples of noir in literature, film, and television, but wherever such examples are found, noir is a hybrid of elements. Film scholars have persuasively argued that noir is not and has never been a genre in its own right. Silver and Ward, for example, suggest that "the relationship of film noir to genre is a tenuous one at best" and conclude that noir is better understood as a cycle than as a genre.[1] Others reject the idea that noir is even a cycle. Steve Neale, for example, argues, "As a single phenomenon, noir, in my view, never existed. That is why no one has been able to define it, and why the contours of the larger noir canon in particular are so imprecise."[2] Noir combines thematic and stylistic features that can be exploited by a variety of genres, including mystery/suspense, detective, crime, science fiction, thriller, melodrama, gangster, and so on.[3] In noir films, we typically encounter a dystopic world where either or both of two things are happening. Either there is something darkly corrupt at the heart of the social order, or the social order is threatened by the criminal or antisocial actions of certain individuals or groups. Consequently, the urban setting in noir films is increasingly identified less with community and more with individual self-interest and/or the systemic corruption of the American dream. Typically, a noir narrative involves a mystery or crime and requires a detective to solve it, although this need not be the case.[4] What becomes necessary in noir narratives, then, is a figure whose actions can resolve the mystery and ensure justice, although such figures are often outside the law as traditionally represented by the police.[5]

Here, we will examine crime detection in *CSI* and discuss how the show deploys various noir conventions, styles, and themes that make it a good example of TV noir. We begin by considering the noir trope of the corrupt city and discussing the sorts of storylines characteristic of *CSI*. Next, we identify it as a procedural noir, focusing in particular on the centrality of scientific procedure and method in *CSI* investigations. We then consider the nature of the investigative team, comparing the *CSI* team to both classical and hard-boiled detectives. We conclude with three case studies that illustrate some of the philosophical themes found in *CSI* programs, including epistemological ones, such as identity and self-knowledge, and moral ones, such as what counts as ethical conduct.

The Corrupt City and *CSI* Storylines

CSI is set in Las Vegas, a city represented as catering to extremes of self-interest and desire. Las Vegas instantiates the noir trope of the corrupt city. It is the sort of place where even some of those charged with upholding the law have selfish motives. For instance, the sheriff is concerned only about the optics of a crime and how they might affect his career, not about justice ("Table Stakes"). *CSI* makes it appear as though Las Vegas is a city where everything is possible and, nearly everyone, whether citizen or tourist, with the money to finance it or the will to achieve it, seems to be pursuing his or her own ends, often by whatever means necessary. Many prominent citizens—for example, the owners of the casinos and even some of the most successful former showgirls—are rich and powerful. At the same time, most tourists can operate anonymously and thus do nearly anything they want without drawing attention to themselves unless they commit a crime. The city is driven by commerce and in particular by the casinos, which both encourage and reflect avarice, desire, and the quest for pleasure. In *CSI*, we find the reworking of a theme that has clearly been established in the genre of the Western. There, the community is considered metaphorically as a garden in the desert, holding out the mythic ideal of a society where law and justice have been established to replace lawlessness and arbitrary violence. In *CSI*, on the other hand, the city is concrete and glass and neon, so it is easy to conclude that the ideal of the garden has been compromised by commerce and human avarice. For example, we typically see the city at night, as in the opening credit sequences, where the casinos and the main strip are ablaze with neon, usually shot from an aerial perspective. When we see it or the surrounding desert in daylight, it is lit by a relentlessly bright sun, with scorching heat to match. Night is when we see the majority of crimes either unfold or be initially investigated, so it is a small step, given the crimes committed in Las Vegas, to acknowledge that our primary access to the city is by means of its dark underside.

The CSI team investigates a range of mysteries, not all of which turn out to be crimes, but when dealing with crime, we find everything from crimes of passion to crimes of cold-blooded premeditation. As CSI Sara Sidle (Jorja Fox) says, "It never ceases to amaze me what people do to each other" ("Crate 'n Burial"). *CSI* plots revolve around events that are at best bizarre and at worst macabre. Consider the cheerleader found dead at night on a high school football field, whose partially eaten body has human teeth marks on it and whose teenage killers are discovered because they become infected with salmonella found in her body ("Let the Seller Beware"); a man in scuba gear is found dead in a tree in the middle of the desert ("Scuba Doobie-Doo"); a murder is discovered thanks to a human eyeball found in a raven's nest ("Got Murder?"); a man with a stake projecting from his head drives miles after the initial accident until his eventual death ("Lucky Strike"); the body of a young women leads to a vampire cult whose members drink human blood ("Suckers"); a car is struck by a severed arm from a female body that has been tied under a bus ("XX"). We have cases of actual and imagined incest. Examples of actual incest include the mother who takes a job as a nurse in a mental hospital to be near her son ("Committed"), as well as an incestuous twenty-something brother-and-sister pair of grifters who kill a prominent socialite who in her youth was a well-known showgirl and feed her body to her piranhas, only to have that crime discovered during the investigation of a young showgirl found dead in the socialite's swimming pool ("Table Stakes"). In addition to these bizarre story lines, *CSI* regularly relies on unexpected and startling coincidences, for example, the death of the one juror whose negative vote has hung the jury turns out not to have involved a crime ("Eleven Angry Jurors").

Given the extremes of human desire and motivation dealt with in *CSI* plots, which suggest a dark side to human nature equally as alarming as the dark side of the city of Las Vegas itself, as well as the frequency of macabre stories, it is perhaps not surprising that the show's dominant tone is one of irony. Its perspective is most regularly found in the quips and throwaway lines delivered as part of the banter among members of the investigative team or as segues to commercial breaks. When the forearm of a man is found protruding from a meat grinder in a packing plant, Gil Grissom (William Petersen) has difficulty extracting it and confesses, "I'm going to need a hand" ("Recipe for Murder"). A more subtle example, which is also typical of the referential dialogue in *CSI*, is Grissom's response to Warrick Brown's (Gary Dourdan) comment, "It's Tom Haviland, the movie star," to which Grissom replies, "*Clark Gable* was a *movie star!*" ("The Accused Is Entitled"). Grissom frequently delivers these ironic remarks, which helps to consolidate his persona as detached from the events that prompt the quip.[6] But Grissom is not the only character capable of irony. One of the bonds between the CSI team members, including Captain Jim Brass (Paul Guilfoyle), is their ability to comment ironically on their investigations. Arguably, irony offers a distance for both CSIs and the viewing audience with respect to the crimes and mysteries under investigation.

CSI as Procedural Noir

CSI is related to both the hard-boiled detective film from the 1940s and the police procedural film. Features of *CSI* that are in part derived from the hard-boiled detective film include the idea of the corrupt city shown primarily at night, detectives who are largely unfazed by crime and the criminal element, and an ironic tone. The parallels are not perfect, of course. The hard-boiled figure can typically take a beating and give one, which does not particularly carry over to *CSI*, although something of this aspect of the hard-boiled persona is seen in Brass. But like the fictional world of most hard-boiled detective films, in *CSI* crime is driven by greed, desire, avarice, and passion, and the protagonist is something of a loner. *CSI* is also indebted to the police procedural film and subsequently to police procedural television programs. The key feature of a *CSI* plot is not a crime so much as a mystery that demands investigation and solution. In the police procedural film, the sort of hard-boiled central detective we associate with *The Maltese Falcon* (John Huston, 1941) or *The Big Sleep* (Howard Hawks, 1946) is frequently replaced by a partnership or team of investigators. Often, we have an older, experienced figure mentoring a younger partner or partners. Perhaps the defining feature of the procedural is that the methods and investigative procedures used in detection are given prominence in solving the mystery. Police procedurals have been a staple of Hollywood television for decades, but few have been noir. What distinguishes *CSI* from typical police procedurals is that it locates itself in the lab. We might even describe *CSI* as a forensic procedural, making procedure and method central to its narratives. A key watchword in *CSI,* which would not be heard in the fictional worlds of *The Maltese Falcon* or *The Big Sleep,* is *science.* Like these film noir predecessors, *CSI* is centrally concerned with determining just what counts as evidence, but as a procedural noir set in the crime lab, scientific evidence is the standard on the basis of which conclusions are reached and mysteries solved. This idea is established early in the series, for example, through phrases such as "The evidence doesn't lie" ("Crate 'n Burial"). To paraphrase Grissom, crime scene investigators cannot speak for the evidence, because the evidence speaks for itself.

One of the recurring motifs used in *CSI* is the hypothetical flash reconstructions of crime events, in which we are shown what members of the CSI team imagine to have taken place during relevant moments of a crime or mystery. These most frequently occur when there is a certain amount of recognized evidence, but when it is not yet clear what it is evidence of. That the reconstructions which illustrate how a crime might have occurred are hypothetical is demonstrated periodically when the CSI team pursues a false lead based on a mistaken interpretation of the evidence. Episodes invariably involve CSIs advancing one or more hypotheses. Finding a father, mother, and two older brothers murdered, Grissom and Catherine Willows (Marg Helgenberger) begin with the entirely wrong hypothesis that the father has been killed trying to save his youngest daughter ("Blood Drops"). In fact, the father is killed by his teenage daughter's boyfriend as the father leaves the bedroom where he has been sexually assaulting his three-year-old, incestuously produced granddaughter/daughter. Grissom ultimately acknowledges that he has misread a situation where the initial hypotheses are so strong and yet so wrong. In such situations, the discovery of a wrong interpretation forces the investigators to produce a better, that is to say, more accurate, account of the evidence and the circumstances that led to the crime. Occasionally we witness competing flash reconstructions, where the evidence is shown to support different interpretations. One illustration of this involves Warrick and Nick Stokes (George Eads) investigating a car accident, where each has a distinct theory of the crime that is consistent with the evidence, but where it turns out that neither of them is right ("Anonymous"). We also occasionally see flash reconstructions by a witness who may be concealing something, by the apparent victim of a crime, such as the woman who appears to have been kidnapped ("Crate 'n Burial"), or by a criminal who seeks to misdirect the investigation ("Lady Heather's Box"). With the exception of the flash reconstructions of most of the autopsy work, there is no guarantee that a flash reconstruction is veridical.

The evidence is used to determine which among conflicting accounts is correct, although success may depend upon having sufficient evidence to determine which of two conflicting stories is true. For example, Sara is unable to determine how Catherine's ex-husband was shot and which of the suspects is telling the truth in the "Lady Heather's Box" episode, and so closes the case because as she says to Catherine, "I had two liars and no murder weapon. I had no choice." The hypothesis that a lactating teenage girl has been impregnated by her father (or for that matter, by anyone at all) is disproved when a medical examination shows she is a virgin suffering from false pregnancy syndrome ("Got Murder?"). We might assume that when someone is killed, the evidence supports the idea that a crime has been committed, but this need not be the case. In fact, when certain hypotheses are tested with the evidence, it is possible to conclude that a man in a raccoon suit who has been poisoned, run over, and shot has nevertheless not been intentionally killed. Rather, as Grissom mordantly remarks, he has just had a bad night, even for a raccoon ("Fur and Loathing"). The central methodological issue of *CSI*, then, concerns how scientific data are narratively restructured into a compelling, persuasive, and accurate account of who did what to whom.[7]

These hypothetical flash reconstructions illustrate the main task of the CSI team, namely, reading the evidence. The significance of the evidence in relation to the mystery or crime may be ambiguous. Any given piece of evidence might figure in multiple interpretations, but an interpretation that is not supported by the evidence is ultimately dismissed. Evidence functions as a system of signs, so the CSIs must determine just what any given sign signifies. The process of reading the evidence involves extrapolations from the scientific data which connect the data into an explanation dealing with the actions, and thus the minds, of CSI suspects. While there are recurring remarks to the effect that the evidence is, as Catherine says, "all we've got," this is not wholly true. What the CSI team has is the best evidence scientific method can produce using sophisticated technologies. These produce the data that then need interpretation, hence the idea of the art of forensic detection. Whether in its classical, hard-boiled, or procedural incarnations, detection works from evidence to narrative explanation by means of good guesswork with respect to the data at hand and the testing of competing hypotheses. While the forensic detection that characterizes *CSI* is much more indebted to the sciences than the sorts of guesses and hunches of classical or hard-boiled detectives, the end result is the same, namely, the CSI investigators use their evidence to construct a persuasive narrative explanation of the motives and actions of their suspects. But the centrality of scientific method and procedure is paramount, given the ultimate objective of CSI investigations: the production of evidence that is, indeed, forensic, which is to say, suitable for presentation in a court of law.

The Investigative Team

Compare the hard-boiled noir detective and the CSI team. The former is a loner, someone who functions on the outer edges of the law because he has all too compelling reasons to think that police officers, police detectives, judges, and so on cannot be relied on to bring about justice. The world of the noir detective is one in which police are slow and likely to follow the wrong leads, and public officials are often motivated either by politics or self-interest. However, being himself an outsider, the noir detective is able to act on his best judgment and his desires: he breaks the law if necessary, he falls in love, he takes a beating if he has to, and he often reasons it out later. The CSI team, by contrast, operates at the center of the criminal investigation and judicial systems and is squarely aligned with the law. So while the detective figures in hard-boiled films and *CSI* are oriented quite differently with respect to the law, both noir films and *CSI* exploit the noir trope of the corrupt city and its crimes. The hard-boiled detective and the CSI team members both operate in fictional worlds whose moral compass has something seriously amiss. In each case, it is the figure of the detective or the crime scene investigator who is able, often just barely, to protect us.

In *CSI,* we have an investigative team, not the single individual we would expect in typical noir films, and the team is mixed in terms of race and gender. The team is led by Grissom, one of the most compelling and yet oddest central characters in recent popular Hollywood television.[8] Grissom is most kindly described as asocial and eccentric. Like someone mildly autistic, he combines an awkward relationship with most other people and a memory that ranges across a huge amount of information, from Shakespeare's plays and Yeats's poetry to arcane details of different kinds of dwarfism ("A Little Murder") or the behavioral characteristics of the bugs he studies. Not surprisingly, he loves opera and crossword puzzles. He is committed to the disinterested and dispassionate stance of scientific research into crimes, however grizzly. He is unmoved by the gruesomeness of a crime, since his primary interest is in figuring out how it was committed. Where a noir detective might be expected to reach a conclusion about the perpetrators of a crime on the basis of an intuition that turns out to be right, Grissom exemplifies an intensification of the cerebral/analytic aspect of the male detective, since his hypotheses are extrapolated from the evidence at hand. In some respects, the character harkens back to classical detectives such as Sherlock Holmes, sharing their acute powers of observation, esoteric knowledge, apparent lack of sexual desire, and cerebral/analytic tendencies.

Unlike his noir counterparts, Grissom normally appears either unable or unwilling to act on his desires. To take one example, at various points in the early years of the series, we sense an attraction between Grissom and Sara. In an early episode, Catherine explains to him that he really should send Sara flowers. While on the phone placing the order, he decides to send a live plant instead of cut flowers, since, as he says, she likes "living things." Yet Catherine has to prompt him to act, and the thoughtfulness of the his gift is undercut by the fact that, rather than taking her the plant himself, Grissom—having difficulty dealing directly with others, particularly in personal circumstances—arranges to have his gift delivered. In a later episode, frustrated, Sara arrives at Grissom's office door and asks him if he wants to go to dinner. She thinks they could eat something and just see what might happen. His answer is an immediate "No." Later still, confronting a middle-aged man who has murdered his younger lover, Grissom—who has thus far let Brass do all the interrogating—interrupts to explain the man's crime and reasoning to him. While apparently talking about the suspect, he is simultaneously talking about his own feelings for Sara, especially his realization that much as he might have wanted a relationship with her, he was unable to act. We are never sure whether Grissom knows or guesses that Sara, who has arrived on the other side of the interrogation room's one-way mirror, overhears the explanation. One of Grissom's most striking characteristics is that, as is frequently pointed out, he is not good with people. That said, he is often at his best with people outside the mainstream—for example, the former model who has become a street person; the woman at the convention of dwarves whom he asks for help in tracking a possible suspect; the autistic clerk who works in a rare book collection where a young woman has been found dead; as well as various members of the deaf community, since he has inherited his mother's hearing loss; and a dominatrix, Lady Heather (Melinda Clarke), whom we will discuss later.

Despite his problems with other people, Grissom is his team's supervisor and he is concerned for their welfare. In a clear departure from the typical classic or noir detective scenario, *CSI* presents us with a group that works collectively to solve crimes. Few noir detectives are initially presented sympathetically—often they initially appear gruff, laconic, and cynical. Both Brass and Grissom come close to following this model. By contrast, the core members of Grissom's team—Catherine Willows, Sara Sidle, Warwick Brown, and Nick Stokes—are sympathetic, thus making it easy for audience members to align themselves with the group. In fact, its extended members, for example, the various medical examiners and lab technicians, are also largely sympathetic. Since *CSI* is focused on investigation and not on the characters' lives outside the lab, it is narratively important that each character has clear but minimal identifying features that recur through the series. Catherine, divorced from an unreliable husband who is eventually murdered, is the single mother of a young daughter and is periodically torn between her job and her child. Prior to joining CSI, she was an exotic dancer who worked in one of the major casinos. She discovers during the series that one of her mother's former lovers, the powerful but shady casino owner Sam Braun (Scott Wilson), is her biological father. Sara drinks more than she should and becomes involved with men who are unavailable, for instance the paramedic Hank, someone she trusts, who she unexpectedly discovers is two-timing her. Warrick has escaped the Las Vegas ghetto but is a gambling addict in a town where temptation is everywhere. Nick is noteworthy for his indiscretions, which include becoming involved with a prostitute and talking out of place, for example, when he inadvertently discloses confidential evidence to the press at the scene of a crime.

While there are moments of stress between different members of the team, these are typically short-lived. Warrick, after a particularly grueling case, might initially feel cold toward Nick, who sits down beside him at a table in one of the Las Vegas casinos. But he gets over his mistaken belief that Nick is there as his minder when Nick says he is just hanging out with his friend. There is occasional professional disharmony, for instance, between Catherine, Nick, and Sara when Catherine insists on handling a case ("After the Show"); between Catherine and Sara when Sara takes over the case of Catherine's ex-husband's death ("Lady Heather's Box"); and even between Catherine and Grissom when he decides to supervise the case of the dead girl in the movie star's bed ("The Accused Is Entitled"). Nevertheless, things ultimately work out. Even when members of CSI argue over jurisdiction in a case, the crime is solved only when all members of the team work together. For instance, when Grissom congratulates Catherine on the job she has done, she says, "I had help" ("After the Show"). Another example is the episode in which Nick sleeps with a prostitute hours before she is brutally murdered ("Boom"), thus making himself the prime suspect in the crime, since his DNA is found on her and he was with her shortly before the time of her death. But the team circles the wagons and works hard to exonerate him. So, despite local problems and occasional rivalries, they are invariably united. The most obvious example of the team working together is, of course, when they rescue Nick after he has been kidnapped and buried alive ("Grave Danger").

One striking difference between noir detective narratives and *CSI* is the presence in the former, but the absence in the latter, of a central femme fatale character.[9] In hard-boiled noir detective films of the 1940s, many detectives encounter tough, sexy, intelligent, and independent women—characters played by such actors as Mary Astor in *The Maltese Falcon* and Barbara Stanwyck in *Double Indemnity* (Billy Wilder, 1944). The femme fatale frequently presents herself, at least initially, as weak, dependent, and in need of a strong man to protect her—all the while busily pursuing her own ambitions and goals. Her actual strength and cunning only emerge when she has trapped the man. Occasionally, the male character is entrapped by her dominant, rather than submissive, persona. Either way, the femme fatale figure poses a distinct threat to her chosen man, whom she is typically intent on manipulating and is frequently willing to set up to take the fall for her. The crux of the problem when two strong characters confront one another—in this case a hard-boiled figure and a femme fatale—comes down to one question: Which will triumph, reason or passion? The femme fatale, initially (and mistakenly) associated more with passion than with reason, in fact uses her reasoning skills to seduce and exploit the detective, particularly when his passion for her at first overrides his reason. The detective, having been won over by passion, needs to find a way for reason to reassert itself and help him extricate himself from the femme fatale's schemes. This dynamic is played out explicitly in Sam Spade's reasoning at the end of *The Maltese Falcon*.[10]

In film studies, there has been much discussion of a so-called crisis of masculinity, focusing on the male fear of confident, assertive, and even aggressive female characters. In *CSI*, the central female characters are members of the CSI team. They use reason to achieve their goals and can also manipulate situations to their own ends, as, for example, when Catherine needs mouth swabs from a group of men at a comedy club after the death of the headliner ("Last Laugh"). While Sara has some of the features typically associated with a femme fatale, it is really Catherine who represents the refiguring of the femme fatale. Tough, smart, sexy women no longer need to pretend to be helpless and in need of a man to rescue them. This shift from the conventions of the hard-boiled detective film has implications for how *CSI* plots work out. Catherine self-consciously takes on the femme fatale role when necessary to gain information from a suspect (for instance, in "After the Show"). Because the role has shifted, the narrative focus that would previously have been directed to a femme fatale is now placed on a suspect and the solution of the mystery. It also means that while Catherine's dress and the angle at which her body is often shown remind us of the female body and the idea of woman as femme fatale, her presence on the CSI team forestalls any development of her as an object of Grissom's desire. She is often shown, however, as a figure of his trust and sometimes gratitude.

Case Studies

To investigate some of the philosophical themes raised by *CSI,* we will examine the episode in which Grissom and his team are challenged by Grissom's former mentor ("The Accused Is Entitled"), the three episodes that feature the serial killer Paul Millander (the pilot episode, "Anonymous," and "Identity Crisis"), and the three featuring the dominatrix Lady Heather ("Slaves of Las Vegas," "Lady Heather's Box," and "Pirates of the Third Reich").

"The Accused Is Entitled" features a movie star who reports a dead woman in his bed after a night of high-stakes gambling at a casino and blames her death on her girl friend, both of whom were picked from a group of adoring fans in the casino and invited to his suite. This episode takes a unique perspective on CSI investigative procedure, since the movie star's lawyer decides, as Grissom remarks, that "when you can't attack the evidence itself, you attack the method of gathering it." The forensic expert hired to attack the CSIs turns out to be Grissom's own mentor, Philip Gerard (Raymond J. Barry).[11] The confrontation between Grissom and Gerard highlights the ethical dimension of forensic investigations in terms of both personal integrity and investigative practice.

As a matter of law, Gerard is entitled to observe everything that happens in the lab as well as to look into the background of everyone involved in the investigation. Moreover, he is willing to exploit any and all foibles of the CSI team. At the pretrial hearing, he helps the defense reveal an error in Nick's collection of evidence, Warrick's gambling addiction, Sara's attraction to Grissom, and Catherine's former life as a stripper; and he even tries to exploit Grissom's hearing loss. The man who helped shape him is willing to portray Grissom's team as unethical, incompetent, and unreliable. As Gerard sees it, the question is not what the facts are or what the evidence is, but what a jury can be persuaded to believe might have happened. His strategy is not to dispassionately assess the evidence but to discredit those who process and interpret it, to introduce doubt as to the veracity and reliability of the CSIs. Gerard is willing not only to discredit the CSI team but also to lead jurors to draw false conclusions, hoping to exonerate his client even if the client is guilty. Gerard deliberately uses his forensic expertise and his reputation to pervert the justice system. In the end, Grissom finds evidence that cannot be discredited, thus defeating his mentor. The conflict between Grissom and Gerard illustrates that there is more involved in forensic investigation than the collection of evidence and the testing of hypotheses. The fundamental difference between the two is that Grissom's commitment to dispassionate analysis of the evidence goes hand in hand with his desire to ensure that courtroom testimony reveals the truth, whatever that is. For Grissom and his team, forensic investigation involves acting ethically—and with the personal integrity Gerard lacks.

Where "The Accused Is Entitled" pits Grissom against his mentor, the three episodes featuring Paul Millander set him against a very complex and calculating serial killer who, it is eventually discovered, has a sophisticated knowledge of forensics and is every bit an intellectual match for Grissom. Millander represents the dark side of forensic knowledge and expertise, using his intelligence to trap Grissom into a set of false assumptions. The theme of identity is examined in a variety of ways in the Millander episodes, often with the trope of the double. There is a doubling of identities and a doubling of events that refer us back to the early traumas that are central to both Millander's identity and to the events around which these episodes are constructed. It is a trope that originates in Millander's own uncertain sexual identity, is developed through Millander's ability to initially outwit Grissom, even assuming his identity, and is resolved by Millander's suicide. We discover the complexities of his sexual identity when it is learned that he was born with ambiguous genitalia. At home, his mother raised him as Pauline, while outside the home, at his father's wishes, he passed as Paul. The trope of the double is bound into Millander's feelings of failure because of Pauline's failure to act, inability to prevent his father's murder—which was staged to look like suicide—and powerlessness to convince authorities the death was a murder. Later, sexual reassignment surgery resolved the ambiguity, but at the expense of Pauline.

The primary crime in the pilot episode is a murder where the victim's body has been staged, deliberately placed in a bathtub with a tape recording of a false suicide note. Grissom and Millander meet when a fingerprint found planted on a murder victim's body is traced back to a Halloween novelty item produced by Millander—a dismembered forearm Millander modeled on himself, including his doubled fingerprints. Only later does Grissom realize this is a calculated move by Millander to bring himself to the attention of the CSI unit with a view to being cleared of the murder: there is reason to think that his fingerprint victim is the result not of his own involvement but of someone instead using the Halloween toy to misdirect the investigation. In "Anonymous," a second murder is staged identically to the first. Aside from their manners of death, there is little to connect the two victims until Sara realizes that they share the same birthday, only one year apart, with the second victim born one year earlier than the first. And if this is a pattern, Grissom appears likely to be next, since he was born exactly one year earlier than the most recent victim. Slowly, it dawns on Grissom that Millander has been setting him up by providing false clues while leaving behind virtually no physical evidence that could connect him to the murders.

In "Identity Crisis," Grissom discovers Millander has again successfully used fingerprints to create an entirely new legal identity for himself as Judge Mason, who explains his supposed resemblance to Millander as a case of their being döppelgangers. Finally, in a bold move, he escapes from custody by passing as Grissom himself, complete with a forged identity card featuring Grissom's name and photograph. "Identity Crisis" concludes with Millander's suicide—staged as the other deaths have been, which Grissom finds too late—along with the prior murder of Millander's mother. Throughout their involvement, Grissom has been at least one step behind Millander. Developed across the three episodes, Millander's actions assert his identity as Paul, as well as his desire to convince Grissom, the figure of authority, of his innocence. He uses his identity as Judge Mason to administer the law as he believes it should be and, indeed, should have been, administered. Finally, the murder of his mother is his final action against her insistence that he be Pauline and his own suicide, his atonement to his father.

The three episodes featuring Lady Heather explicitly introduce the noir femme fatale figure and explore Grissom's interest in and attraction to her, while simultaneously dealing with seemingly abnormal sexual behavior. That Lady Heather is a dominatrix is an inspired variation on the theme of the femme fatale. The typical noir femme fatale is someone hiding behind a disguise, using her wits to try to secure some desired end. Lady Heather, by contrast, seems completely identified with her role as dominatrix. She is strong, independent, powerful, and sexually iconic—with her black hair, red lips, charcoaled eyes, and fetish clothes. She has built what even Brass admits is a very successful business around sexual fantasy and role-playing. While Lady Heather's business is not criminal, it certainly focuses on unconventional aspects of sexual desire and pleasure, notably on clients' desires for either dominance or submission. Investigating the murder of one of Lady Heather's dominatrixes in "Slaves of Las Vegas," Brass asks, "Were there any disturbances last night? Did you hear screams?" to which she replies, "It's when I don't hear screams that I start to worry." Lady Heather combines a quick, analytic mind with a nice sense of irony.

When we are first introduced to her, Lady Heather is not a suspect but a striking individual the CSIs meet in the course of investigating the murder of one of her employees. Grissom immediately notices her ability to assess people, to guess their desires and fears, to understand what motivates them. Her powers in this regard are a central part of what attracts Grissom to her, even when she directs her ability to read people toward Grissom himself. What makes Lady Heather so compelling to Grissom is her insistence that she *knows* him. While part of his attraction to her involves an aspect of sexual desire, what primarily motivates him is a deeply repressed desire to know and be known. The intimacy they share is arguably not primarily sexual but rather intellectual, something like a meeting of minds. For someone usually so inscrutable, it is remarkable to Grissom how quickly and accurately Lady Heather understands him. As she remarks over afternoon tea, "The most telling thing about people is what frightens them," and what most frightens Grissom, she recognizes, is that anyone should actually know him.

The complex relations between intellect and passion, reason and desire, are examined in the three episodes which bring Grissom together with Lady Heather. In "Slaves of Las Vegas," one might well imagine that she is using her analytic abilities to seduce him. Most uncharacteristically, in "Lady Heather's Box," he confesses to her that he is "losing his balance" and then puts first one hand on her face and then his other. He says to her, "You can always say stop," and she replies, "So can you." This refers to the convention of dominance and submission, where it is the submissive who ultimately holds power, since he or she can end any action by simply saying, "Stop." That Grissom and Lady Heather acknowledge this between themselves suggests that neither is in a particular role—both cannot be dominant, for example—but rather that they are each willing to accept the other's sense of when it is time to stop. The convention increases the intimacy they share and takes it beyond the standard expectations of Lady Heather's S&M fetish fantasy dominion.

The apparent resolution of the Lady Heather and Grissom saga occurs in season 6's episode "Pirates of the Third Reich." Here, the gruesome story involves the death of Lady Heather's daughter, Zoe. Heather immediately turns her analytic abilities to the solution of her daughter's death. She quickly identifies a potential murderer and works to draw the police's attention to him. In this episode, the femme fatale, who characteristically works by means of reason, switches over to passion. Producing a condom with the semen of the man suspected of killing her daughter, Lady Heather tells Grissom that she is trying to help him by providing him with evidence he can use against her daughter's killer. Members of the CSI team wonder how a bereaved mother could have sex with the man she believes killed her daughter. Grissom responds that revenge is an act of passion. Whatever has gone on between them before, in this episode Lady Heather is distanced from Grissom. In fact, this distancing began in the previous episode. When, in "Lady Heather's Box," Grissom apologizes for treating her as a suspect, Lady Heather coldly remarks that "apologies are only words."

In "Pirates of the Third Reich," after investigating the house of the suspect, an identical twin who the CSIs believe has killed his sibling and adopted his identity, Grissom learns that Lady Heather's daughter had been captured by someone intent on conducting arcane and macabre scientific experiments based on the Nazi desire to create a perfect Aryan race. Heather's daughter would have been the perfect Aryan woman, except that she had one blue eye and one brown one. The episode concludes with Grissom tracking down Lady Heather, who has previously stated that she would be willing to kill her daughter's murderer if she could find him (and Catherine has echoed the sentiment). He finds her in the desert flaying her daughter's killer with a long whip. Grissom finally gets the whip away from Heather by repeatedly saying, "Stop." The coded word ends the drama in this episode.

The cliff-hanger of season 6, unresolved as of this writing, seems to suggest that Grissom has recovered from his attraction to Lady Heather and decided in favor of Sara instead. Identity, self-knowledge, the unknown, ethics, and responsibility are philosophical themes that fit well with the noir elements of *CSI* and suggest the focus of interest that can be found throughout the many episodes of this unique program.

Notes

1. Alain Silver and Elizabeth Ward, *Film Noir: An Encyclopedic Reference to the American Style,* rev. and exp. ed. (1979; Woodstock, NY: Overlook, 1988), 3.

2. Steve Neale, *Genre and Hollywood* (London: Routledge, 2000), 173–74.

3. Silver and Ward suggest that even certain comedies, for instance several made by Preston Sturges during the war years, are part of the noir cycle. See their discussion in *Film Noir,* 331–33.

4. For example, films that feature noir themes and style might involve a mystery but no detective, as can be seen in various noir crime films, such as *Double Indemnity,* where detectives might be present but are not central to the narrative. A more recent example is *Dark City* (Alex Proyas, 1997), a noir sci-fi mystery where the detective figure (played by William Hurt) is peripheral to the solution of the mystery. We discuss noir influence in science fiction in "What is it to Be Human? *Blade Runner* and *Dark City,*" *The Philosophy of Science Fiction Film,* ed. Steven M. Sanders (Lexington: University Press of Kentucky, 2007).

5. For additional discussions of whether noir is a genre, style, cycle, or something else, see the essays in Mark T. Conard, ed., *The Philosophy of Film Noir* (Lexington: University Press of Kentucky, 2006).

6. Steven M. Sanders discusses the noir protagonist as ironist, with Bogart and Mitchum as examples, in "Film Noir and the Meaning of Life," in Conard, *The Philosophy of Film Noir,* 100–101.

7. It must be acknowledged that the process of scientific investigation is tremendously compressed in CSI. In the series, a team of four or five does work that would require many more people and doubtless much more time. What the series is trying to do, of course, is to sustain the narrative thread without bogging down in too many subplots. That said, we recognize that *CSI* does not serve as an accurate model of forensic science as it is actually practiced.

8. Another poorly socialized, brilliant, obsessive, gruff protagonist, this time a doctor, is played by Hugh Laurie in *House*—though it is fair to say that the figure of a doctor with no bedside manner is a staple of television programs based on the practice of medicine, with such characters appearing in drama (*St. Elsewhere, ER*) and comedy alike (*M*A*S*H, Becker*).

9. The obvious exception to this general point is the character of Lady Heather, to whom we will return.

10. For more on reason versus passion in *The Maltese Falcon,* see Deborah Knight, "On Reason and Passion in The Maltese Falcon," in Conard, *The Philosophy of Film Noir,* 207–21. See also Aeon J. Skoble, "Moral Clarity and Practical Reason in Film Noir," in the same volume, 41–48.

11. As Aeon J. Skoble had pointed out, there seems here to be an ironic reference to Richard Kimble's nemesis, Lieutenant Philip Gerard, in the television program *The Fugitive.* The figure of Philip Gerard in *CSI* does not care about the law qua institution as *The Fugitive*'s Gerard does and lacks precisely the sort of integrity Lieutenant Gerard represents.

DETECTION AND THE LOGIC OF ABDUCTION IN *THE X-FILES*

Jerold J. Abrams and Elizabeth F. Cooke

The truth is out there.
　　　—*The X-Files*

Alien Noir

Film scholars agree that classic film noir emerges most prominently in the early 1940s with *The Maltese Falcon* (John Huston, 1941) and *The Big Sleep* (Howard Hawks, 1946), and lasts until *Touch of Evil* (Orson Welles, 1958), setting the basic template: a hard-boiled detective in trench coat and fedora investigates a murder, interviews suspects, encounters a dangerous and beautiful femme fatale, navigates through a labyrinth to solve a mystery, and kills the killer. From the 1940s to the 1970s, however, as society began to change, film noir did, too (becoming neo-noir). Social issues, like race and gender, start to play a much stronger role, as Foster Hirsch points out in *Detours and Lost Highways: A Map of Neo-Noir.*[1] And so did the transition from the modern city center to postmodern suburbia, as Edward Dimendberg argues in *Film Noir and the Spaces of Modernity.*[2] More recently, though, since the 1980s and 1990s, culture has become saturated with high technology, setting the stage for a new fusion of science fiction and noir, which Paul Sammon calls "future noir."[3] We might, however, further subdivide this category into "alien noir" and "cyborg noir," where cyborg noir would include, most prominently, Ridley Scott's *Blade Runner* (1982).[4] Cyborg noir films are noir detective stories in which the criminal or the detective (or both), is somehow fused with cyborg technology. Alien noir, by contrast, includes those works in which human detectives investigate crimes committed by aliens and human/alien conspiracies. Here we may safely put *Dark City* (Alex Proyas, 1998), certainly the film *The X-Files: Fight the Future* (John Bowman, 1998), and *The X-Files* TV series (1993–2002), created by Chris Carter.

The *X-Files* Mythology

The *X-Files* "Mythology" refers to the central storyline running through the series (though not every episode involves this storyline). Special Agents Fox Mulder (David Duchovny) and Dana Scully (Gillian Anderson) are detective partners who work in a division of the FBI known as the X-Files. This section studies cases that are filed under "X" because they fall outside the scope of the FBI's regular investigation units, most of them regarding paranormal activity. There is, however, one case (or system of cases) that underlies all the others in scope, danger, and plot. This is the mythology plot, according to which Scully and Mulder search to uncover the U.S. government's conspiracy to conceal the existence of extraterrestrials. After the alien spaceship crashed at Roswell, New Mexico, in 1947, the aliens contacted a group of world elites, The Syndicate, to negotiate a deal: assistance in alien colonization of Earth, in exchange for the elites' survival. The Syndicate will usurp world power for the aliens through the Federal Emergency Management Agency. As Dr. Alvin Kurtzweil (Martin Landau) puts it: "FEMA allows the White House to suspend constitutional government upon declaration of a national emergency" (*The X-Files: Fight the Future*). The emergency will be a viral holocaust, and quickly all governmental powers will be turned over to the shadow government. Virtually all human life on the planet will be wiped out, except for a select population, which will include The Syndicate and its members' families. They will, however, be reengineered as human/ alien hybrid clones, which is why Mulder's father, Bill Mulder (Robert Donat), allowed the aliens to abduct Fox Mulder's sister, Samantha Mulder (younger: Vanessa Morley; older: Megan Leitch), when she was eight and he was twelve.

This work of hybrid cloning is being advanced, in part, by former Nazi scientists who came to the United States after World War II, as part of Project Paper Clip. This project, as Mulder puts it, was "our deal with the devil. The U.S. government provided safe haven for certain Nazi war criminals in exchange for their scientific knowledge" ("Paper Clip"). Only, now, rather than engineering a master race, men like Victor Klemper (Walter Gotell) are using DNA from a cryonic alien fetus to engineer a "slave race"—slaves to the aliens. The Syndicate purposefully keeps the work slow, to stall for as much time as they can—even though an ultimate timetable has been set. They also secretly use the alien DNA to work on a vaccine, to prevent the holocaust altogether. At the same time, and certainly with as much difficulty, The Syndicate must ensure the absolute secrecy of the conspiracy from the entire world, while always keeping a watchful eye on Agents Mulder and Scully, who are quickly closing in on the truth.

Mulder and Scully as Sherlock Holmes and Dr. Watson

The Mulder-Scully relationship is modeled on Sir Arthur Conan Doyle's characters of Sherlock Holmes and John Watson. And both Mulder and Scully are quite aware of the similarity. For example, Scully says, "So Sherlock, is the game afoot?" And Mulder responds: "I'm afraid so, Watson" ("Fire"). This line comes from Conan Doyle's "The Adventure of the Abbey Grange," in which Holmes says, "'Come, Watson, come!' . . . 'The game is afoot.'"[5] Scully's right: Mulder *is* Holmes. He even *looks* like Holmes: well-dressed, tall, thin, and languid. Mulder also enjoys lying around watching TV, as Holmes lounges and listens to music; and both are entirely brilliant (Mulder, in fact, has "a photographic memory") ("Fire").[6] The scenery of *The X-Files* is also very Holmesian, a point made by director Rob Bowman: "Because of the fog, or the overcast conditions a lot of the time, rain, [*The X-Files*] maintained a bit of Sherlock Holmes feel to it for me."[7]

Scully is also right that she plays Watson to Mulder's Holmes. She is even a medical doctor, just like Watson. Her role as doctor is significant because physicians are detectives, too, in a way; they read signs on the patient and detect the cause, sometimes a disease, but sometimes a murder. Scully is also—as she correctly notes—almost always two steps behind Mulder, just as Watson is to Holmes. "What I'm thinking, Mulder," says Scully, "is how familiar this seems. Playing Watson to your Sherlock. You dangling clues out in front of me one by one. It's a game, and . . . and, as usual, you're holding something back from me. You're not telling me something about this case" ("Fight Club"). Scully can follow Mulder, because she is a detective—she is simply very close to the hard empirical evidence (mulling it over slowly). While Mulder's mind has already skipped steps ahead to an almost always bizarre conclusion: it is a vampire, or a monster, or a devil, or an alien. Scully, on the other hand, thinks like we do, and we the viewers are meant to identify with her character, just as we identify with Watson. Just as we learn about Holmes's genius through Watson's questions, Scully asks our questions, and Mulder provides the brilliant answers.

Mulder and Scully as Noir Detectives

As a neo–Sherlock Holmes, however, Mulder is also a very noir version of the classic detective (just as Scully is a very noir Watson). Of course, there are no hard and fast rules about what makes a noir detective, but there are several elements common among many noir stories. Among these, first, the lead character (or characters) is typically a detective. And essential to virtually all noir detective stories is the idea of the labyrinth. In fact, the classical myth of the labyrinth is the ancient ancestor of the detective story. In this tale, Ariadne gives Theseus a sword and a "clue of thread" to navigate the labyrinth and slay the Minotaur within it. From mythology to noir, Theseus becomes the detective; the labyrinth is now the detective quest; the Minotaur is the villain; Ariadne becomes the femme fatale, and can, in noir, come in two forms: one good, the other bad; and finally, the "clue of thread" becomes the "thread of clues." In *The X-Files,* Theseus is Mulder; the labyrinth is the alien–U.S. government conspiracy; Scully is the *good* Ariadne, while Special Agent Diana Fowley (Mimi Rogers)—Mulder's past lover, whose mind is like Mulder's—is the *bad* Ariadne; and the Minotaur is the alien race, which, like the classic Minotaur, is hidden. Only now, they are also hidden in space, which lends an additional very noir element to *The X-Files:* namely, a very dark screen.

The labyrinth theme is also extended from the external world of space to the internal one of the mind. Scully and Mulder must navigate the mazes of their own (often unreliable) memories to discover the clue to the alien-government conspiracy—a theme that places *The X-Files* squarely in a tradition of noir films known to film scholars as "amnesia noirs." In the early 1940s, there were several amnesia noirs, for example, *Somewhere in the Night* (Joseph L. Mankiewicz, 1946), *Spellbound* (Hitchcock, 1945), and *Crack-Up* (Irving Reis, 1946), with a standard plot: a noir detective with amnesia investigates not only his external surroundings but equally his own mind for signs that will show who he is and what happened to him. Today, most amnesia noirs use retrograde amnesia. The detective cannot remember who he is and must discover what happened, for example, *Angel Heart* (Alan Parker, 1987), *The Machinist* (Brad Anderson, 2004), *Dark City,* and *Blade Runner:* Rachel (Sean Young) has false memories, "implants"; and so does

Rick Deckard (Harrison Ford). At least one amnesia noir, that is, *Memento* (Christopher Nolan, 2000), has used anterograde amnesia. The detective has a well of solid memories but cannot form any new memories. So, every five to ten minutes, it is all gone. *The X-Files,* however, is a distinctly lacunar amnesia noir. Mulder must fill in a missing gap (a "lacuna") of memory from of one night when he was twelve and saw his sister abducted by aliens. (But then again, maybe Mulder just overlaid a repressed memory with boyish fantasies of little green men from outer space.) Mulder is driven by this memory of Samantha's alien abduction and the hope that one day he can find her. And he knows that the truth of her whereabouts lies half in the X-Files themselves and half in his own mind. So, just as he studies the science of the paranormal, he also examines his past, and he undergoes regression hypnosis for clues. Scully, however, is skeptical of Mulder's amnesia and the very idea of regression hypnosis, as well as aliens and government cover-ups; that is, until her own apparent alien abduction, when she is struck with lacunar amnesia as well. Struggling with the gap of memory, she, too, engages in regression hypnosis—though, again, she is consistently skeptical. Indeed, as in any great amnesia noir detective story, there are, within *The X-Files,* at least two detective searches: one for the villain (aliens and government conspirators), and the other for the detective's own mind. And as the quest proceeds, we hear both Mulder and Scully (separately) and very often describe their experiences with amnesia in that cool voice-over detective narration so common to noir cinema.[8]

Mulder and Scully and Clifford and James

In exploring their respective amnesias Scully and Mulder are, indeed, quite different. In fact, in exploring virtually every case, Scully and Mulder use distinct detective methodologies for getting at the truth. And at the end of the episodes, we get summaries of these methods as they narrate the reports of the cases they have just investigated. Here we get their two perspectives and explanations of the same phenomena—the believer and the skeptic—while leaving the viewer to ponder the truth about what is *really* out there. What emerges in this point-counterpoint dialectic between Mulder and Scully is precisely the idea that perspective matters. Our beliefs and commitments condition our understanding because they condition how we select and interpret data. For, with no absolutely neutral point of view, seeing something is neither the beginning nor the end of the matter. Scully believes in the method of science, so she refuses to trust anything she sees unless it is based in empirically testable evidence. While Mulder believes without evidence—and comes to see everywhere what he already believes—he almost seems to believe out of passion alone. Indeed, seeing is *not* believing: rather, in *The X-Files,* believing is seeing.

The same tension between belief and evidence played out over a century ago between the American pragmatist William James (1842–1910) and the British philosopher William Clifford (1845–1879). In his 1879 essay, "The Ethics of Belief," Clifford argued that it is simply immoral ever to believe anything on insufficient evidence, despite the comfort it may provide.[9] Belief is not about private pleasure but should be included in our duties to humankind. So, for example, one may want very badly to believe in fate, and such a belief may even lead to a much happier life for the individual who holds it. But one has no right to hold this belief and, in fact, does a moral injustice to one's fellow man doing so. One bad belief leads to another, and soon an entire generation holds many unfounded, even ridiculous ideas: witches, crystals, astrology, numerology, and extraterrestrials. Future generations then labor under so many (often dangerous) illusions that they have to slowly weed out the various unsupported beliefs of their traditions. We owe it to future generations not to corrupt the pool of collectively evolving beliefs in the here and now. We are *only* morally permitted to maintain, and—most importantly—to transmit to children and students those beliefs that hold up to rigorous scientific testing and examination from the entire critical community. So, Clifford argues, we are morally obligated *not* to believe when there is no evidence and to suspend judgment, even if that means suspending it indefinitely. And when we search for evidence, it is paramount that we do so without a belief already in place. We should be open to whatever the inquiry itself suggests. Clifford thinks that to investigate something about which one has already made up his mind is not to investigate honestly; the genuine inquirer must be a true agnostic on the matter. Of course, this is also Scully's view: she is willing to believe, but *only* with hard evidence. And if she happens to witnesses what science cannot support or handle, she will even doubt her own senses and remain in a state of doubt. This is the only honest, scientific thing to do. And she has no problem living up to that ideal.

But James recognizes in Clifford's methodology an internal problem. Rather than based on evidence, Clifford's cautious ethics of belief is, in fact, based in passions—specifically the passion of fear: fear of being wrong, fear of trying out difficult ideas because it risks error. So, ultimately, his anti-passion epistemology itself rests upon the very passions it seeks to circumvent and dispel from belief. Of course, this is not to say that James is an unscientific philosopher. In fact, his entire philosophical system is based in contemporary evolutionary theory. But, as James sees it, there are limits to this scientific approach, and he attempts to make room within his system for the reasonableness of holding beliefs without hard evidence.

What Clifford overlooks is that when one encounters a genuine possibility, *"our passional nature not only may, but must, decide,"* as James puts it.[10] From time to time we find ourselves forced to choose between two live (or credible) hypotheses, and whatever decision we make will be momentous because we will not likely get a chance to reverse our decision. And in these cases, we *must* suspend Clifford's demand for evidence. James himself has in mind a belief in a personal God, for which (many reasonable people hold), there is no solid scientific evidence to convince the skeptic. Nevertheless a belief in God, as James sees it, is credible, and indeed momentous—rather than trivial (in that a personal relationship with God changes the way a person lives her life). Faced with this possibility, we simply cannot suspend judgment, as Clifford suggests, waiting for the scientific community to amass evidence (which may or may not come) over hundreds of generations.

Now, of course, James knows we risk error in "willing to believe"; but this is a relatively minor risk, considering what we may lose by suspending belief. We can hardly (positively) pursue the truth of what may be, if we are only concerned with avoiding error. Each of us must choose for herself—*not* for future generations, as Clifford claims. Ultimately, though, according to James, such an impassioned choice without evidence has its consequences for future generations as well. For, it is our mutual respect for one another's personal struggle with belief that fosters the moral tolerance so essential for an open society—indeed for all the free-thinking members of future generations (in stark contrast to Clifford's position).

We see this Jamesian view in Mulder, who *also* has a personal interest in an otherworldly being (or beings), that is, the aliens, and the evidence for which is hardly scientific. Nevertheless, Mulder (like James) "wills to believe"—evident on his office poster: "I WANT TO BELIEVE" is printed over a blurry UFO image hovering over a forest. Driven by this passionate will, Mulder pursues a truth *he already believes.* And it is simply beyond him why Scully *cannot* believe:

Mulder: Why do you refuse to believe?
Scully: Believing's the easy part, Mulder. I just need more than you. I need proof.
Mulder: You think that believing is easy? ("Nisei")

But Scully is right here. Believing *is* easy for Mulder. For him, in fact, nothing seems easier than believing. After all, he believes in the sea monster "Big Blue" ("Quagmire"), reincarnation, the extraterrestrial impregnation of zoo animals ("Fearful Symmetry"), even an extinct dog called the Wanshang Dhole, which developed human-like intelligence ("Alpha")—and almost every other mythical monster the writers can think of. As Scully puts it, Mulder "believes without question," which drives her a little crazy. And yet, regardless of how far-fetched Mulder's beliefs are, when he employs them in his detective work, somehow he is almost always right on target:

Scully: Mulder, can't you just for once, just . . . for the novelty of it, come up with the simplest explanation, the most logical one, instead of automatically jumping to UFOs or Bigfoot or . . . ?
Mulder: Scully, in six years, how . . . how often have I been wrong? No, seriously. I mean, every time I bring you a new case, we go through this perfunctory dance. You tell me I'm not being scientifically rigorous and that I'm off my nut, and then in the end who turns out to be right like 98.9 percent of the time? I just think I've . . . earned the benefit of the doubt here. ("Field Trip")

Of course, Mulder's point is a good one. He *is* almost always the one to crack the case, at least in terms of the mysterious phenomenon. But Scully raises a good question, too, because he seems to avoid logic in favor of the least plausible explanation. And it is hardly an adequate response merely to note that he tends to be right. She wants to know what he is doing when he "automatically jumps to UFOs or Bigfoot" as an explanation, rather than the "most logical one." In fact, it is fair to say that Mulder has no idea what he is doing when he jumps to the right answer. He does not really know if or how his method is logical or whether it is intuition, or creative imagination, or perhaps some form of paranormal faculty that he alone possesses.

The Logic of Abduction—the Other "Abduction"

What Mulder is doing, however, is using a logic that all detectives use, and which is called the "logic of abduction" (which is meant in a logical, different sense than "aliens stealing bodies").[11] Perhaps we should not blame Mulder for not knowing what he is doing, because really no detectives—brilliant as they appear to be—have the slightest clue what they are doing. Even the best of them, Sherlock Holmes, mistakenly identifies his logic as "deduction." The logic of abduction was pioneered by American philosopher Charles S. Peirce (1839–1914), making Peirce one of the most important philosophers of detective work.[12] The standard logical form of abduction is as follows:

THE LOGIC OF ABDUCTION
[Premise 1: *Result*] The surprising fact, *C,* is observed;
[Premise 2: *Rule*] But if *A* were true, *C* would be a matter of course;
[Conclusion: *Case*] Hence, there is reason to suspect that *A* is true.[13]

Or, in layman's terms, abduction is the logic of how we make guesses. As Peirce puts it, "abduction is, after all, nothing but guessing."[14] It works like this: Everything seems normal, and then suddenly you are surprised. Anything can do it—your door is ajar, or the doormat has shifted, or a boot print appears on your floor (and you do not wear boots). You want to explain these surprises, these anomalies. So, you advance a hypothesis, a guess: "If someone broke in, then these anomalies would be a matter of course; therefore, there is reason to suspect a break-in." Granted, this has not been established; it is just a guess worth considering, just the best explanation you can come up with—something to start you on your way to further investigation, to test whether your guess is right. It could be that a family member or a friend is paying you a surprise visit, or perhaps something else. But your reasoning to the best explanation—narrowing the possibilities down to what you think is most likely—is this generation of the abduction.

Or, consider another abduction example that Scully makes. Scully and Mulder are hiding the first successful alien-hybrid clone, Cassandra Spender (Veronica Cartwright), in Mulder's apartment. Suddenly, FBI agents in chemical suits bust in, seal off the building and take all three away to a quarantine facility, because, they are told, everyone may be susceptible to a biohazard. Mulder and Scully wait in a room (after showering), and Special Agent Diana Fowley enters. Then Scully makes the abduction that the whole biohazard claim was a lie. Scully says, "No one is sick or infected here. I mean, I assume that, based on you walking in here dressed to the nines offering apologies masquerading as explanation" ("One Son"). If people were sick or infected, then Agent Fowley would still be in her chemical suit, rather than ready for a dinner party. So, Scully is right. Fowley is lying. But, in fact, Scully is wrong about her thought being the result of an assumption: it is actually the conclusion of an abductive inference:

SCULLY'S CLOTHING ABDUCTION
[Premise 1: *Result*] The surprising fact, *C* [Agent Fowley is without a
    gas mask and "dressed to the nines" in a quarantine situation], is
    observed;
[Premise 2: *Rule*] But if *A* [this is *not* a quarantine situation and
    Fowley is lying] were true, *C* would be a matter of course;
[Conclusion: *Case*] Hence, there is reason to suspect that *A* is true
    [Fowley is lying].

Actually, this is a distinct form of the logic of abduction, one of three developed by the contemporary philosopher and Peirce scholar Umberto Eco.[15] In "Horns, Hooves, Insteps: Some Hypotheses on Three Types of Abduction," Eco expands Peirce's logic of abduction and distinguishes between "overcoded," "undercoded," and "creative" abductions (each using the same logical form above).[16] The difference is in how the second premise comes about. Overcoded abductions are the easiest: the rule "is given automatically," and no searching for the right hypothesis is required.[17] Agent Scully's abduction about Agent Fowley is an overcoded abduction. Undercoded abductions are harder: you *search* for the rule most "plausible among many," like Scully does in all her autopsies (because if you need an autopsy in the first place, then the abduction is not obvious).[18] Mulder also uses undercoded abductions, for example, he guesses that Gibson Praise (Jeff Gulka) is telepathic (can read minds), from a tape-recording of Gibson who barely avoids being shot at a chess match. Everyone else in the room thinks it obvious that Gibson missed a bullet from a sniper by pure chance, and Mulder knows that is a possibility, but he asks for a replay of the tape because he knows it is also possible that something more than chance is at work—and Gibson has given away some very subtle clues.

With creative abductions, however, the rule is invented. In "Field Trip" (one of the best non-Mythology *X-Files* episodes), Mulder and Scully notice that they are hallucinating, and yet they have taken no drugs. Typically, we noted, it is Mulder who makes the giant leaps forward—which is true (no doubt about it). But we cannot help noting that one of the best creative abductions in the entire series is made by Scully. She actually synthesizes three different rules: Some mushrooms are massive; some are hallucinogenic; and some plants are carnivorous, such as pitcher plants and Venus flytraps. Fusing these three (and remembering they saw mushrooms earlier), Scully creatively abducts that they are now being slowly digested underground, inside a gigantic hallucinogenic mushroom, and must now make their way out.

SCULLY'S CREATIVE MUSHROOM ABDUCTION

[Premise 1: *Result*] The surprising fact, *C* [We are both hallucinating, since our field trip where we saw mushrooms, but have taken no drugs], is observed;

[Premise 2: *Rule*] But if *A* [We are being digested within a giant underground hallucinogenic mushroom] were true, *C* would be a matter of course;

[Conclusion: *Case*] Hence, there is reason to suspect that *A* is true.

After making their way out of the underground mushroom and cleaning up at home, Scully and Mulder report to Assistant Director of the FBI Walter Skinner (Mitch Pileggi), who is impressed with their escape. Mulder, however, is still in doubt as to their success, based on two results. First, he asks Scully, "Can you name me one drug that loses its effect once the user realizes it is in his system?" And second, "We were covered in hydrochloric acid. Yet look at our skin. Nothing." Now Mulder makes the abduction (which is "undercoded" because Scully's rule—the possibility that they could be inside a giant mushroom—has already been created): "Scully, . . . we never escaped. We're still trapped underground" ("Field Trip").[19]

MULDER'S UNDERCODED MUSHROOM ABDUCTION

[Premise 1: *Result*] The surprising fact, *C* [Our escape seems causally problematic; and further we have no burn marks from the acid], is observed;

[Premise 2: *Rule*] But if *A* [We only *think* we've escaped, and we are still being digested underground] were true, *C* would be a matter of course;

[Conclusion: *Case*] Hence, there is reason to suspect that *A* is true.

Detective Semiotics and the "Absence Sign"

The surprising fact that sets these abductions in motion (the "result"), is always a sign—or, what in detective stories is called a "clue"—a point that brings us back momentarily to the myth of the labyrinth (central to all detective stories). Remember, Ariadne gives Theseus a "clue" of thread so that he can enter the labyrinth and then find his way back out after killing the Minotaur. As the detective story evolved through Sherlock Holmes and noir, the "clue of thread" became transformed into the "thread of clues" (as we noted). In the myth of the labyrinth, the clue represents a series of coded signs that the detective creates—and these then serve as a form of artificial memory (intentionally logged memory by the detective), which is really only useful on the way out of the labyrinth. Think, for example, of Hansel and Gretel using stones and breadcrumbs to lay down a clue to find their way out of the forest labyrinth (the witch, of course, is the Minotaur). In the hard-boiled detective story, however, the clue represents a series of coded signs that the detective does not so much *create* as *discover*. And they do not form so much an artificial memory leading out of the labyrinth and away from the Minotaur, as they do a trail of codes, typically unintentionally left by the Minotaur/villain, leading progressively into the labyrinth and toward the villain. And rather than Ariadne's string, which need only be followed blindly out of the labyrinth, the detective clue must be studied and placed into the abductive syllogism at every turn of the labyrinth.

The study of these detective signs is called "semiotics" and, once again, is a field pioneered by Peirce. According to Peirce, virtually all of our thinking takes place in terms of a flow of signs, one into the next and the next, without end. And, typically, the form of transition is precisely the logic of abduction. So, in effect, as Peirce sees human beings, we are all essentially highly evolved detectives. We are always spotting signs, like clouds for rain, the slight curl of a mouth for approval or understanding, the subtlest innuendo to convey what is being said between the lines. Only, evolved as we are, we are mainly unconscious of the thousands of tiny codes we detect and abduct on a daily basis. What separates the great detectives, like Edgar Allan Poe's Monsieur Auguste Dupin and Sherlock Holmes and Fox Mulder, from people like us is that the method of reading signs and drawing abductive inferences is, for them, not unconscious, but conscious and deliberate and self-controlled (even though, as we noted, they are not aware of the specific logical form of abduction).

These signs take many forms. But in terms of detective work—which was very close to Peirce's heart—one particular kind of sign, the index, is the most important. The index is a sign that signifies its object physically, like a footprint signifies a foot, or a thermometer signifies heat (by being affected by that heat).[20] And, once again, building on Peirce's philosophy of detective work, Eco adds to his semiotics—developing three kinds of detective (indexical) signs. These are "imprints" (one-to-one, point-for-point signs, e.g., fingerprints); "symptoms" (not so much point-for-point, but tandem signification, e.g., the black oil/alien virus expresses itself in the decomposition of body tissue within the host); and "clues," which are objects deposited (e.g., Morley cigarette butts deposited by the Cigarette Smoking Man [William B. Davis]).[21] Naturally, Scully (the physician) is concerned with medical symptoms. And certainly Mulder studies these, too. But it seems more often that he is concerned with a unique kind of sign, one that is a little underdeveloped in the literature on semiotics—and even seems to fall outside of Eco's (Peircean) taxonomy. In effect, Mulder often detects the sign of "nothing," or what we might call the "absence sign." A situation arises, and something is missing, but just what that is, Mulder and Scully cannot yet tell. Consider the following dialogue.

> Scully: Well, nothing about it makes sense. We've got three deaths of
>   identical victims, no bodies, a virtual non-suspect . . .
> Mulder: Sounds just like an X-File.
> Scully: You don't even know who sent that information. ("Colony")

Scully points out that they have no evidence in the crime, and that nothing makes sense about that lack of evidence. Yet, from Mulder's perspective, the lack is precisely why the case *does* make sense, from the perspective of *The X-Files,* placing it right within his realm of semiotic expertise. After all, consider Mulder's study of alien villains, compared to ordinary earthly criminals. Usually, when a detective tracks a human villain, the signs are blood, hair, DNA, fingerprints, footprints, et cetera. But aliens do not really have blood (they have a black oil inside them, which is semi-sentient and capable of moving or burying itself—making itself absent); nor do they leave human prints; and there is no public database on their DNA, pictures, travel habits, or goals. In fact, the clue they usually leave is a sign of absence. They take bodies without a trace: Samantha Mulder, Fox Mulder, Scully, and Cassandra Spender.[22] Of course, a victim or a bystander would remember all the necessary details, but the aliens actually wipe the memories of all their victims, leaving nothing but a sense of loss of memory (again, a sign of absence). They even stop all the surrounding clocks. For example, Mulder says, "We lost nine minutes" ("Pilot Episode"). Indeed, examples of this "absence sign" abound throughout *The X-Files*. We may even take our mushroom example above: Consider that second undercoded (not creative) abduction that Mulder makes. He notices that there is an absence of signs, an absence of burn marks from the hydrochloric acid that has been digesting his flesh and Scully's. These signs are missing, when they should be present.

Now, returning to Eco's triad of subcategories of Peirce's index, it is not entirely clear where to place the absence sign. As we noted, the absence sign seems to fall outside the imprint-symptom-clue triad, at least on first glance. But on second glance, one possibility is to conceive it as itself a kind of clue, an object deposited. Only, here, with the absence sign, our clue is not an object deposited; rather, it is an object removed, making it a kind of inverted clue. With the clue, the object (being deposited there, in a given place) is traceable to the agent. But with the absence sign, it is harder to trace. There is less to go on, because you do not have the object in hand; in fact, that is what you are looking for.

Mulder Thinks Outside the Paradigm

This point also returns us to Scully's and Mulder's debate over their respective methodologies. It is clear they both use detective semiotics and the logic of abduction. But why is Mulder almost always the one who makes the really creative leaps of thought and almost always the one who can read the harder signs (like the sign of absence)? He was the one who knew right away that they were still inside the mushroom, that nine minutes missing meant alien encounter, and that the U.S. government had systematically undermined the American public (and the entire world) for decades, ever since Roswell.

Perhaps part of the reason that Mulder is so good, and Scully lags behind, is that he is able to think more creatively—he is able to extrapolate widely from various scientific data (while Scully is not), but, more importantly, he is able to think beyond the given scientific framework of today. This ability is evident even in the series' pilot episode, when Mulder and Scully meet for the first time. He has read her undergraduate thesis on Einstein and tells her he likes it, but that, unfortunately, in most of the X-Files cases, the laws of physics do not apply. In fact, most of the cases Mulder works on are well beyond the pale of what the scientific community takes to be true or reasonable.

To put it another way, Scully is still operating within what Thomas Kuhn, in *The Structure of Scientific Revolutions,* calls a "paradigm," or a set of acceptable explanations as a way of practicing science.[23] And, as far as Mulder is concerned, that paradigm is a little outdated. Kuhn says there are two stages of science: "revolutionary" (e.g., Aristotle, Galileo, Darwin, Freud, Einstein), in which a paradigm is established, and then "normal science." Once a paradigm is in place, certain ideas are no longer in question; they are just taken for granted, and normal science simply fills in the paradigm. So, for example, Watson and Crick discover the DNA double helix (which is certainly very revolutionary), but the generations who fill in the genomes of humans, pigs, flies, et cetera, are working from within a paradigm, filling it out rather than challenging it. And if an anomaly arises within the theory, typically the scientist ignores it or forces it into the paradigm, since it is more than inconvenient to give up the entire paradigm for just a few anomalies. But if enough anomalies build up, a crisis state arises and science is ripe for a paradigm shift or revolution. In these times, competing theories are on an equal footing until one paradigm gains support and wins out. And then the process begins all over again.

Here we should point out that Kuhn's views on science are somewhat controversial. Many philosophers think the idea of paradigm shifts is too relativistic because the choice of a new theory, according to Kuhn, is not rational. The crisis state does not contain within itself a vision of the new paradigm, which guarantees improvement. Rather, a new paradigm is established for reasons of power, control, and authority. Yet, it is hardly necessary to reject Kuhn's idea of how normal science is done as opposed to revolutionary science, even if one does reject the relativism or irrationality of theory choice. After all, most scientists will tell you quite frankly that sometimes the work is slow and tedious, and they certainly do not throw out a theory based on a few anomalies. They will also say that a Galileo or Darwin comes along rarely, which is not exactly controversial.[24] And there is, in fact, a way to conceive paradigm shifts as a little more rational. Eco, for example, claims that these shifts are perfect examples of creative abductions, which provide logical explanations of the problematic anomalies.

With that in mind, it seems clear that Scully represents the dominant scientific paradigm. If she cannot explain something using current science, she will dismiss it or suspend judgment, noting that an explanation eventually will come. For example, with Eugene Victor Tooms (Doug Hutchison), who fits into tiny spaces, like pipes ("Squeeze" and "Tooms"), Scully has no explanation, so she suspends judgment (rather than reasoning creatively). Mulder, however, is never satisfied with what the paradigm leaves out or science's dismissal of anomalies, a point made by Mulder's informant "Deep Throat":

> Deep Throat (Jerry Hardin): Mr. Mulder, why are those like yourself, who believe in the existence of extraterrestrial life on Earth, not entirely persuaded by all the evidence to the contrary?
> Mulder: Because, all the evidence to the contrary is not entirely dissuasive.
> Deep Throat: Precisely. ("Deep Throat")

Anomalies show that something is possible, and that is enough for Mulder's considerations—even enough for belief.

Scully, however, does come to believe as the seasons progress; and this (using Kuhn's model) is because the anomalies build up within the paradigm and create a crisis state. By the middle of the series, she is ready for a paradigm shift and sees Mulder initiating it. Indeed, Mulder has been quite ready for a paradigm shift since he was twelve. And he knows, too, that paradigm shifts follow a pattern. For just as alien science now looks crazy within our current paradigm, so, too, did Galileo to his contemporaries. And someday, Mulder knows too well, alien science will be just as common and foundational as the heliocentric solar system is today. He also knows that, far from the accountant type of scientist, who dutifully fills in the paradigm, it is, rather, the extremely passionate and obsessive—sometimes even religious (seemingly unscientific)—scientist who changes the way we see things, a man, in fact, just like Mulder.

Indeed, Mulder almost seems beyond paradigms altogether. After all, when we consider the incredible number of possible explanations to which Mulder opens himself, he seems to be the most revolutionary scientist of them all. He is open to almost anything: UFOs, telepathy, astrology, precognition, miracles, demons, shapeshifting, body-jumping, astral projection, stigmatas, aliens, monsters, werewolves, renegade alien bounty hunters, witches, ancient myths, anything that is possible, no matter how unlikely. And this openness to anything is why Mulder is perfect for the "X"-Files—again, these are cases filed under "X" for unclassifiable, unable to be fit into the FBI's paradigm. So, like any dominant paradigm, the FBI relegates the X-Files (as a set of strange anomalies) to the margins (out of sight, out of mind: in the basement). And Mulder (also marginalized) examines these obsessively, without ever worrying how fit them into the dominant paradigm.

Return to the "Will to Believe"

This point about Mulder's pursuit of wacky marginalized ideas, of course, also returns us to Mulder's will to believe. And, again, he pursues these ideas—down in the basement bowels of the FBI, and in spite of all the ridicule of his colleagues—because deep down and on a personal level (because of losing his sister), he wants to believe. This is the motor driving Mulder beyond those merely overcoded and undercoded abductions (at which Scully is so adept), and into the wilder side of the imagination, where he can see other extraterrestrial worlds (and make novel and creative abductions). Indeed, Mulder knows what James knows: believing helps us to see what might otherwise be overlooked. Wanting to believe, or *willing* to believe, can grant us access to certain truths that otherwise may not appear so concretely (and may easily fall outside our paradigm). We must trust first, and then other truths can be discovered.

Examples abound throughout *The X-Files*. First, Mulder (immediately) believes in Clyde Bruckman's (Peter Boyle) psychic ability to tell when and how people are going to die ("Clyde Bruckman's Final Repose")—which leads him (and Scully) to solve a case. Second, Mulder believes it is possible that a genetic mutant consumes human livers, hibernates for years, and can squeeze into the smallest spaces—which allows Mulder to see the man's fingerprints, which look inhuman (completely stretched out) and are placed where no human could possibly travel, for instance, the inside of a small air vent. Third, he accepts without question the existence of the Moth Men, a species of humanity, perfectly adapted over hundreds of years to the Everglades ("Detour")—and this aids in their analysis of their situation. In each of these cases—and virtually every episode of *The X-Files*—Mulder's extreme will to believe provides him with many more hypotheses to select from to form his creative abductions, with a better explanation than the one Scully (and "normal science") comes up with—better because it explains more of the anomalies.

Scully and Mulder as One Mind

On the other hand, however, while Scully is often two steps behind, she is hardly a sideshow to Mulder's genius—she is, in fact, quite integral to it. For, it is her constant analytic counterpoint that keeps his head on straight—helps to keep him level and clear, forcing him to translate his wild creativity into rigorous rationality. In doing so, she very often saves him from being too trusting and too willing to believe. For example, she immediately spots the forged alien spaceship photograph leaked by Deep Throat, intended to throw Mulder off the trail of an alien autopsy—when Mulder would like nothing more than to believe he finally has proof positive of alien visitations to Earth. Nor is Scully's intelligence and value lost on Mulder: "As difficult and as frustrating as it's been sometimes," he tells her, "your goddamn strict rationalism and science have saved me a thousand times over. You kept me honest. You made me a whole person" (*The X-Files: Fight the Future*).

Mulder's right, and he recognizes in Scully what James sees in Clifford: the will to believe and extreme caution are equally integral to the discovery of truth. Indeed, there are, according to James, two goals of inquiry: one, to seek truth, and the other, to avoid error. Logically speaking, these should work together. But, in practice, they do not. Searching for new and creative hypotheses to explain strange phenomena is searching for truth. But worrying too much about mistakes, while we are brainstorming, will not help. That is the second stage, where we test hypotheses and examine empirical results.

And it is precisely here that Mulder, in his search for truth, needs Scully and her correction of error and extreme caution in the search for evidence. This cautious error correction helps Mulder refine his search, making him ever more systematic and careful in his analysis. At the same time, Scully gradually comes to see the limits of her own scientific methodology. While she never gives up on the scientific method, she does, however, come to expand her field of vision. She begins to open her paradigm to the things of Mulder's world, ultimately seeing with her own eyes hard evidence of the truth that Mulder has long known about aliens, conspiracy, and the end of the world. In fact, by the end of the series, after Mulder has been abducted by aliens, it is left to Scully to explain to Agent John Doggett (Robert Patrick)—someone just as skeptical as Scully used to be—that "Gibson Praise . . . is part alien" ("Without").

For the philosopher, this is the true arc of the story of *The X-Files*, underlying the massive mythology plot of alien conspiracy, how two minds, one wild and creative, and the other empirical and analytic, are fused into one—into a "whole person," as Mulder puts it. Mulder sharpens his wild imagination on Scully's hard empirical method, while Scully opens her mind more and more to the various political and metaphysical possibilities at work behind the scenes. As this whole person emerges, moreover, a greater noir detective does, too—one who sees more and more deeply into the truth (as the seasons unfold), and the arc of the mythology reaches its climax. Yet, somehow, even this whole person must necessarily fall short of the task. For, with all their powers of mind and their mutual trust in one another, they are ultimately led to a place that neither expected, where even reason cannot help them. Indeed, here they come up against the very limits of their own methodologies, in the face of the greatest terror they can possibly imagine. And it is here where they must leave their abductive logic and intricate detective semiotics behind and embrace a strange kind of faith—though not for any of the reasons Scully used to hold, and despite all of Mulder's arguments against them. The aliens are coming, and there is absolutely nothing they can do—but hope (blindly) in what, they do not know.

Notes

We would like to thank Aeon J. Skoble and Steven M. Sanders for reading and commenting on an earlier draft of this essay. Of course, any mistakes that remain are our own.

1. Foster Hirsch, *Detours and Lost Highways: A Map of Neo-Noir* (New York: Limelight, 1991), 14.

2. Edward Dimendberg, *Film Noir and the Spaces of Modernity* (Cambridge: Harvard University Press, 2004), 255. See also Jerold J. Abrams, "Space, Time, and Subjectivity in Neo-Noir Cinema," in *The Philosophy of Neo-Noir,* ed. Mark T. Conard (Lexington: University Press of Kentucky, 2006).

3. Paul M. Sammon, *Future Noir: The Making of Blade Runner* (New York: Perennial, 1996).

4. See also *Paycheck* (John Woo, 2003) and *Minority Report* (Steven Spielberg, 2002).

5. Sir Arthur Conan Doyle, "The Adventure of the Abbey Grange," in *The Complete Sherlock Holmes* (New York: Barnes & Noble, 1992), 636. The line originally comes from Shakespeare, *Henry V,* III.i.2: "The game is afoot," in *The Complete Works of William Shakespeare* (New York: Avenel Books, 1975), 500. We are grateful to Richard White and Clarinda Karpov for pointing this out to us in conversation.

6. It is unclear whether Mulder shares Holmes's madness (based more or less on

the madness of Edgar Allan Poe's Monsieur Auguste Dupin). Perhaps the closest we come to an answer is in "Grotesque." Here he must find Agent Bill Patterson (Kurtwood Smith), who trained him in the art of seeing madness but who has since gone completely mad. Now, Mulder must explore his own insanity to solve the case. He says: "We work in the dark. We do what we can to battle with the evil that would otherwise destroy us. But if a man's character is his fate, this fight is not a choice, but a calling. Yet sometimes the weight of this burden causes us to falter, breaching the fragile fortress of our mind, allowing the monsters without to turn within and we are left alone, staring into the abyss . . . into the laughing face of madness."

7. Rob Bowman commentary, "Threads of My Theology," *The X-Files Mythology,* Disc 4: *Abduction,* DVD, directed by Bowman et al. (Beverly Hills, CA: Twentieth Century Fox, 2005).

8. As the seasons press on, and new detectives are added, Special Agent John Doggett (Robert Patrick) also has amnesia (retrograde)—wakes up in a dirty town in Mexico with no idea how he got there or who he is—and now must discover both his identity and who took his memories away ("John Doe").

9. William Clifford, *The Ethics of Belief and Other Essays* (1878; New York: Prometheus Books, 1999).

10. William James, "The Will to Believe," in *The Will to Believe and Other Essays in Popular Philosophy* (1896; New York: Longman, Green, 1927), 11

11. Umberto Eco and Thomas Sebeok, ed., *The Sign of Three: Dupin, Holmes, Peirce* (Bloomington: Indiana University Press, 1983). See also Jerold J. Abrams, "From Sherlock Holmes to the Hardboiled Detective in Film Noir," in *The Philosophy of Film Noir,* ed. Mark T. Conard (Lexington: University Press of Kentucky, 2006). Sometimes Scully and Mulder come close to discussing their methods; but these approximations seem haphazard at best. For example, Scully says, "Yeah, I was sure of the facts as I had deduced them scientifically" ("Patience"). Of course, she is not deducing anything. And Mulder notes: "I'm guessing that's what he said" ("The Goldberg Variation"). But, again, this is hardly a Dupin or Holmes-type self-analysis of method.

12. Peirce is arguably—and almost always credited as—America's greatest philosopher. In addition to being a master logician (pioneering the logic of abduction, and the logic of relatives, along with Augustus De Morgan), he was also a mathematician, a chemist, and the inventor of the philosophy of pragmatism, a philosophical worldview based in the Darwinian evolution of ideas as signs. This philosophy would t become popularized by William James, John Dewey, and, later, Hilary Putnam and Richard Rorty.

13. Peirce, "Pragmatism as the Logic of Abduction," in *The Essential Peirce, Selected Philosophical Writings,* Vol. 2: *1899–1913,* ed. the Peirce Edition Project (Bloomington: Indiana University Press, 1998), 231. Some versions of abduction may be said to affirm the consequent (If P then Q; Q; ∴ P), which is a fallacy of the deductive syllogism. But no one here is claiming that abduction, like deduction, is valid—nor are we claiming that abduction is deduction, or even like it. Abduction, like induction, is invalid; true

enough—but it works very well. And besides, it is precisely the logic used by all detectives, fictional and real, and it is the logic used in all scientific discovery.

14. Peirce, "On the Logic of Drawing History from Ancient Documents," *The Essential Peirce,* 2:107.

15. For many, Eco is best known as the novelist who wrote *The Name of the Rose* (1980), trans. William Weaver (New York: Harcourt Brace, 1984). In Peirce circles, however, he is one of the top abduction and semiotics scholars. See for example, his *A Theory of Semiotics* (Bloomington: Indiana University Press, 1976); *Semiotics and the Philosophy of Language* (Bloomington: Indiana University Press, 1984); *Kant and the Platypus: Essays on Language and Cognition* (1997), trans. Alastair McEwen (New York: Harcourt, 1999); *The Limits of Interpretation* (Bloomington: Indiana University Press, 1994); and "Unlimited Semeiosis and Drift: Pragmaticism vs. 'Pragmatism,'" in *Peirce and Contemporary Thought: Philosophical Inquiries,* ed. Kenneth Laine Ketner (New York: Fordham University Press, 1995).

16. Eco, "Horns, Hooves, Insteps," in Eco and Sebeok, *The Sign of Three,* 206–7. Eco also develops a theory of "meta-abduction," which is strongly intertwined with creative abduction: "Meta-abduction. It consists in deciding as to whether the possible universe outlined by our first-level abductions is the same as the universe of our experience" (207).

17. Ibid., 206.

18. Ibid.

19. Quotations taken from Red Wolf's *X-Files Episode Guide,* http://www.redwolf.com.au/xfiles/season06/6abx21.html (accessed July 5, 2006). One of the weaknesses in the character of Mulder as a detective (in the same line as Sherlock Holmes) regards what Peirce calls the "musement state." Musement is a meditative and contemplative state, which in Holmes is typically drug-induced. In this state, the mind rearranges clues in various orders to allow the best abduction to present itself. Mulder does not seem to engage in it. He drinks once in the film, but he is clearly not musing. Nor does he take drugs. He does like to zone out in front of the TV, but that is not quite musement, either. In fact, Mulder often appears almost *too* quick to make the abduction, and certainly this is what is so jarring to Scully. Right out of the blue, Mulder will look at a few signs and guess correctly: it was the aliens, or the vampires, or the Moth Men.

20. According to Peirce, when we are reading a sign, we must grasp what it signifies, that is, the object of the sign. There are three basic kinds of sign-object relation: symbols, icons, and indexes. Symbols are conventional signs: we just agree that "&" signifies "and," "%" means "percent," and "@" means "at." Iconic signs, by contrast, signify their objects by resemblance: "☺" signifies "happy" or "smiling"; "☼" signifies "sun," because the sign "looks like" the object; maps, diagrams, and portraits are the same. Indexes have an even closer relation to their objects because they signify by physical connection. And these are signs detectives study.

21. Eco, "Horns, Hooves, Insteps," 211.

22. Of course, it is true that "nothing disappears without a trace," as Albert Hosteen (Floyd "Red Crow" Westerman) says—a sentiment echoed by the Cigarette Smoking Man ("Anasazi"). But these traces are often so faint, and the causes so strange—and, more often than not, both are covered up or destroyed by the government (as in the 1947 Roswell crash).

23. Thomas S. Kuhn, *The Structure of Scientific Revolutions,* 2nd ed., enlarged (1962; Chicago: University of Chicago Press, 1970), 10, 174–210.

23. Eco, "Horns, Hooves, Insteps," 207.

24. Here we should point out that bringing Peirce and James together (as well as Kuhn and Eco) is a creative fusion intended to reveal what Mulder does. It is an important point to note because, in fact, Peirce and James disagreed on so much in their respective philosophies. Peirce was a realist and believed that logic, signs, and numbers lay at the foundation of thought and reality; while James was more antirealistic, far less logical, far less semiotically driven, and believed that material flux lay at the core of reality and that radical empiricism was the way to know it. Indeed, while the two were friends and colleagues, after Peirce invented pragmatism, James took it and popularized it (wrongly, in Peirce's view). So, Peirce renamed his method "pragmaticism," claiming that such an ugly name would keep it safe from kidnappers. Nevertheless, there are elements of their theories that come together rather nicely, particularly with regard to the logic of abduction, especially evident in Mulder's method. We are grateful to Steven M. Sanders for bringing this to our attention.

Part 4

AUTONOMY, SELFHOOD, AND INTERPRETATION

Kingdom of Darkness: Autonomy and Conspiracy in *The X-Files* and *Millennium*

Michael Valdez Moses

> The judges of normality are present everywhere. We are in the
> society of the teacher-judge, the doctor-judge, the educator-
> judge, the "social worker"–judge; it is on them that the universal
> reign of the normative is based; and each individual, wherever
> he may find himself, subjects to it his body, his gestures, his
> behaviour, his aptitudes, his achievements. The carceral network,
> in its compact or disseminated forms, with its systems of
> insertion, distribution, surveillance, observation, has been the
> greatest support, in modern society, of the normalizing power.
> —Michel Foucault, *Discipline and Punish*

Mr. (and Ms.) Noir

In Michel Foucault's influential account of the rise and consolidation of modern society, the individual soul, if it can be said to exist at all, is the easily manipulated product of an all-pervasive and interlocking set of disciplinary institutions and administrative bodies, a "carceral archipelago" consisting of prisons, schools, hospitals, psychiatric clinics, the army, social-welfare agencies, the police, and the courts. For most Americans, Foucault, like Orwell before him, would seem to describe the realities of Stalin's Russia or Hitler's Germany (rather than modern France), but in any case not those of the United States of America, whose citizens historically understood their nation as a bastion of individual liberty and freedom. And yet, at the turn of the last millennium, a mass viewing audience in the United States (and around the globe) sat transfixed each week before televised images of America as the quintessential disciplinary society. To be sure, Chris Carter's two most successful shows, *The X-Files* (which ran from 1993 to 2002) and *Millennium* (1996–1999), regularly presented their chief protagonists—Fox Mulder, Dana Scully, John Doggett, Monica Reyes, Frank Black, Emma Hollis, and Lara Means—as resolutely heroic in their efforts "to fight the future," to defend a traditionally American conception of individual freedom and personal autonomy against those agents of darkness, whether mundane, extraterrestrial, or supernatural, who would impose upon the American people and the rest of the world a compulsory disciplinary order. And yet, what may prove most memorable about these two television shows is not their wildly imaginative use of alien abductions, extraterrestrial bounty hunters, genetically engineered super-soldiers, satanic agents, angelic manifestations, prophesies of the coming apocalypse, or even the sudden worldwide celebrity of David Duchovny and Gillian Anderson, but rather an uncompromising vision of postwar (and post–Cold War) America as a kingdom of darkness, a fallen republic in which political rights are routinely violated, a nation in which the realm of individual autonomy is both increasingly circumscribed and fatally imperiled.[1]

Given their dark vision of postwar America, it should come as no surprise that both of Carter's shows are deeply influenced by classic film noir. Featuring protagonists who are current or former FBI agents, both series play off the well-established conventions of gritty and hard-boiled crime and espionage films that came to prominence in the 1940s and 1950s and which include such classics as *The Maltese Falcon* (John Huston, 1941), *Laura* (Otto Preminger, 1944), *The Big Sleep* (Howard Hawks, 1946), *Out of the Past* (Jacques Tourneur, 1947), *The Third Man* (Carole Reed, 1949), *The Asphalt Jungle* (Huston, 1950), and *Touch of Evil* (Orson Welles, 1958). While it is impossible to offer a single formula that would fit every episode of the two series (which ran for 201 and 67 episodes respectively), both shows feature intrepid investigators whose attempts to solve mysterious, bizarre, and often grisly crimes lead them to uncover a vast conspiracy involving governmental agencies, religious organizations, business interests, and nonhuman forces (extraterrestrial interlopers, satanic powers) who attempt to control the lives of ordinary citizens. The quest to discover the truth leads Carter's protagonists on a labyrinthine journey through an underworld of crime, deceit, danger, and paranoia, a dark realm populated by illegal immigrants, street hustlers, prostitutes, exotic dancers, sexual deviants, the destitute, the insane, disabled vets, alcoholics, junkies, assassins, spies, mystics, fortunetellers, misfits, circus freaks, black marketers, disgraced government officials, petty criminals, religious fanatics, adolescent runaways, computer hackers, and conspiracy nuts, to name only a few of the more commonly encountered types. And yet, as with the detectives of classic film noir, Carter's protagonists belatedly discover that at the organizational hub of the underworld are the very people and institutions that ostensibly represent the cause of law and order, public respectability, and moral rectitude. The protagonists of *The X-Files* and *Millennium* thus come to embody that peculiar ethos of cynicism and selfless devotion to the truth, moral tolerance, and heroic self-sacrifice that often (but not always) defined the heroes of classic film noir, Bogart's Sam Spade and Philip Marlowe (*The Maltese Falcon, The Big Sleep*) Joseph Cotten's Holly Martins (*The Third Man*), and Charlton Heston's Ramon "Mike" Vargas (*Touch of Evil*).

Film critics and historians have long insisted that classic film noir is defined less by its generic plot or stereotypical characters than by its distinctive visual style and narrative techniques (in part because film noir encompasses so many disparate genres: detective and crime vehicles, espionage and psychological thrillers, and at a later stage of its development science fiction and horror films). In particular, critics have emphasized the importance of high-contrast black-and-white cinematography (rooted in German expressionist films of the silent era), obtuse or disorienting camera angles (including the hero's-eye-view), flashbacks, and confessional voice-over as among the most distinctive features of classic film noir. Both *The X-Files* and *Millennium* make generous use of these techniques: an entire episode of *The X-Files* is shot in high-contrast black and white ("The Post Modern Prometheus"), while segments of many other episodes of both shows utilize stylized black-and-white cinematography as a means of evoking the feel of America in the 1940s, '50s, and early '60s ("Musings of a Cigarette-Smoking Man," "The Curse of Frank Black," "Midnight of the Century," "Seven and One"). More generally, both shows helped change the look of American television in the 1990s by employing a distinctive style of high-contrast lighting, the frequent use of minimally lit scenes (recall the signature shots of Mulder, Scully, Black, and Hollis armed with flashlights investigating darkened interiors), a washed-out color palette, and the frequent use of jarring or unusual camera angles (including low- and high-angle shots and the hero's eye view) that consciously evoke the visual texture of classic film noir. Perhaps most conspicuously, both shows make routine use of flashback and voice-over (confessional and otherwise) to frame or propel the narrative of many episodes. It thus should come as no surprise that in a punning homage to film noir, Frank Black, the hero of *Millennium,* is reintroduced in the first episode of season two as "Mr. Noir" ("The Beginning and the End").

But if *The X-Files* and *Millennium* aimed to evoke classic film noir, both shows redefined the genre for the 1990s. In at least two crucial ways, the two series broke with convention. First, whereas the heroes of classic noir were typically single (and sexually promiscuous) male protagonists who preferred to work alone, the protagonists of Carter's shows are married and devoted to wife and child (Frank Black; his wife, Catherine; and his daughter, Jordan) or paired with a partner of the opposite sex (Mulder and Scully, Doggett and Reyes, Black and Means, Black and Hollis). In contrast to their classic noir predecessors, Carter's protagonists locate the emotional center of their lives in their family relationships or in a (not necessarily sexual) partnership that has the potential to become the basis of a new family (Mulder and Scully). While Carter's shows occasionally play with the classic formula of the sexually experienced gumshoe seduced by a femme fatale, or in Scully's case, an *homme fatal* ("3," "Never Again"), *The X-Files* and *Millennium* consistently represent either family or a faithful (heterosexual) partnership as the primary source of value in the lives of their protagonists. This is never clearer than when family relations and partnerships are routinely threatened by external forces and institutions (which is nearly always the case in the two series).

Second, the conspiracies uncovered by the heroes of classic noir were almost always local and urban in character and scope. The locus classicus of 1940s and 1950s film noir is "the city." The urban dimension of these films is often announced by their very titles: *Stranger on the Third Floor* (Boris Ingster, 1940), *The Asphalt Jungle* (significantly subtitled *The City under the City*), *The Naked City* (Jules Dassin, 1948), *Night and the City* (Dassin, 1950), *Sunset Boulevard* (Billy Wilder, 1950), and *Pickup on South Street* (Samuel Fuller, 1953).[2] The hero of classic noir might uncover an elaborate criminal conspiracy, but the network of corruption only very rarely extends beyond the boundaries of the city in which he lives and works. (And insofar as the web of crime traverses the city limits, it is generally not the business of the detective to follow leads outside those limits.) By contrast, the conspiratorial networks uncovered in *The X-Files* and *Millennium* turn out to be, at the very least, *national* in scale and, indeed, upon closer examination seem part of a *global* and even *cosmic* plot. The systemic evil onto which Carter's heroes and heroines stumble is thus emphatically not a local problem; the federal government of the United States is deeply implicated. And arrayed behind a corrupt national government are global and cosmic forces—shadowy international networks, extraterrestrial forces, satanic powers. The peculiar darkness of Carter's most successful shows thus stems at once from their more sentimental appreciation of the domestic world of marriage, family relations, personal friendship, and romantic (heterosexual) love, as well as from their far more comprehensive and pessimistic assessment of all that lies beyond the narrow arc of light that illuminates the private sphere of our natural life. The embattled refuge of domesticity and personal freedom is represented in iconic fashion by the "yellow house" into which Frank Black, his wife Catherine, and their young daughter, Jordan, move in the pilot episode of *Millennium*. And it is the place from which Frank and his family are ultimately driven by the forces of darkness.

G-Men

Defenders of the necessity and legitimacy of state power have often contended that civil society (the world of voluntary associations and private affiliations) can only flourish with the establishment of a strong sovereign power (a government). Some contemporary defenders of what is called "communitarianism" insist that the health and well-being of communal life must and should be supported by the benign efforts of the state. Their contention has a long and distinguished pedigree, dating back at least to the sixteenth and seventeenth centuries, when the political philosophers Jean Bodin and Thomas Hobbes laid out their highly influential arguments on behalf of sovereign power. In his magnum opus, *The Leviathan* (1651), Hobbes contends that prior to the establishment of civil government the natural condition of man was one of endless war and complete insecurity of life, liberty, and property. As he puts it, "It is manifest, that during the time men live without a common Power to keep them all in awe, they are in that condition which is called Warre; and such a warre, as is of every man, against every man."[3] For Hobbes, the state of nature lacks all the advantages, resources, and refinements of civilized life:

> In such condition, there is no place for Industry; because the fruit thereof is uncertain: and consequently no Culture of the Earth; no Navigation, no use of the commodities that may be imported by Sea; no commodious Building; no Instruments of moving, and removing such things as require much force; no Knowledge of the face of the Earth; no account of Time; no Arts; no Letters;

no Society; and which worst of all, continuall feare, and danger of
violent death; And the life of man, solitary, poore, nasty, brutish,
and short.[4]

According to Hobbes, all the good things in human life depend first upon
the prior establishment of sovereign power, that is, on the creation of an
absolute government that wields a monopoly on coercive force and to
which all of its subjects owe near total obedience. (The individual has the
right to try to preserve his life if the sovereign attempts to take it, but,
paradoxically, Hobbes nonetheless insists that the sovereign legitimately
exercises absolute power over the lives of its subjects, including the power
of life and death.)

But if seventeenth-century political philosophy helped provide the
groundwork for the creation of the modern state, it also gave birth to a political philosophic tradition that criticized notions of absolute sovereignty
and attempted to place strict limits on the emergent powers of the state. In
his *Second Treatise of Civil Government* (1689), John Locke directly challenges Hobbes's conception of the "state of nature" and sharply distinguishes
it from the "state of war" that Hobbes describes. In Locke's view, man is by
nature a social animal who forms social institutions, makes contractual
agreements, and establishes mutually beneficial relationships prior to and
without need of a common government. Hobbes and Locke agree that
men in their natural condition are both free and equal, but in contrast to
Hobbes, Locke argues that a "Law of Nature" (the rule of reason among
free and equal men) governs the state of nature. Because man is by nature
free and possessed of reason, he is theoretically and historically capable
of forming mutually beneficial contracts and personal affiliations prior to
the creation of government. Indeed, it is only because he wishes to better
ensure his natural rights to life, liberty, and property that, in Locke's view,
man voluntarily consents to form civil government in the first place. For
Locke, the only legitimate forms of government are based on the consent
of the governed and guarantee the freedoms and rights already found in
man's natural state. In brief, Locke contends that civil society (one in which
a government holds sway) must be based on and protect the privately initi-
ated affiliations and associations freely entered into by man in his original
natural condition. Contra Hobbes, a legitimate government neither abolishes
nor contravenes the laws of nature. For Locke, a government, if it is to be
legitimate, must build upon and guarantee those natural freedoms, social

affiliations, and voluntary contracts that already exist (though somewhat more precariously) in natural society.[5]

Locke's writings deeply influenced the founders of the American republic, including James Madison, Thomas Jefferson, and Thomas Paine. Paine, in particular, radicalized and gave clear and forceful expression to the classical liberal or libertarian elements within Locke's writings. In the famous opening of his revolutionary tract of 1776, *Common Sense,* Paine declares that

> some writers have so confounded society with government as to leave little or no distinction between them; whereas they are not only different, but have different origins. Society is produced by our wants and government by our wickedness; the former promotes our happiness positively by uniting our affections, the latter negatively by restraining our vices. The one encourages intercourse, the other creates distinctions. The first is a patron, the last a punisher. Society in every state is a blessing, but government, even in its best state is a necessary evil; in its worst state an intolerable one.[6]

In part 1 of his *Rights of Man* (1791), a defense of the French Revolution in the days before the Terror, Paine reiterates Locke's basic notion that all civil rights are based on preexisting natural rights and that the sole purpose of legitimate government is to secure those rights more fully and surely than they would have been in man's original natural condition: "Man did not enter into society to become *worse* than he was before, nor to have less rights than he had before, but to have those rights better secured. His natural rights are the foundation of all his civil rights. . . . Every civil right has for its foundation some natural right pre-existing in the individual."[7] In part 2 of the same work (1792), Paine insists that the advantages of a "civilized community" originate chiefly in the free associations and natural and voluntary affiliations among men rather than in government:

> A great part of that order which reigns among mankind is not the effect of government. It had its origin in the principles of society and the natural constitution of man. It existed prior to government, and would exist if the formality of government was abolished. The mutual dependence and reciprocal interest which man has in man, and all the parts of a civilized community upon each other, create that great chain of connection which holds it together. . . . In fine,

society performs for itself almost everything which is ascribed to government.[8]

Our brief excursus into the history of classical liberal political philosophy will help us recognize one of the most striking features of *The X-Files* and *Millennium:* in the America of the 1990s depicted in these two shows, the world of voluntary associations, of private contracts and affiliations, of un-regulated human action that exists outside of and prior to the establishment of state power has become so attenuated and desiccated as to have almost disappeared. Consider the occupations of the primary characters of both shows—Frank Black, Lara Means, Emma Hollis, Fox Mulder, Dana Scully, Monica Reyes, and John Doggett—as well as many of the more important secondary characters who appear regularly throughout the series: Walter Skinner, CGB and Jeffrey Spender, William Mulder, Diana Fowley, X, Alex Krycek, Arthur Dales, Maria Covarrubias, Deep Throat, Peter Watts, Barry Baldwin, Bob Bletcher, and Bob Giebelhouse: all of them work for or have worked in some capacity for the government (chiefly the federal govern-ment) or its affiliates. Even Catherine Black, the most conspicuous omission on this list, works for social services, a department of the municipal Seattle government. It is a running joke that the goofiest, most socially inept, and isolated group of characters in either show—Byers, Frohike, and Langly—the self-styled Lone Gunmen, are virtually the only regularly recurring characters *not* working for the government (unless we include Jordan Black, who, being under age ten, is perhaps just a tad too young to be employed full time by the Feds). Of course, even the Lone Gunmen spend their time obsessively monitoring the activities of the government in lieu of pursuing their per-sonal lives. In short, characters not immediately identifiable as pathetic (if lovable) misfits demonstrate that they are capable of normal social relations (a pretty tenuous claim in the cases of Fox Mulder and Frank Black) only insofar as they work or have worked a government job. Theirs is a world in which, if you don't work for the state, you are not a normal adult. If you are not a government employee, you are most likely, and almost by definition, a child or a lunatic (whether benign or maleficent). And even children are not wholly immune to the social demands of government service; consider Gibson Praise, the young telepathic savant held captive and forced into service by the government/conspiracy of Elders in *The X-Files.* In its second season, *Millennium* repeatedly used the tag line: "This is who we are"; and who we are, it turns out, are government servants.

"Trust No One"

In 1835 and 1840, the most important work of the great French political thinker Alexis de Tocqueville appeared in two volumes. A philosophic reflection on his visit to the United States in the early 1830s, *Democracy in America* records Tocqueville's observations on the novel political experiment that was America, a regime founded on classical liberal principles articulated by the likes of Locke, Jefferson, Madison, and Paine. Among a myriad of brilliant insights into the genius of American democracy, Tocqueville noted with favor the superabundance in early-nineteenth-century America of "associations of civil life":

> Americans of all ages, all conditions, all minds constantly unite. Not only do they have commercial and industrial associations in which all take part, but they also have a thousand other kinds: religious, moral, grave, futile, very general and very particular, immense and very small: Americans use associations to give fêtes, to found seminaries, to build inns, to raise churches, to distribute books, to send missionaries to the antipodes; in this manner they create hospitals, prisons, schools.[9]

Tocqueville concludes that the very health of American, indeed of all democratic government, depends crucially on its plenitude of voluntary (nongovernmental, purely private) industrial, moral, religious, intellectual, and political associations: "In democratic countries the science of association is the mother science; the progress of all the others depends on the progress of that one. Among the laws that rule human societies there is one that seems more precise and clearer than all the others. In order that men remain civilized or become so, the art of associating must be developed and perfected among them in the same ratio as equality of conditions increases." According to Tocqueville, the freedoms of political and civil association are interdependent. Where one declines or is prohibited, the other will also degenerate or cease to exist.[10]

But if the robust health of the American republic in the 1830s is to be measured by the vigor of its voluntary associations, what are we to say about the state of American society in the 1990s? If *The X-Files* and *Millennium* were accurate gauges of our civic health, then American democracy at the end of the millennium would appear to be on life support. As Rod Serling might say, consider, if you will, both what is and, more importantly, what is *not* present in the world portrayed in these two television shows. What is nearly as conspicuous as the fact that the chief characters all work for the government or its affiliates is that they tend to be unusually devoted to their jobs. Both shows feature workaholics (Mulder, Scully, and Black) who repeatedly risk their personal happiness and private lives for the sake of their professional objectives. Frank Black's marriage nearly dissolves as a result of his devotion to his job; Mulder maintains an immaculate bachelorhood as he pursues his investigations of the X-Files; Scully finds it difficult to spend time with her family during the holidays, much less to settle down and have her own family, once she joins Mulder in his obsessive quest for the truth. Rarely in either of the two shows do the principal characters spend time with friends or associates with whom they do not work. In the only episode ("Dead Letters") in which Frank and Catherine invite a non-relative to a meal at their home, their guest is Jim Horn, a former FBI profiler and candidate for the Millennium Group. After he fails to get the job, he is never heard of again. In a seriocomic episode of *The X-Files* ("Arcadia"), Mulder and Scully go undercover as "Rob and Laura Petrie" (the names of the main characters on *The Dick Van Dyke Show*), a married suburban couple who move into a new upper-middle-class gated community; of course, the agents are acting, and none too persuasively. Mulder is amusingly inept as the guy next door and Scully dutifully annoyed in her unaccustomed role as devoted wife and homemaker. Neither welcomes the task of mixing with or entertaining their neighbors, and in fact the two spend most of their time trying to keep their new "friends" in the community from entering the house they've staked out.

It is remarkable how infrequently in *The X-Files* and *Millennium* we see any of the main characters engaged in the activities of civil associations. Carter's protagonists are not members of local sports clubs; they don't attend concerts or perform in amateur musical groups; they don't volunteer time for charitable organizations; they don't participate in the activities of local business associations or trade groups; they rarely, if ever, attend or throw parties.[11] The one notable exception seems to be their rather strained relations with religious organizations. Both Dana Scully and Frank Black occasionally attend Mass, and several episodes of the two shows revolve around their respective struggles with religious faith. But even these civil associations are frayed: Scully resists the entreaties of her priest and family to return to the rituals of the Catholic Church (though she does seem to renew her belief in its doctrines); Black attends services for the sake of his wife and daughter, and on one occasion seeks out the advice of Catherine's priest ("Seven and One") but professes to lack conviction in the teachings and practices of the Church.[12] In short, Carter's heroes and heroines, like the criminals they pursue and the acquaintances they make, tend to keep to themselves. Their personal attachments are limited to members of their immediate families and to those with whom they work.[13] To cite a pop-sociological phrase that described the apparent decline in American civil associations in the 1990s: it's not so much that Mulder, Scully, and Black go "bowling alone," as that they don't go bowling at all.[14]

The Carceral Archipelago and the Panoptical Regime

It would be difficult to name a television show that appeared before *The X-Files* and *Millennium* in which a greater number of governmental departments, agencies, projects, and entities were either directly represented on screen or alluded to in the course of the action. I confess to never having had the patience to compile a comprehensive list of them, but even a cursory review of a few episodes of *The X-Files* and *Millennium* provides a prolific number of encounters with or references to the FBI, Department of Justice, Department of the Treasury, Department of State, Department of the Interior, Department of Agriculture, Department of Transportation, Department of Defense, Secret Service, CIA, NSA, OSS, BATF, DIA, U.S. Army, U.S. Air Force, U.S. Navy, U.S. Marines, U.S. Coast Guard, Navy SEALS, Strategic Air Command, NORAD, U.S. Customs Service, INS, NTSB, FAA, CDC, NASA, NIH, IRS, DEA, EPA, USPS, SEC, Federal Reserve, U.S. Census Bureau, U.S. Marshals, National Parks Service, U.S. Fish and Wildlife, Federal Forest Service, National Weather Service, Federal Statistics Center, DARPA (Defense Advanced Research Projects), Manhattan Project, Project Paper Clip, Project Grill Flame, MK ULTRA, United Nations, Mexican Federal Police, Canadian Mounted Police, European Space Agency, NYPD, LAPD, California Highway Patrol, Mississippi Department of Corrections, Washington, D.C., Violent Crimes Unit, Boston Transit Police, Baltimore Animal Control Office, New Jersey Sanitation Department, and, last but not least, the great Satan: FEMA (featured in the movie, *The X-Files: Fight the Future*). Of course, the omnipresence in Carter's shows of a few super-sinister federal agencies with a particular fondness for black helicopters, swat teams, special ops, and hazmat suits shouldn't blind us to the fact that a truly vast and pervasive network of everyday institutions run, funded, or regulated by local, state, and national governments is everywhere in evidence. Consider, if you will, just how many episodes are set in prisons, public schools, court rooms, psychiatric clinics, publicly supported hospitals (especially VA and military hospitals), jails, day care centers, federally run academies and training schools (Quantico), government laboratories, government-supported universities, government-supported research facilities, government-supported museums (especially anthropological and natural science), federally protected Indian lands, military bases, refugee camps, POW camps, national (or state) parks and forests, satellite and weather-tracking facilities, space-flight centers, military vessels and aircraft, geological research stations, government-run nuclear reactors, and the post office. (The list could easily be expanded.) The landscape and setting of the shows thus tend to feature places under direct government control. There are few places in the imaginative geography of the two shows that are not, in some sense or another, part of what Foucault would call the carceral archipelago. Free space is in short supply.

Interestingly, elected representatives, those "servants" of government through whom the voice of the people is supposed to be heard, almost never appear on screen and always prove ineffectual. (Senator Matheson shows up in a few episodes of *The X-Files* but is unwilling to speak officially or publicly about the abuses of federal power.) A crucial component of liberal democracy, the legislative branch and its public forum, in which matters of concern to the people are supposed to be deliberated by their elected representatives in open session, is almost invisible.[15] Bill Clinton and Janet Reno's official portraits appear hauntingly in the background of numerous sets, omnipresent icons of federal power. But Clinton, the man behind the portrait, much like Big Brother, is more or less irrelevant to the actual business of government as it is carried on in *The X-Files* and *Millennium.* It is a shadowy army of bureaucrats, government agents, and unelected officials who wield the apparently limitless sovereign power of the state over the citizens of the republic. In the world of *The X-Files* and *Millennium,* Lincoln's famous characterization of the United States as a government of, by, and for the people seems far less credible than the theory that aliens are abducting American citizens in advance of planetary colonization. As the political economist and social theorist Joseph Schumpeter once remarked: "The freely voting rational citizen, conscious of his (long-run) interests, and the representative who acts in obedience to them—is this not the perfect example of a nursery tale?"[16]

Agent or patient, investigator or perpetrator, witness or suspect, victim or bystander, the characters of *The X-Files* and *Millennium* are almost always deeply engaged with the machinery of government and are very often its products. Take for example, "The Judge," an episode in the first season of *Millennium*. At the request of Lieutenant Bob Fletcher, and assisted by Detective Bob Giebelhouse and Cheryl Andrews (former FBI agent and expert pathologist for the Millennium Group), Frank Black assists the Seattle Police Department in hunting down a serial murderer who is dismembering his victims and sending their body parts seemingly at random through the mail. The perpetrator of the crimes is a disgruntled former judge who feels the legal system has failed to uphold the law; he now practices his own form of vigilante justice. Strictly speaking, the judge doesn't actually commit the murders but instead delegates them to a killer, Carl Nearman, who has been recently released from prison and who operates under the patronage and protection of the judge. Nearman disposes of the remains of his dismembered victims by feeding them to the hogs kept by the judge on his secluded farm. When Nearman fails to carry out a sentence exactly as set forth by the judge, the latter recruits another ex-con, Bardale, to execute him. Catherine Black, who works for Seattle social services and helps counsel crime victims (including Annie Tisman, who has received a severed tongue in the mail), provides her husband with a crucial clue that advances the investigation. Evidently, all but one of the judge's victims are former employees of the judicial or prison system, and they include a corrupt police officer, Jonathan Mellen, whose false statement led to the wrongful conviction of Annie Tisman's husband, who died in prison. Ultimately, Frank solves the crime and interrogates the judge. The latter hints that he is in league with the devil (his name is "Legion," the appellation of demons who, after being exorcised by Jesus, possess a herd of swine and plunge to their deaths).[17] The judge implies that Frank should come to work for him, or at any rate for the (Satanic) power he represents. Despite the judge's oblique hints of responsibility, the Seattle Police have insufficient evidence to keep him in custody. After the judge's release, Frank finally tracks down Bardale, who confesses to killing the judge in the interim and feeding his body to the swine.

"The Judge" neatly encapsulates the political-theological mythos of *Millennium* (and, I would argue, of *The X-Files* as well). Protagonists and antagonists are at once agents and products of the disciplinary order of the state. Their lives are entirely circumscribed by the institutions of government: the courts, the penal system, the police, social services. Even an apparently innocent victim of the judge, Jonathan Mellen, turns out to be a corrupt former cop, and Annie Tisman's husband, who was genuinely innocent, dies as a prisoner in a state-run penal institution. To be sure, one might claim that the Millennium Group is not really an arm of the government; it is only acting in a private consulting capacity. But, of course, the members of this elite group are all ex-FBI agents, and the group's only clients, it would seem, are local, state, and federal agencies. Like the conspiratorial Elders of *The X-Files* (a.k.a. The Firm, The Consortium, and The Syndicate) who are in league with alien colonizers, the Millennium Group operates with the tacit consent and full cooperation of national, state, and local governments. (Its members have, for example, unlimited access to all FBI and NCIC—National Crime Information Center—databases.) If the government and the Group are not one and the same, they are, in any case, engaged in a deeply collusive and corrupt partnership.[18]

Of course, the Millennium Group and Seattle Police Department claim to respect the rule of law and insist that they strictly adhere to the procedures and protocols of a legal system that protects the rights of citizens. Thus, they appear to be unequivocally opposed to the disgruntled judge, who aims to impose his own absolute and (supernaturally sanctioned) form of justice. But, as fans of *Millennium* will surely acknowledge, the extra-legal privileges and prerogatives exercised by the judge are precisely those claimed by the Millennium Group (and its various subsects, affiliates, and competitors: Owls and Roosters, the Family, Odessa). Though it works alongside or in the shadow of government officials, the Millennium Group routinely operates outside the positive law, according to a divine sanction and special revelation given to its members alone, a special dispensation the uninitiated (which is to say, virtually all citizens) do not fully comprehend and can never challenge. The group is ultimately interested in control, in sovereign power—the power to determine the end time, the power to kill by releasing a man-made plague on the population, the power to control the lives of all those who are not among its initiates, the power to direct the lives even of its own elite members. "The Judge" thus suggests that the rule of law, which Frank, the Millennium Group, and the Seattle Police Department claim to uphold, is sinewless, so vitiated by the arbitrary manipulations of state authorities and their nefarious (if unacknowledged) partners as to undermine any faith in the positive justice of legitimate government. Indeed, the horrific crimes committed by the judge are motivated precisely by his conviction (never seriously challenged) that the legally administered system of justice in America has utterly failed.

Lest I seem too hasty in criticizing the good intentions of the Seattle Police Department and Frank Black, consider the investigative methods on which Mr. Noir relies. He can see crimes committed from the perspective of the perpetrator. Frank is of interest to the FBI, the Seattle Police, and the Millennium Group because he can get inside the heads of psychopathic serial killers and sexual predators. Whether a blessing or a curse, his visionary talents make him uniquely valuable to the state and its affiliates. He unites the mind of the criminal with the mind of the sovereign authority; in his head the two become one. Frank's special powers enable the Seattle Police Department and the Group to look for evidence and build a case only after they have determined who is guilty. Like Mulder's hunches and intuitions, Frank's visions allow him to bypass the objective methodology of criminal science and the legal niceties of due process. Though we never doubt the accuracy of Frank's visions or Mulder's uncanny insights, nor the honesty and moral integrity of either sleuth, we cannot be certain that in their eagerness to serve justice and discover the truth, these dauntless crusaders have not (at least unwittingly) helped circumvent or violate the law they are pledged to uphold. Consider how routinely Mulder engages in warrantless searches of private property and personal effects, fails to inform suspects of their legal and constitutional rights, employs excessive force in apprehending suspects, threatens and sometimes abuses those under his custody (Krycek seems particularly in need of improved legal counsel in this respect), and takes a wildly expansive view of federal jurisdiction (what exactly are the grounds for federal involvement in a missing persons case in the gated community of "Arcadia"? Under what authority do FBI agents investigate irregular weather patterns in a small Kansas town in "The Rain King"?) If Frank is comparatively more attentive to the procedural rights of suspects, and far more reluctant to employ force in the performance of his duties (he refuses to carry a weapon), he is even less inclined to offer objective evidence and empirically verifiable reasons for suspecting an individual or pursuing his criminal investigations.[19] Even more insistently than Mulder, he expects his partner and colleagues simply to trust his instincts. But even if we allow that both Frank and Mulder are ultimately devoted to justice and faithful to the spirit, if not always the letter, of the law, the same cannot be said of those whom they serve. The government and its cohorts seek not justice or truth but power. And what could enhance the power of government more than a tool that allows it to identify those who defy its laws and challenge its sovereignty even when demonstrable proof of their guilt or solid empirical evidence of their identities is lacking? Frank Black provides the ultimate shortcut for a prosecutorial government authority. He is that unique thing: the panoptical spy who can see into the minds of the enemies of the state.

If I seem to have misrepresented or distorted Mulder or Frank's roles, consider "Exegesis," a crucial episode in the mythic arc of *Millennium,* in which Black uncovers the existence of "Grill Flame," a secret government program run by the CIA and the Pentagon. The program has made use of remote viewers, psychic spies who can "project themselves outward and down to a predetermined target." During the Cold War, these remote viewers enabled the U.S. government to learn about advanced Soviet weaponry.[20] Many years after Grill Flame was apparently terminated (or was it only driven underground?), the most talented of the remote viewers, "512," a.k.a. "Mildred Carson," and her daughters are being hunted by the Millennium Group, who fear that the women can remotely view what the Group does in secret. When Frank finally encounters the elderly woman, 512 gnomically tells Frank: "*You see.*" At first he fails to comprehend, but when she gently directs him to see, and he experiences one of his visionary moments, he and we understand that, like 512, he is a remote viewer, a psychic spy who has been employed by the government and its shadowy affiliates.[21] According to Mildred, these men, whom Frank knows (government or former government men, the Millennium Group), "thought they could control the world because they had their fingers on the button." With the waning of the Cold War, there are "no enemies, no wars, no need for them." But these men "can't accept that, can't stop." This deeply revelatory episode suggests that there are not two opposed systems of justice—one positive, legitimate, and state-sponsored, and another, arbitrary, cruel, and vengeful—but just one corrupt system that masquerades as two. It is much like the moment in *1984* when O'Brien reveals to Winston Smith that Big Brother has written the "subversive" book of Emmanuel Goldstein, that Oceania is in league with its ostensible global enemies, Eurasia and Eastasia. The sovereign world of government and the outlaw world of criminal activity are, in fact, one and the same, and both are given over to the works of the devil.[22]

Fugitives

In the dark world of *The X-Files* and *Millennium*, the ultimate objective of the governmental conspiracy is to reduce all individuals to docile subjects. Not only would the government surveil its entire population, it would also reduce each individual to a mere number (like "512"), case load, or file. One of the most shocking, if oft-repeated, revelations in both shows is the discovery that the government monitors, tests, tracks, and records the lives of its citizens. Knowledge is power, and the government is nearly omniscient, or so the shows would suggest. Whole mountains in West Virginia have been hollowed out to accommodate paper files, DNA samples, and medical records of every citizen of the United States; the Millennium Group has access to computerized data bases that allows it to locate every citizen, monitor her every purchase, listen in on his every conversation. What the government wants is not merely to control the recalcitrant but to make each and every citizen into its own "merchandise," its own product, its own creation.

One measure of the unnaturalness of government power, of its inhuman aims, is its overt hostility to the one institution that unquestionably precedes its establishment and which it cannot claim to have created: the family. Perhaps that is why both shows so prominently and regularly feature genetic experiments, human cloning, in vitro fertilization, artificial insemination, and scientifically engineered human-hybrid life forms. The ultimate aim of conspiratorial government in these shows is to create a brave new world in which even the family would owe its biological existence to the sovereign power. The family would cease to be a natural phenomenon and become merely another government sponsored program, a group of genetically altered test subjects dependent upon the government rather than one other for their material and emotional sustenance. A people of, by, and for the government.

But if *The X-Files* and *Millennium* are inspired by the likes of Orwell's *1984* and Huxley's *Brave New World* (if not more distantly by Foucault's *Discipline and Punish*), neither show is ultimately as despairing about the future. Indeed, two of the most memorable taglines of *The X-Files*, "Fight the Future" and "Resist or Serve," are calls to arms. In the spirit of resistance, Carter's shows are populated by a wide array of marginal, isolated, and sometimes deeply misguided, but nonetheless courageous individuals who fight for their independence. It is among this shadowy counterforce of conspiracy theorists, social outcasts, political crazies, and subversives that Carter's heroes find allies, friends, and fellow travelers. If *The X-Files* and *Millennium* often tempt us to dismiss the likes of the Lone Gunmen as mere techno-geeks unworthy of our respect, both shows lead us to sympathize with their revolutionary fervor. If such characters seem ridiculous, it is partly because they represent the anachronistic ethos of a bygone era, one in which an odd assemblage of inventors, cranks, conspiracy theorists, ne'er-do-wells, agitators, and amateur soldiers fought to establish an independent American republic.

"Collateral Damage," which aired during the third season of *Milllenium,* vividly represents the revolutionary sentiment that still agitates a disillusioned American citizenry at the turn of the last century. In this episode, Frank encounters Eric Swan (James Marsters of *Buffy* fame), a disgruntled Gulf War veteran-cum-antigovernment radical. Believing that the Millennium Group in collusion with the U.S. Army has used him to test secretly a weapons-grade biotoxin on his fellow soldiers in Kuwait, Swan kidnaps Peter Watts's daughter to force the government and the Group to acknowledge their responsibility for the deaths of so many innocent men. In a deft touch that slyly evokes the radical political heritage of the American revolution, Swan operates under a memorable nom de guerre: "Thomas Paine." Swan/Paine's fate is ultimately a tragic one: his justifiable outrage against the atrocities committed by the government leads him to acts of terrorism—he exposes an innocent civilian (Watts's daughter) to the same deadly biotoxin (a microplasma flavivirus known as the Marburg Variant) that killed his men. Though he succeeds in extracting a confession from Peter Watts that the U.S. Army and the Group are responsible for the needless slaughter of American soldiers in the Gulf, he is, in a deeply ironic twist, killed by the very woman he has held hostage. Even so, the tragic culmination of Paine's violent life ultimately lends a greater urgency and resonance to his political message: resistance is possible; the conspiracy that would enslave the American people is not invulnerable; the struggle for traditional freedoms and liberties must not be abandoned.[23]

If Carter's heroes avoid the fate of "Thomas Paine," and never succumb to the temptations of terrorism, they nevertheless also evade the destiny of Winston Smith, who betrays Julia and learns to love Big Brother. Mulder, Scully, and Frank never surrender to the powers that be and never betray their partners and loved ones.[24] To be sure, these heroes and heroines ultimately pay a terrible price for their courage, fidelity, and independence. They must endure the merciless destruction of their friends, allies, and—most particularly—families. Mulder's sister (in at least one version of the story) is abducted by the government/aliens (or given to them as a hostage by William Mulder) and never returned to her family. His father is assassinated, and his mother may have committed suicide or been killed by the government. Government agents gun down Scully's sister. Scully herself is stricken by cancer and rendered incapable (for a time) of bearing children. She later discovers a biological daughter, Emily (created by the Consortium/government from ova extracted from Scully during her abduction), only to lose the child just as suddenly. After Scully's ability to conceive is miraculously restored, the alien-government alliance seeks to terminate her pregnancy and threatens to abduct or kill her infant son, William. Fearing for his life, Scully ultimately decides to give her baby for adoption. Frank's wife is abducted and assaulted by a killer whose movements are carefully tracked and monitored by the Millennium Group and she ultimately succumbs to a biologically engineered plague they unleash. In the original series finale, Frank flees Washington, D.C., with his daughter, Jordan, fearing that the Group seeks to kidnap, injure, or kill her.

As I have noted, the heroes and heroines of the two shows tend to neglect their families because they are obsessed with their work. But, over the course of several seasons, Fox Mulder, Dana Scully, and Frank Black all see that the center of the lives, their realm of individual autonomy, their very humanity is to be found within the family. Lamenting the death of his wife and the destruction of his family in "Borrowed Time," Frank confesses, "You're talking about the only great thing that happened in my life." Mulder and Scully ultimately become lovers and Scully bears a son (though the precariousness of their existence and Scully's fear for William's safety prompt her to give him up to adoptive parents). In the end, Mulder and Scully, Frank and Jordan become fugitives from the state. Both shows end where *The Fugitive* begins, with the main protagonists on the run from the governmental powers and conspiratorial forces that seek to keep them in their thrall. Their families having been nearly destroyed and many of their friends killed, the heroes and heroines of the two shows finally go underground, eluding their pursuers, and holding fast to the undying dream of a future that promises a natural and free existence: a life beyond the outermost limits of the kingdom of darkness.

Coda: A Noir World Order

Murray Rothbard's libertarian critique of the illegitimacy of the modern state captures the subversive spirit that animates both *The X-Files* and *Millennium*: "The State is an inherently illegitimate institution of organized aggression, of organized and regularized crime against the persons and properties of its subjects. Rather than necessary to society, it is a profoundly antisocial institution which lives parasitically off of the productive activities of private citizens."[25] Film noir has always offered a dark vision of authority. Even so, Carter's two shows mark a significant transformation of film noir that occurs in wake of the Cold War. Since the genre rose to prominence in the 1940s as a world war gave way to a cold war, it should come as no surprise that the form undergoes a dramatic transformation with the fall of the Berlin Wall and the collapse of the Soviet Union. In a unipolar world in which the specter of communism has begun to fade from the scene, it is to be expected that critical attention should focus on the one remaining sovereign superpower occupying the geopolitical landscape: the U.S. government.

As noted, Carter's shows feature new sorts of noir heroes and new forms of conspiratorial forces against which these heroes struggle. Our analysis allows us to connect these generic innovations with the new global reality that characterizes the post–Cold War era. The defeat of communism and the Soviet Union was supposed to herald a global flowering of freedom and democracy. Such hopes were premised on the conviction that the U.S. government was fundamentally different from, indeed the very opposite of its Soviet counterpart. But both the *X-Files* and *Millennium* offer a deeply unsettling and revisionist account of the Cold War, one in which the United States and the Soviet Union (as well as their defeated fascist German and imperial Japanese antagonists) appear as mirror images of one another, competitors and conspiratorial partners who made and broke tactical alliances to suit their strategic ends. In Carter's shows, the Cold War ends not in the triumph of freedom over tyranny but merely in the victory of one absolute and despotic power over its rivals. The end of history would appear to offer not the coming to consciousness of human freedom, but the endless reign of what Nietzsche famously called the "coldest of all cold monsters," the final victory of the sovereign state that seeks only to increase its power at the expense of the individual.[26]

The X-Files and *Millennium* accordingly mark a fundamental shift in political and social consciousness. Classic film noir tended to portray money and greed as the root of all evil. Reflecting left-of-center and anticapitalist sensibilities, classic noir films typically presented political corruption as the outgrowth of criminal activity that was morally indistinguishable from ordinary commercial enterprise. City politicians were corrupted by the criminal and business interests who bribed them. Some classic noir films, particularly those made by central and eastern European émigrés inspired by socialist ideology, implicitly endorsed a dramatic transformation of the economic order and the end of an exploitative class system. Other more politically centrist vehicles suggested that top-down political reform was needed to free America of corrupt government officials and the criminal elements who manipulated them. The key to reform in either case was combating the corrupting influence of money and material interest in modern American political life.

However, in the post-communist era of the 1990s, the old left critique of capitalism seems hopelessly antiquated and beside the point. For in the neo-noir world of *The X-Files* and *Millennium,* material interests seem, at most, of secondary or incidental importance. While the members of the Consortium are wealthy and politically influential, they are not concerned with increasing their profits. The members of the Millennium Group, who live in middle-class comfort or even rustic simplicity, cannot be bought off. The government officials with whom they collude are not on the take. These neo-noir conspirators hunger not for financial gain but for absolute global sovereignty. Their dominion now extends to the inhospitable deserts of the American Southwest, the arboreal wastes of Siberia, and the empty reaches of Antarctica. As Mulder traverses the remote corners of the earth, he inevitably finds that that conspiratorial forces have been there before him.

The neo-noir world order in *The X-Files* and *Millennium* thus seems darker and more completely forsaken than that urban jungle of classic film noir. In Carter's shows, there is no longer a higher government authority to which the citizens of the corrupt and crime-ridden city might appeal for assistance. There is no place left on earth entirely free from the influence of the powers that be. The very notion of political and economic reform seems risible. The virulent and uncompromising nature of the neo-noir conspiracy precludes negotiation, amelioration, or appeal to common interests. In *The X-Files* and *Millennium,* the big-government remedies of old-time populists and socialists of the Cold War era are revealed to be not the solution but the problem. Carter's heroes and heroines reject not the ideals of truth, justice, and freedom but the notion that government, especially big government colluding with its clients and cohorts, offers the means by which these traditional American ideals can be realized. Mulder, Scully, and Black learn not to evade political responsibilities but to resist the illegitimate claims that the state makes on them. They become not apolitical but antipolitical figures. Their heroic statures grow even as their actions and sensibilities become increasingly anarchistic. Fugitives one and all, they seek a future for themselves and those they love free from the tyranny of government authority. The state that they look for is not one found on any contemporary political map but is one traversed by nomads who recognize and revere the autonomy of free individuals.

Notes

1. Throughout this essay I refer to *The X-Files* and *Millennium* as "Chris Carter's shows." While Carter is listed as "creator" of both shows, served as executive producer, and wrote and directed many episodes, the two shows are nonetheless the collaborative work of a great many people in the cast and crew. While it is impossible for me to list even all of the most significant contributors, I would like to mention a few of the principal writers for *The X-Files:* Vince Gilligan, Darin Morgan, Glen Morgan, John Shiban, Frank Spotnitz, and James Wong; and two of its producers, Rob Bowman and Kim Manners. The staff writers of *Millennium* include Marjorie David, Michael Duggan, Erin Maher, Michael Perry, Kay Reindl, and the aforementioned Glen Morgan and James Wong, who are generally credited for assuming creative control of the series in its second season. Two directors who contributed significantly to the success of the show are Thomas J. Wright and Paul Shapiro. Neither series would have achieved its level of success without its leading actors and actresses: David Duchovny (Fox Mulder), Gillian Anderson (Dana Scully), Mitch Pileggi (Walter Skinner), Robert Patrick (John Doggett), Annabeth Gish (Monica Reyes), Lance Henriksen (Frank Black), Megan Gallagher (Catherine Black), Terry O'Quinn (Peter Watts), Kristen Cloke (Lara Means), and Klea Scott (Emma Hollis).

2. The urban setting of film noir continues to be evoked by the titles of more recent examples of the genre: *Chinatown* (Roman Polanski, 1974), *L.A. Confidential* (Curtis Hanson, 1997), and *Dark City* (Alex Proyas, 1998).

3. Thomas Hobbes, *Leviathan* (1651; Cambridge: Cambridge University Press, 1991), 88.

4. Ibid., 89.

5. See in particular, John Locke, chapters 2 and 3, *The Second Treatise of Civil Government,* in *Two Treatises of Government* (Cambridge: Cambridge University Press, 1988), 269–82. For an illuminating discussion of the continuing importance of Locke's theories of natural right and natural law for an understanding the original meaning of the U.S. Constitution, see Randy E. Barnett, *Restoring the Lost Constitution: The Presumption of Liberty* (Princeton: Princeton University Press, 2004), 70–75, 323–31.

6. Thomas Paine, *Common Sense,* in *Political Writings,* ed. Bruce Kuklick (Cambridge: Cambridge University Press, 1989), 3.

7. Thomas Paine, *Rights of Man,* part 1, in *Political Writings,* 86 (emphasis Paine's).

8. Thomas Paine, *Rights of Man,* part 2, in *Political Writings,* 165.

9. Alexis de Tocqueville, *Democracy in America,* trans. and ed., Harvey C. Mansfield and Delba Winthrop (Chicago: University of Chicago Press, 2000), 489. Tocqueville here mentions the creation of those institutions that Foucault considers "carceral" or "disciplinary." But, of course, Tocqueville means to describe the private and voluntary origins of hospitals, prisons, and schools that only subsequently become part of the state apparatus.

10. Ibid. 492; for the vital and necessary connection between political and civil association, see vol. 2, part 2, chap. 7, 496–500.

11. Even pet ownership, hardly the most socially demanding of activities, seems beyond the capacity of the chief characters. Benny, the dog Frank gives to Jordan, and Queequeg, Scully's Pomeranian, appear briefly and almost as quickly disappear from the shows. (Queequeg is eaten by a lake monster after only his third appearance in an *X–Files* episode). When Frank buys Jordan a bird, it doesn't survive even a single episode. Mulder barely manages to keep his fish fed when he's away on assignment.

12. Both shows tend to be particularly suspicious of evangelical Protestantism and especially of small Pentecostal sects (though there are exceptions). The Catholic Church, which Hobbes refers to in *The Leviathan* as "the Kingdom of Darkness," also comes in for its share of criticism, especially in *Millennium,* where the Church is shown to be inextricably entangled with the Millennium Group ("The Hand of Saint Sebastian," "Owls," "Roosters," "Anamnesis"). An entire essay deserves to be written on the representation of the Catholic Church in *Millennium* as a forerunner of the modern disciplinary state.

13. As far as I can determine, Scully goes on only two dates in the course of nine seasons ("Jersey Devil," "Never Again"), though prior to being assigned to the X-Files, she maintained two romantic relationships, the first with one of her teachers at medical school ("All Things") and the second with an FBI instructor while she attended Quantico ("Lazarus"); she vacations alone in "Chinga," as does Mulder in "Never Again."

14. "Bowling Alone," was the title of an article that propelled Robert Putnam, a self-described "obscure academic" (and a professor of sociology at Harvard University), into semi-celebrity in 1995. He worked out the main thesis of his article in greater detail in his book, *Bowling Alone: Restoring the American Community* (New York: Simon and Schuster, 2001).

15. Walter Skinner attends a congressional committee hearing in "Redux II," and Scully testifies before the Senate Select Subcommittee on Intelligence and Terrorism in "Terma" and "Tunguska" ; however neither of the hearings leads to any kind of legislative response to the matters raised in the X-Files.

16. Joseph A. Schumpeter, *History of Economic Analysis* (New York: Oxford University Press, 1954), 429.

17. See Luke 8:26–39.

18. In "Skull and Bones," Peter Watts describes the Millennium Group as a "private" firm that "subcontracts" for the FBI. In the same episode, Frank is asked about the

Group: "Are they the government?" He replies, "Not exactly." His interlocutor presses him: "Do they work for the government?" He concedes, "Sometimes." In "Collateral Damage," Eric Swan/Thomas Paine claims that the Group "does what the government can't do"; I take him to mean that the Group does on behalf of the government that for which government officials wish to disclaim responsibility.

19. Wayne Nederman, who tags along with Mulder and Scully to get the flavor of their work for a film script he's working on in "Hollywood A.D.," wryly sums up their methods: "No warrants. No permission. No research. You're like studio executives with guns."

20. Fans of the show may be surprised to discover that "Grill Flame" (a.k.a. "Sun-streak," "Center Lane," and "Star Gate") was a highly classified CIA sponsored program devoted to the study and deployment of RV (remote viewing) and related psi phenomenon that began in the early 1970s. Located at first at the Stanford Research Institute and then at the Science Applications International Corporation, both in Menlo Park, California, the program was initially directed by Dr. H. E. Puthoff, from 1972 to 1985. The first acknowledgment by the federal government of the existence of the program came in 1995 as a result of Executive Order 1995–4-17, which greatly increased pressure on the government to respond to requests under the Freedom of Information Act. For Puthoff's own account of the early years of the program see H. E. Puthoff, "CIA-Initiated Remote Viewing at Stanford Research Institute," *DIA Coordinate Remote Viewing Manual*, http://www.crvmanual.com/docs/hp95.html (accessed April 25, 2007).

21. Mulder becomes a remote viewer in "The Sixth Extinction I"; obviously Grill Flame and the government use of psychic spies had a particular fascination for the creator, producers, and writers of *The X-Files* and *Millennium*.

22. An exchange between Frank and conspiracy-theory radio talk-show host Art Bell in "Collateral Damage" suggests that Black appreciates the Orwellian character of his employers:

> Art Bell: "Mr. Black, a lot of my listeners consider you the enemy."
> Frank: "Me?"
> Art Bell: "FBI, NSA, CIA, government. I let them talk, that doesn't mean I agree with them."
> Frank: "Sometimes *I* agree with them."

23. It is notable that the two shows cast a number of contemporary American political activists and critics of the federal government in small roles: Don Gifford, writer and producer of the documentary *Waco: Rules of Engagement*, appears as a news announcer in "The Rain King;" Art Bell, host of a 1990s AM call-in talk show that featured discussion of antigovernment conspiracy theories, appears as himself in "Collateral Damage;" and Floyd Red Crow Westerman, a Lakota activist and member of AIM (American Indian Movement), appears in six episodes of the two shows ("Anasazi," "Paper Clip,"

"The Blessing Way," "Biogenesis," "The Sixth Extinction II: Amor Fati," and "A Single Blade of Grass").

24. Admittedly, Lara Means is driven insane by her involvement with the Millennium Group in the finale of season two and Emma Hollis appears to have sold out to the Group in the series finale of *Millennium*; however, the arc of Carter's shows generally allow for the possibility that such characters might recover or redeem themselves. The cancellation of *Millennium* at the end of its third season necessarily renders such a turn of events mere speculation on my part.

25. Murray N. Rothbard, *The Ethics of Liberty* (New York: New York University Press, 2002), 187.

26. Friedrich Nietzsche, *Thus Spoke Zarathustra*, in *The Portable Nietzsche*, ed. and trans., Walter Kaufmann (New York: Viking, 1968), 160.

THE PRISONER AND SELF-IMPRISONMENT

Shai Biderman and William J. Devlin

Know Thyself

When we discuss the cinematic realm of noir, what exactly are we talking about? Literally, the word "noir" means dark. But what is so dark about these cinematic features to constitute them as films noirs? Typically, such features are dark in their imagery and content. Visually, most noir is characterized by dark scenery, tilted angles, black-and-white film to sharpen the contrast, and gloomy atmospheres. Meanwhile, their content is characterized by moral ambiguity, usually emphasized by the leading character—the dark hero who exemplifies the existential qualities of disturbance, complexity, anguish, and despair.[1]

Quite often, we find that this angst-ridden character is a private eye (though for our purpose, it is better to see him as a private I). The audience enters the noir scene by adopting the eye of the I, so to speak. As we follow the private eye through his perspective, we come to discover the darkness—the misapprehension, ambiguity, and confusion—of the world as seen (or known) through the eyes of the main subject. As viewers, we are led to take the point of view of the noir hero, to see reality from his perspective and identify with him. We share his engagement with the world and share the epistemological and ethical questions he encounters. We immediately grow to learn (due to the noir elements) that it is not easy being the noir hero: the world seems a grim and confusing place, and the moral and epistemological questions we ask are met with ambiguous answers (and sometimes with no answers at all). The ambiguity and darkness of reality projects itself on the protagonist. It is not just reality that is unknown and ambiguous—the protagonist himself is, as well. His moral standing is in doubt; he skeptically questions what he knows and does not know. In other words, his entire self—and not just the mystery case at hand—is under examination.[2]

Questions of selfhood can be fruitfully explored through film noir. Such questions include: How do we construct our self-identity? Am I free to create my own conception of selfhood? Is selfhood merely a fiction? Selfhood is one of the most elusive concepts in the western tradition: it is necessarily presupposed and yet it eludes analysis. On the one hand, the self can be interpreted as an active ontological entity that engages the world and directs individuals in their actions. For instance, René Descartes claimed that the self is an active thinking entity—it is the only thing of which one can be certain and so provides the starting point for all of our investigations. On the other hand, the self can be interpreted as a passive linguistic apprehension insofar as it is simply a name ascribed to the collection of experiences that one can have. David Hume, for example, held that the self is a fictitious concept; when one looks inside oneself, there is no self to be found, only a bundle of impressions. At best, the self is a passive container that receives these impressions through experience. But there is no active enduring agent, as Descartes maintained. Whether we take the self to be something that is active or passive, however, we use the notion of selfhood to refer to the particular person one is—that which persists though time, that which makes us unique and distinguishable from one another, et cetera.[3]

The self thus takes center stage in noir. In this essay, we discuss the issue of selfhood with reference to an out-of-the-ordinary private eye. He is not a detective but a secret agent. But his selfhood suffers the most acute withdrawal when he is deprived of his freedom through imprisonment. This imprisonment is not simply a case where our private eye is behind bars. Rather, not only is he stripped of his physical and actual freedom of action, but also, and more importantly, he is losing his conceptual freedom as a self—one who has the freedom to reflect and to define himself. As we shall see, such imprisonment leads our hero to confront the ambiguity of his selfhood and therefore the ambiguity and uncertain nature of the concept of the self. This existential engagement with selfhood, accompanied by a psychedelic cinematic atmosphere, allows us to call him a dark noir hero.

In the 1960s television series *The Prisoner,* a man we presume to be a newly retired agent of some branch of British intelligence is gassed and awakens in an isolated island community called "the Village." As a prisoner of the Village, he discovers that his imprisonment on the island requires his conformity: all members are assigned numbers and follow the rules of the Village, which is guarded by the various Number 2s, who enforce conformity and answer ultimately to the elusive and mysterious Number 1. With his thought and action constrained, our imprisoned agent is outwardly stripped of his identity, as he is now only known and referred to as "Number 6." With his conceptual freedom for self-definition in jeopardy, Number 6 turns to his only solution: rebellion. Introspectively, he rebels by fighting for his conceptual freedom: "I am not a number, I am a *person.*" Physically, he rebels through various attempts to thwart authority and escape from the Village.

Let us follow our noir hero, Number 6, through his reorientation of self-understanding as a prisoner, his physical and introspective rebellions, and his apparent escape from the Village to help us understand the philosophical questions concerning selfhood: What does it mean to be a person, exactly? What is the noir take on selfhood? What does Number 6's discovery tell us about the notion of individuals as authentic beings? What does it say about the modern world? What can we, as modern human beings, learn from *The Prisoner* about our relation to the modern world?

"Be Seeing You"

When we first take up the question of selfhood—that is, what it is to *be* a self—it may be tempting to confine our attention to the physical dimension. This dimension concerns the physical, corporeal features of individuals. It deals with the things about our nature that make us palpable creatures driven by needs, urges, and inclinations and that give us particular constitutions or temperaments, for instance, more or less energetic, lethargic, passionate, or apathetic. Our selves on this level, including whatever consciousness we have of them, are housed in our bodies and are shaped by the body's needs. In this section, then, let us investigate what *The Prisoner* tells us about the material dimension of selfhood through the physicality of the Village.[4]

The Village appears to be a retirement community for former secret agents. And while the villagers may not have initially welcomed their enforced residency, nearly all of them have come to accommodate themselves to the Village and to conform to its rules and regulations. As Number 2 explains to Number 6, "They didn't settle for ages—now they wouldn't leave for the world." But this village is not established as a way of saying thank you to the agents for all of their years of service; on the contrary, the powers that be (Numbers 1, 2, and others) have more devious intentions—namely they seek to extract information from the villagers about their experience as agents.

The general method used to pull information from the agents is to eliminate their freedom for self-identity by limiting their physical freedom. Each person is robbed of this freedom through the suppression of his or her material selfhood. The Village suffocates and extinguishes unique urges, inclinations, temperaments, and personalities by enforcing conformity throughout the community: they must dress according to the Village dress code; they must awaken at a prescribed hour ("Rise and shine"), retire at "lights out," come to a halt when Rover appears, and even act as pawns in a game of chess. But unlike the black-and-white contrasts typical of film noir, the village's visual aspect is one of psychedelic colors, festivals, music, and parades. All villagers are given uniforms characterized by their vibrant colors of red, blue, and yellow (as opposed to the dark colors of Number 6's original personal outfit—a charcoal-gray suit, black shirt, and black shoes—which he wears in the first and last episodes of the series). Nevertheless, these colors are specifically used to help disarm the existential anguish and isolation triggered by the demand for conformity.

Furthermore, the Village is structured so that all villagers are constantly watched. The community is filled with hidden cameras that watch a person's every move, which are managed by a supervisor who operates the control center hidden within the Village. There are a multitude of wardens and guards to keep the residents' behavior in check, with the most famous warden being the dreaded Rover, a roaming weather balloon that guards the Village from rebellious behavior. Once someone falls out of step, Rover pounces upon the rebel, absorbing the person's face (so the becomes faceless, thereby eliminating his facial, physical self-identity), suffocating him, and leaving him either unconscious or dead. Through these tactics, it becomes clear that one of the central characteristics of the Village is that "Big Brother" is watching you, or "seeing you."

While the elusive Number 1 is the leading authority figure of the Village, he is completely hidden from the residents, and his identity remains mysterious. Number 1 aside, the key figure in retrieving information is Number 2. While we do see various Number 2s, their identities are also mysterious, since each Number 2 is replaced in almost every subsequent episode (and sometimes within a single episode). Each person who serves as Number 2 has the same role, so that what is important (for purposes of carrying out the mission of the Village) is that the functions of that role are carried out, not who serves in the role in any particular episode.[5]

Each Number 2 contributes to breaking a prisoner's spirit though various techniques and games that elicit and exploit confusion, apprehension, and ambiguity, so often found in film noir. Whether it is duping the prisoner into participating in rigged democratic elections, creating a faux London scenario to deceive him into thinking he has escaped, monitoring dreams, transplanting the prisoner's mind into another's body, leading the prisoner to believe that he is not himself, but is rather a double agent, or using various spies in the Village to double cross him, the goal of each plan is the same: wear down the prisoner, mentally and physically, so he can no longer trust anyone in the Village, not even himself. Such a breakdown would lead one to conform to the society and "freely" give up the information that Number 2 wants to retrieve.

Thus, by installing fear and paranoia that one is being watched and that escape is futile, the villagers' physical freedom, including their ability to construct their own material selfhood, has been eroded so that they now blissfully conform to the rules of the society: they have been brought around to the Village's way of thinking and simply volunteer the wanted information. That is, through the physical conformity set up by the external structure of the Village, the residents become conditioned to think ways that cause them to lose their conceptual freedom to reflect upon and define their own selfhood. With this freedom lost, they not only physically conform to the Village, but they mentally conform to the rules and ideas of the society. With both physical and conceptual freedom lost, one's individual selfhood is obliterated. The villagers are now more like what Friedrich Nietzsche calls "the herd" or existentialist philosophy typically refers to as "the crowd." The villagers no longer have a unique selfhood—they are "inauthentic" insofar as they now think, talk, and act in accordance with society. By losing their freedom over their control of their behavior and their physical existence, they have lost their individuality.

"I Am Not a Number! I Am a Free Man!"

As we suggested in the introduction, those who are in power in the Village focus their attention on the new resident, Number 6, since he has the most valuable information. "The information in your head is priceless," he is told by Number 2 in "Arrival." "I don't think you realize what a valuable *property* you've become. A man like you is worth a great deal on the open market." And so, the treatment of Number 6 follows the various methods of treatment toward prisoners of the Village: deprive him of his physical freedom so that his material and conceptual notions of selfhood wear away and he becomes one of the crowd and provides them with his priceless information.

But Number 6 does not respond as expected. Physically, he vies for his freedom. He refuses to go along with their bizarre reality. He tells his captors: "I am not a number!" He is adamant about refusing to share any information: "I have nothing to say. Is that clear?" He defiantly and arrogantly remains detached from the Village's communal functions and uncooperative with Number 2 and the wardens. All the while, he verbally slaps the authorities in the face with his sarcastic and acerbic wit. For instance, in "Free for All," when Number 2 asks him if he will run (in the upcoming elections), Number 6 responds, "Like the blazes; first chance I get." That is, escape from the prison is always at the forefront of his mind. But his escape is not simply one of individual resistance—Number 6 intends to overpower the authority of the Village by destroying this society altogether: "I'm going to escape and come back . . . come back, wipe this place off the face of the earth, obliterate it" ("Chimes of Big Ben").

Throughout the series, we thus see Number 6 constantly trying to escape his imprisonment. But given the tight security—the "Big Brother" surveillance—of the prison, all of his attempts to free himself are ultimately thwarted. Whether he tries to run, sail, drive, or fly out of the Village, all of his escapes are foiled under the watchful eye of Number 2, Rover, the wardens, and spies. Still, given his constant attempts to flee, we see that Number 6 is unique not only because he has priceless information but also because of his undying resistance to conformity. Number 6 is now recognized as "a challenge," "a subject proving exceptionally difficult" to break down.

Still, despite his relentless drive toward physical freedom, the life within this imprisoned society cannot help but affect his behavior. Still conceiving himself as a free man, Number 6 is seen as an outsider by those who have taken on the herd mentality of the Village. To the crowd and the authority figures, the Village is not a world that erases identity but instead the ideal vision for the best possible society. As Number 2 explains in "Chimes of Big Ben," "What in fact has been created? An international community. A perfect blueprint for world order. When the sides facing each other suddenly realize that they're looking into a mirror, they'll see that this is the pattern for the future." From their point of view, Number 6 is an anarchist who does not want to acknowledge the benefits of the discipline that the Village, the ideal society, provides. As we see in Number 2's characterization of Number 6 in "Dance of the Dead," Number 6 is at best a dreamer who lives in his own world and has gone mad.

The Authentic Number 6

While the villagers believe Number 6 has no values, Number 6 maintains that he has "different values." He is thus estranged from the world around him; he displays the freedom to create his own self-identity, a freedom which is now foreign to the villagers. And so, our dark hero is all alone in a world that appears upside down, a world where, through his eyes, everyone else has gone mad.

Notice, however, that Number 6's steadfast recognition of himself as a free man, and his subsequent isolation from the crowd, is not simply a characteristic of his material self. He is not just maintaining physical freedom and physical isolation; rather, he is vying for the conceptual freedom to preserve his own self-identity, independently of the world of the Village. This freedom leads us to a second dimension of the self, namely the reflective one. This dimension concerns the human capacity to make both the world, and our own existence as a self, objects of our active reflection. Under this dimension, my selfhood is my ability to reflect upon myself. Here, we turn a kind of mirror not only on phenomena in the world, including our own bodies and our social relations, but also inward, on our own consciousness, as we place ourselves at a distance from our own being so as to examine, judge, regulate, and revise our self-identity. The self on this level is understood as an active agent of its own realization, establishing order among its attitudes and beliefs, and giving direction to its actions. It appears to be (how far or how justifiably so is not in question at this point) self-constituting or self-made: we are what our attention to ourselves makes us be.

Since human beings are reflective creatures, we can theorize about the disappearance of our own ability to reflect upon, and to independently maintain, our self-identity. We find that this becomes the central concern for Number 6. It is not merely the physical imprisonment that bothers him because, really, the Village *is* much like a vacation resort: there is a lovely shoreside, scenic mountains, daily activities, free room and board, et cetera. The real problem with the Village is that it aims to erase the reflective dimension of the self—the villagers no longer think for themselves, and those who do are threatened by Rover or even by execution as rebels to the society. Number 6 is aware that the Village eliminates the reflective dimension of the self, and it is this dimension, this freedom of the self, that he wishes to maintain throughout his imprisonment.

This explains why Number 6 is seen as an outsider to the villagers and why Number 6 sees the world of the Village as an upside-down one. Number 6 is much like Socrates, insofar as he does not simply conform to the rules of society. He is the gadfly of the Village, who challenges the unreflective obedience that everyone else displays. At times, his challenges can be acerbic, such as when he talks to the crowd in "Free for All": "Unlike me, many of you have accepted the situation of your imprisonment, and will die here like rotten cabbages." At other times, however, his challenge indicates his appeal to the reflective nature of the self, such as when he again talks to the villagers in "A Change of Mind," telling them, "You still have a choice. You can still salvage your right to be individuals, your rights to truth and free thought. Reject this false world of Number 2 . . . reject it *now!*"

Likewise, Number 6's emphasis on the reflective dimension of selfhood relates him to both Descartes and Immanuel Kant. Number 6 follows Descartes insofar as the self, as an active thinking entity, is the only thing of which we can be certain: while the Village, its citizens, and its authority figures are deceptive and so cannot be trusted, Number 6 trusts his firm belief that he is an active thinking being and a free man. Kant emphasizes the reflective aspect of human beings, which helps to ground moral decisions. As rational agents, we decide how to act ethically. With Number 6's understanding that he is a free, rational being, he uses his reflective aspect of selfhood to determine how he should act in the Village. His notion of selfhood grounds his decisions for escape and his resistance to giving information.[6]

Furthermore, by maintaining his active reflective selfhood, Number 6 is isolated because he is unwilling to simply follow the herd mentality. Here, he displays what existentialism calls "authenticity." The authentic individual is aware of this reflective aspect of the self—he realizes that his existence, his being, is a being-in-question. The human being is unique among all other beings insofar as his being can be reflected upon, solidified, revised, etc. As Jean-Paul Sartre puts it, the human "existence precedes essence." The human being is a being who comes to exist in such a way so that he is thrust into the world. As a being-in-the-world, or a self that cannot be completely separated from the world, the human being must create his own essence for himself—he has the freedom to create his own self-identity. The authentic individual is thus the one who is aware of his reflective, malleable nature, acknowledges his freedom for self-definition, and lives a life that does not conform to the steps of the crowd but rather mirrors his own creative abilities.[7]

Number 6 is existentially an authentic individual because he is aware of, and utilizes, the reflective aspect of the self. While he is forced into this prison, and so is thrust into the world of the Village, he uses his reflective nature to determine how he should create his essence in this bizarre existence. How should he act? How should he treat his supervisors? How should he relate to the Village crowd? Here, Number 6 acknowledges that his being is a being-in-question. His reaction to this new world further indicates his authenticity. Understanding that he is a being-in-the-world, Number 6 knows that his freedom is in jeopardy as this Village-world can deceptively strip him of his willingness to create his own self-identity, by pulling him into the crowd. With the determination to avoid collapsing into the faceless crowd, Number 6 creates his essence in the village-world as one of defiance. Physically and conceptually, he aims to maintain his freedom and his self-hood on his own terms: "I will not make any deals with you. I've resigned. I will not be pushed, filed, stamped, indexed, briefed, debriefed or *numbered!* My life is my own." Thus, despite the attempts to brainwash and mentally program him, Number 6 continues to maintain his freedom to create his own self-identity, both on the material and reflective levels of selfhood.

"Six of One"

Throughout the series, Number 6 is portrayed as the existential, authentic individual who refuses to submit to the rules and conformist ideals of the Village. He maintains his physical and reflective freedom and so is able to hold onto his selfhood in both the material and reflective dimensions. But there is a third dimension of selfhood investigated in *The Prisoner,* namely the relational one. This dimension concerns the social and cultural interaction of the self. Here, one turns to the common connections and involvements that give us collective identities and shared orientations and values, making us people able to use a specific language or idiom and marking us with its particular styles of description, categorization, and expression. In this perspective our selves are what our relations with society, and relations with others, shape us or allow us to be. It thus includes the roles we play within society that contribute to the overall social good. While we find examples of this dimension of selfhood throughout the show—Number 6's role as a candidate for the position of Number 2, his planned coup d'état, Number 2's role of carrying out the mission of the Village, the villagers' role as cogs in the wheel of the machine of the Village (or pawns in a chess game)—the relational dimension is most strongly emphasized at the end of the series.

In the last two episodes, "Once Upon a Time" and "Fall Out," Number 6 undertakes his final attempt to free himself from the Village. Realizing that all of the best efforts to retrieve information from Number 6 have failed, Number 2 decides that there is only one final method left, the method of "degree absolute": Number 6 and Number 2 are to be locked in a room together for one week, where each will challenge the other until one of them finally breaks down and is conquered. After a grueling week of mental, emotional, and physical dueling, Number 6 defeats Number 2, thus killing him. With this victory, Number 6 is granted his desire to meet Number 1.

But before he can meet Number 1, Number 6 is requested to attend the council of the Village, led by its president, where it is said that the Village is facing a "democratic crisis" concerning the "question of revolt." In "Fall Out," Number 6, now held in esteem, is given the high throne to watch the proceedings, as the council determines the fate of two rebels. The first rebel, Number 48, represents the rebellion of "uncoordinated youth," frowned upon by the Village, since it is "against *any* accepted norm," a "rebellion against nothing it can define." The second rebel, a resurrected Number 2, represents the rebellion of authority, discouraged since it is a case of "an established, successful, secure member of the establishment, turning upon, and biting, the hand that feeds him!" Both rebellions are deemed "dangerous" since they "contribute nothing" to the society.

In the trial of the rebels, Number 48 and Number 2 are evaluated in terms of their relational selves. How do they connect or relate to the society of the Village? What do their rebellious actions say about, and do for, the society in which they live? As the president of the council suggests, their behavior is negative—they relate poorly to their social environment insofar as they provide nothing that benefits the good of the whole. Whether they are rebelling for no particular reason or betraying the society that provided them with their authority and power, their reactions are intended to ultimately dismantle, and so destroy, the society: their social relations "are nonproductive and so must be abolished!"

But this does not mean that society frowns upon every form of rebellion in terms of social relations. On the contrary, the trial concludes by examining the third form: namely, the rebellion of Number 6. From the perspective of the Village and the council, Number 6 is "a revolutionary of a *different* caliber," since he has "revolted, resisted, fought . . . overcome coercion . . . for the right to be a person, someone, an individual." Number 6's revolution is not to be frowned upon by the Village; instead "he must no longer be referred to as 'Number 6,' or a number of any kind," since "he has gloriously vindicated the right of the individual to *be* an individual." That is, Number 6 has fought a "private war" to maintain his relational independence of selfhood and overcome the "materialistic efforts" of the Village to reduce his selfhood to crowd conformity. Ultimately, Number 6 has prevailed and so maintained his self-identity as "a *man,* a man of steel." And so his persistence is a rebellion that conveys a value upon society: by living the authentic life, he serves as "an example" to all other members of society as to how to live. The council and the Village acknowledge that Number 6 is living a life that is authentic and pure, and so his behavior can teach everyone else how to live. Not only are they thankful of Number 6's actions, since he has "convinced them of their mistakes," but they also would like him to "lead them" and take the authoritative position of the Village. Such a celebratory stance toward Number 6 provides a positive interpretation of his relational selfhood: he is construed as having the role of leader who benefits the society of the Village by being an example for all.

Thus, even if rebellious, the relational dimension of the self is central to one's self-definition, as one's material and reflective dimensions meet through one's social interactions with one's environment. And so it seems that our noir hero, Number 6, is ultimately triumphant, since he now has the power to control the Village and lead this world in the direction he sees fit—into a new world where everyone can exhibit their physical and conceptual freedom to create their independent self-identity.

"Half a Dozen of the Other"

But then, all of a sudden, "Fall Out" seems to take a 180-degree turn. In perhaps the most bizarre scene of the most bizarre episode of this bizarre world of the Village, the noir element of confusion, apprehension, and ambiguity explosively returns to the forefront of the series. Number 6 meets Number 1, only to find that he *is* Number 1. Our dark hero, resolute to maintain his free self-identity, and the antihero, the overseer who attempts to break down all self-identities, are one and the same. This revelation twists not only the plot of the series but also the notion of the self, as it hinges upon the relational dimension of selfhood.

In "Fall Out," not only is the world of the Village that we've come to know twisted, but the analysis of selfhood applied to Number 6—his material, reflective, and relational self—is turned on its head. If Number 6 is Number 1, how are we to now make sense of his physical and conceptual pursuit of freedom, his determination to maintain his reflective self, and his personal revolution as the correct educative relation to society? It seems rather inane to say that Number 6 is an authentic individual because he is rebelling against himself. But what is the correct thing to say about selfhood in *The Prisoner,* if we maintain that Number 6 and Number 1 are the same person?

To be sure, "Fall Out" is the most peculiar episode of *The Prisoner*—one that leaves the viewer in confusion, trying to bridge this episode to the rest of the series both cinematically and philosophically. The standard approach to understanding the final episode (and the apparent identity between Number 6 and Number 1) is to separate it from the other sixteen by interpreting "Fall Out" as a surrealist romp that is hyper-allegorical and should not be taken literally. Thus, the apparent identity between Number 6 and Number 1 is not literal, since it is a logical impossibility for the same person to occupy two places at once. Since Number 6 and Number 1 do, indeed, occupy differ-ent places at once (e.g., Number 1's mask is pulled off by Number 6 who is standing in front of him), it cannot be the case that Number 6 and Number 1 are identical. This interpretation thus marks "Fall Out" as an episode to be treated independently of the noir realism of the entire series. We accept that its cinematic features are radically different from the series as a whole, that a completely literal interpretation of the identity connection between Num-ber 6 and Number 1 leads to a logical contradiction, and that, to an extent, this episode is disjunctive from the others. But even given this cinematic separation, we would like to use this episode, and its chaotic collection of metaphors, to flesh out a view of selfhood that stands in a stark contrast to the conception we have examined thus far. This is not to say that the entire series should be interpreted by "Fall Out"; rather, we are interested in using "Fall Out" to further the landscape of selfhood that we are investigating. Thus far, the entire series, and our philosophical coverage of it, can be un-derstood as an odyssey: it is a journey of a man seeking a solid definition of selfhood. We now dare to offer an interpretation that puts aside the series' central theme of authentic selfhood and look at this separate final episode.

Here, we can interpret this episode as philosophically arguing that there is no self: the odyssey of Number 6 to discover his selfhood is hopeless, since self is a fictitious concept.[8]

The identity of Number 6 as Number 1 leads us to an overall critique of the concept of selfhood. This stems from the relational dimension of the self and ultimately holds that the self as a free and independent individual is a fictitious concept. As we shall see, this critique argues that there is no completely independent individual; rather, people are dependent upon society in forming their personal identity. How we create ourselves (in the existential hopes of authenticity) stems from the social views and values of the society in which we are raised. This suggests we cannot completely escape conformity altogether; that is, we are not as free as Number 6 seems to believe.

This critique of selfhood is brought about by postmodernist philosopher Michel Foucault. Foucault's claim that we are not free to create our own unique self-identity, independent of society, stems from his analysis of the modern prison, an analysis befitting of the Village. He maintains that the modern prison is characterized by its use of three different techniques to control prisoners. First, there is hierarchical observation. Prisoners are always monitored, and by different groups of guards who serve under, and report to, a higher figure of authority. In the Village, there is around-the-clock surveillance of the villagers, which is managed by the supervisor at the control center. The supervisor reports to Number 2, who, in turn, reports to, and works under, Number 1.[9]

The second technique is normalization, in which prisoners are not physically punished to reprimand them for their behavior; rather, they are reformed through imposed social norms. They are retrained on how to properly behave and function in society. We see such a normalization process in the Village through the villagers themselves. The villagers contribute to the attempt to correct Number 6's deviant behavior and reform him by helping him come to live by the Village's standards and norms. The villagers have already been conditioned through the process of normalization. They do not wish to escape, they obey the commands of Number 2, and they joyously participate in the activities that the hierarchy provides for them, such as playing as human chess pieces and participating in elections.

The final technique of modern prisons is examination, a method of control that incorporates both of the previous techniques. Here, the prisoner is tested and examined to determine whether he has been properly conditioned to follow the norms of society. The results of these examinations are written down so that authorities have detailed information about each prisoner and his progress for functioning in society. In the Village, we see that the authorities have a full documentation of Number 6's life—everything from his history as a secret agent to how many lumps of sugar he likes in his tea has been recorded. Likewise, he is continuously examined so they can retrieve the priceless information he is keeping secret. Here, the success of these exams is dependent upon whether or not Number 6 has been conditioned to follow the social norms of the Village. Thus, in line with Foucault's analysis, the Village follows each of the three techniques of the modern prison.

But Foucault does not think that these techniques are confined to the prison. Instead, they are analogous to those found in modern society. Modern society is structured so that there is a hierarchy of observation (insofar as there is an overarching method of surveillance and reports to higher authoritative figures), an implicit normalization process (insofar as there are social norms set down in society, which are imposed upon its citizens), and examinations (insofar as one is educated and tested on how to properly function in society). These methods are valuable to those who run modern societies, according to Foucault, because they produce knowledge about the citizens, which enables authority to further control their behavior. Since knowledge enhances control, these methods are useful for maintaining order and the preservation of power.

With these methods of control implemented in society, however, we come to see that the notion of an individual having the freedom to create his own unique self-identity, one that covers the material, reflective, and relational dimensions, is impossible. No matter how we create our self-identity, Foucault maintains, there is a society that lies behind it. That is, we create our selfhood through our society, through our social influences, so that our self-definition is completely dependent upon that society. Our entire construction of our selfhood follows the goal of Jeremy Bentham's *Panopticon,* a prison structure designed so that no inmate can see another, but every inmate is visible to the monitors located in a central tower.[10] While the monitors do not always observe every inmate, the structure imposes the idea that they can view them at any time. Since the inmates do not know when exactly they are being monitored, they continue to behave properly. That is, this prison is self-monitored, or internally monitored, by the inmates themselves. Here those who are controlled, the prisoners, remain under control because of their own mental constraints: the controlled and the controller are one and the same. Likewise, our construction of selfhood is so deeply entrenched in society that we believe we have the freedom to create ourselves in any way we'd like, but in fact we are fooling ourselves. Ultimately, we are conditioned and trained to think and act in a way that follows the rules, regulations, and philosophical ideas of the society in which we are living. So, for instance, in a society that encourages the idea of freedom, we create a self-identity that suggests we are free. But this freedom is not something real, as it is not an image created independently of society. Our society always lies behind and helps guide the construction of selfhood. Thus, for Foucault, the self is dead because any definition of selfhood is un-free insofar as it is derivative of society.

Using Foucault's extension of the three techniques of control to modern society and the notion of selfhood, we can see how the identity between Number 6 and Number 1 flips the original portrayal of selfhood in the series completely upside down. If Number 6 is the prisoner who is being monitored, and Number 1 is the highest figure in the hierarchy of observation which is monitoring Number 6, and if Number 6 and Number 1 are identical, then Number 6 is like Bentham's panopticon-inmate: the process of monitoring and controlling the behavior of the inmate is all done internally. Once again the controller and the controlled are identical. Number 6 is simply monitoring himself, so the push for conformity to society comes from within himself.

While this may suggest that his entire imprisonment in the Village is a figment of his imagination, insofar as everything is occurring in his head, the Village becomes a metaphor for the modern society in Foucault's terms. Just as Number 2's greatest dream is to use the "perfect blueprint" of the Village to structure the whole world, so that there is "a Village of the world," so too Number 6's internal monitoring becomes a mirror of how societies are structured in the world. That is, the Village follows the structure of the panopticon, which, for Foucault, constitutes the paradigm for modern society's use of self-discipline for power and control.

Since the Village is a metaphor for society, Number 6's ideal of freedom—both physically and conceptually—is hopeless. Number 6 can never achieve the kind of freedom he believes he can, since his physical escape from the prison only brings him to the prison of the modern world, and, conceptually, he can never have the freedom to create his own self-identity, since his notion of selfhood will always be dependent upon the society in which he lives. Whether he emphasizes the material dimension of the self, so he follows what he thinks are his independent inclinations, attitudes, and desires; or the reflective dimension of the self, so that he thinks he is creating his own self-identity; or the relational dimension of the self, so he follows his behavior toward others, Number 6 cannot be an existentially authentic being that exhibits absolute freedom. All creations of the self, from all dimensions of the self, will be derivative from society.

Across the Landscape of Selfhood

From start to finish, the journey of Number 6 in *The Prisoner* is a journey across the landscape of selfhood. From the construction of the Village, to the defiant demeanor of Number 6 and his attempts to escape, to the identity of Number 6 as Number 1, the series explores various dimensions and interpretations of selfhood. This exploration centers on the noir hero, and through his own perspective we are led through the noir elements of misapprehension, confusion, and ambiguity, in terms of both Number 6's attempt to escape the prison and our philosophical attempt to define selfhood. Has Number 6 successfully escaped the Village at the end of the series? Or is this apparent escape another deception brought on by the authority of the Village? Likewise, does Number 6 have the freedom to create his own self-identity, whether it is in terms of the material, reflective, or relational dimensions of selfhood? Is Number 6 the existential authentic being? Or is he an inmate of modern society, as Foucault would maintain, and so constructs his self-identity through social influence and control? Ultimately, *The Prisoner* maintains its noir elements throughout, as it leaves us in our dark state of misapprehension, confusion, and ambiguity in both cases until the bitter end.

Notes

We would like to thank Steven M. Sanders and Aeon J. Skoble for their enthusiasm and hard work in reading and providing insightful and helpful comments on previous drafts of this essay.

1. Some identify film noir with a historical cycle, specifically 1941–1958. For us, however, noir is not a historical claim but an essential one—it is essentially characterized by a certain style and a certain content. In this sense, we have neo-noir, which extends beyond the historical period of classic noir (and is new in the historical sense) or, alternately, will manage to renew something else while maintaining the overall

essence (e.g., to deal with the same moral grimness but with psychedelic colors). For further discussion of the cinematic nature of noir, see Aeon J. Skoble, "Moral Clarity and Practical Reason in Film Noir," in Mark T. Conard, ed., *The Philosophy of Film Noir* (Lexington: University Press of Kentucky, 2006), 41–48. See also Conard's introduction to the volume and his essay, "Nietzsche and the Meaning and Definition of Noir," 7–22. In the same work, for the claim that noir is defined within a particular cinematic period, see Jason Holt, "A Darker Shade: Realism in Neo-Noir," 23–40.

2. Epistemology is the branch of philosophy concerning the nature, sources, and limits of knowledge. In this case, we are concerned with the knowledge of the world and introspective knowledge of ourselves. Ethics is the branch of philosophy that concerns systems of values organized in the lives of groups or individuals, moral notions of right and wrong, and principles of moral action.

3. For Descartes' notion of the self, see his work *Meditations on First Philosophy*, ed. and trans. George Heffernan (Notre Dame, IN: University of Notre Dame Press, 1990). For Hume's critical stance toward such a notion, see his *Treatise of Human Nature*, ed. L. A. Selby-Bigge (Oxford: Clarendon, 1896).

4. For further discussion on the material dimension of the self, see Jerrold Seigel, *The Idea of the Self: Thoughts and Experiences in Western Europe since the Seventeenth Century* (Cambridge: Cambridge University Press, 2005), 3–44.

5. Notice that while each Number 2 can appear radically different—Number 2 may be short or tall, soft-spoken or boisterous, male or female, et cetera—we usually identify them as Number 2 by their one identical physical feature: namely, the button that depicts a Penny Farthing bicycle and the number "2." Once we see an individual wearing this button, we infer that it is indeed "the new Number 2" and that this person carries out the mission of the Village.

6. For Kant's view of ethics, see his *Grounding for the Metaphysics of Morals*, trans. James W. Ellington (1785; Indianapolis, IN: Hackett, 1981).

7. See Jean-Paul Sartre, *Existentialism and Human Emotions*, trans. Bernard Frechtman (New York: Philosophical Library, 1957), 9–51

8. Given the bizarreness of "Fall Out" and all of its metaphors (the use of the Beatles' song "All You Need Is Love," the council singing "Dry Bones" along with Number 48, the globe that Number 1 is holding, the gorilla mask on Number 1, Number 1's escape from the Village via a rocket, etc.), this episode is open to a wide array of interpretations. Whether one holds the view that the show challenges the hippie counterculture movement of the 1960s, the theory that it is Patrick McGoohan's response to the public attention toward the series, or one TV critic's derogatory idea that the episode is meaningless and at best an ego trip by McGoohan, "Fall Out" is so complex and metaphorical that it is open to several different interpretations. Since we quite enjoy it and its chaotic explosion from the other episodes, and since it is the finale of the series, we find it important to consider what this episode can reveal about the question of selfhood.

9. This argument from Foucault is sketched throughout his various texts. See his

Madness and Civilization, trans. Richard Howard (New York: Pantheon Books, 1965); *The Archaeology of Knowledge,* trans. Alan Sheridan (New York: Harper and Row, 1972); *Discipline and Punish,* trans. Alan Sheridan (New York: Pantheon Books, 1977); and *The Foucault Reader,* trans. and ed. Paul Rabinow (New York: Pantheon Books, 1984).

10. For further reading on Bentham's panopticon, see his "Panopticon," in *The Panopticon Writings,* ed. Miran Bozovic (London: Verso, 1995), 29–95.

TWIN PEAKS, NOIR, AND OPEN INTERPRETATION

Jason Holt

Any fan of *Twin Peaks* who encounters Goya's lithograph *The Sleep of Reason Produces Monsters* (1803) cannot help but see an obvious connection to the landmark TV series; whether series creators David Lynch and Mark Frost had this connection in mind is of little importance. The lithograph depicts a sleeping figure slumped over a desk. From behind, almost out of view, the somnolent head, emerging from an indeterminate place that seems not quite real, are the so-called monsters identified, together with their cause, in the title: creatures far more sinister than their appearance would normally suggest, many of them winged things, owls. The owls in *Twin Peaks* play a similar symbolic role, have a comparable significance. These are not, in either case, the wise Minervan creatures of Western European culture or native North American folklore. Instead they augur ill, harbingers of bad times hooting evil tidings. "The owls," to follow the series motif, "are not what they seem." Indeed.

Evoking a dark, existential atmosphere is one of the hallmarks of film noir, and while it would be wrong, for many reasons, to call Goya's etching "lithograph noir," the application of "noir" to *Twin Peaks* seems far less inapt, not least because it comes much closer to respecting the historical dimension of the term. Purists might demur from using the term beyond the borders of cinema, and even, within these bounds, with reference to films falling outside what is generally regarded as the cycle of classic film noir, 1941–1958. But one of the guiding assumptions of this volume is that it might be fruitful to view certain small-screen works through the dark lens of those classic films that so clearly influenced them. *Twin Peaks* is no exception; it would not have been possible without film noir. The influence is incontrovertibly strong, the show's noirish tendencies as many as they are diverse. Juxtaposing *Twin Peaks* with the conceptual apparatus of film noir will help foster a greater appreciation of the former and, as side benefits, a richer understanding of the latter and of interpreting artworks generally.

The question is less whether *Twin Peaks* is noir—it almost certainly is not—and more a matter of why and how its undeniable noirishness falls short of pure noir. *Twin Peaks* is rarely if ever discussed by film critics or theorists as a series noir, and this is understandable, despite the substantial influence of the film type on the series. True, *Twin Peaks* has been called noir, for example, in the *New York Times,* and this reflects the recent trend of using the term "noir" more and more liberally.[1] This practice is especially annoying when the label is applied carelessly, overlooking noir's hard-boiled metaphysics, its commonsense, darkly realistic, naturalistic worldview. Arguably the key reason why *Twin Peaks* is merely noirish, and not actually noir, is that it deliberately leaves, even forces, the metaphysics and, correspondingly, the interpretation of it, wide open. Openness of interpretation, by which I mean the multiple interpretability of art, is apparently inconsistent with noir, which is somewhat puzzling. The open interpretability of *Twin Peaks* gives it its aesthetic piquancy, without which the series would surely be inferior. Yet noir, which seems by contrast to *close* interpretation, is hardly aesthetically impoverished as a result.

I will first examine various noir elements in *Twin Peaks*. Next, I will address *Twin Peaks* and noir metaphysics respectively, to explain in greater detail why, despite its noir elements, the series is not noir. By implication, then, I will chasten overly liberal uses of the term "noir." Then I will argue that open interpretation à la *Twin Peaks* is aesthetically desirable and that, appearances notwithstanding, the best films noirs also exhibit, though in a more limited form than this show does, multiple interpretability. In championing open interpretability as aesthetically desirable generally, I will identify its source in what I call the "omissive" aesthetic, the art of leaving some things, some important things, out of art, or including them only implicitly.

Shades of Noir

Twin Peaks comprises thirty episodes. The pilot was released, with additional footage inconsistent with the series proper, as a movie, *Twin Peaks* (David Lynch, 1990). The series was later followed by the film prequel *Twin Peaks:*

Fire Walk with Me (David Lynch, 1992). The series consists, ancillary and relatively minor plotlines aside, of two consecutive narratives that focus, in the bizarre, dreamlike logging town of Twin Peaks, on FBI special agent Dale Cooper (Kyle MacLachlan). The telos of the first arc is to solve, and in a sense resolve, the murder of homecoming queen Laura Palmer (Sheryl Lee), who, it turns out, was killed by her abusive father Leland (Ray Wise). The second pits Agent Cooper against his former partner and arch nemesis, Windom Earle (Kenneth Welsh), whose vendetta against Cooper is ultimately undone not by Cooper but by the dark forces he seeks out to fulfill his own dark purposes. The arcs dovetail around BOB (Frank Silva), the malevolent presence/psychological symbol under whose influence Leland abused and murdered his daughter and who issues from the Red Room/Black Lodge/White Lodge to which Earle seeks and ultimately gains access.[2]

On the surface, these two major plotlines are classic noir crime stories (crime being essential to noir), thus providing a first taste of the noir elements in *Twin Peaks*.[3] The Laura Palmer investigation is more or less a textbook example of the noir quest narrative, in which the hero, typically a private investigator or cop, is brought into a mystery already in progress. He must rely on his special skills and own code of values if he is to crack the case and avoid the dangers along the way. Likewise, the Windom Earle plot is a standard former-partner-turns-bitter-enemy-and-the-stakes-could-not-be-higher story. Though some of the more minor plotlines are far from fitting such classic noir patterns, others fit, almost to the point of cliché, the femme fatale pattern, in setup and development if not in resolution. Other plotlines in the series are similarly noir.

In keeping with the narrative patterns of noir are the classic character types they require, such as the trench-coated investigator in the labyrinthine world of crime. Agent Cooper fits the bill to that extent, and although his tragic end distinguishes him from his classic predecessors, it puts him in company with Jake (Jack Nicholson) from *Chinatown* (Roman Polanski, 1974) and other neo-noir counterparts. Still, Cooper appears to be too lighthearted a character, too oddball—with often quasi-mystical investigative techniques—to qualify as an updated Sam Spade or legitimate heir to Philip Marlowe.[4] Even the noir patter is left to his FBI colleague Albert (Miguel Ferrer). Similarly, the town of Twin Peaks is positively teeming with actual, virtual, would-be, and will-be femmes fatales. Almost every resident woman has the tell-tale trappings, allure, poses, and behaviors, in fashionable fashion, of the true noir bad girl. For most, there is at least one requisite sap, one sucker, although, admittedly, the femme fatale mystique seems less intrinsic to the female characters in *Twin Peaks* than a stylized aesthetic veneer. Along with lawmen, femmes fatales, and the saps who love the latter, sundry criminal lowlifes and highlifes complete the ensemble.

Speaking of stylization, many of the stylistic elements of film noir are liberally sprinkled throughout *Twin Peaks*. Cooper's Dictaphone communiqués to the never-seen Diane evoke the classic noir voiceover, a device used partly, then as now, for the benefit of the audience, although the device was mostly phased out during the neo-noir period. The use of low-key and high-contrast lighting is taken directly from the noir handbook, not to mention subjective and canted angle shots during psychologically or dramatically intense scenes, somewhat disoriented and disorienting, both. Among various different stylistic parallels, two deserve special mention. First, a certain style of jazz music recalls the noir mindset, even, and sometimes especially, where the setting itself does not: both when jazz is used to complement a scene, as with the sax soundtrack to Sheriff Truman's (Michael Ontkean) shadowy, slow-motion drinking binge, and more strikingly as a motif, as with Angelo Badalamenti's oft-recurring "Freshly Squeezed." Second, the use of reflected images, mirror images in particular, to problematize the identity of the reflected subject, is straight out of versions of psychological noir stories, even where the reflection is far from realistic, as in the Leland-BOB and series-closing Cooper-BOB sequences.

Another element of noir in *Twin Peaks* which cannot be ignored is the dark, somber mood, in effect the existential atmosphere that conveys a tragic sense of life, of meaninglessness, the inevitability of despair. In early noir films this sensibility reflected an increasingly pervasive undercurrent of anxiety and uncertainty in American culture during and after World War II. In *Twin Peaks* this feeling is grounded in the main narrative threads but also significantly maintained and heightened by establishing and closing shots of various town and forest nightscapes to the accompaniment of downbeat Badalamenti music. These include slow panning shots across windswept conifers and still shots of traffic lights with no one in the streets to follow them, the Roadhouse, the RR Diner, and the unremitting waterfall of the Great Northern Hotel.

To some extent, the existential mood of *Twin Peaks* might be seen as undercut by the frequent juxtaposition of such atmospheric shots with more quirky, humorous scenes, which sometimes cross the line into absurdity. Two remarks are in order here. First, the presence of humor, especially dark or absurd humor, has never been inconsistent with a general existential outlook. Indeed, the absurd, both tragic and humorous, is taken to be a fundamental phenomenon by many existential thinkers and writers. Take, for instance, Albert Camus' fiction and philosophy or Samuel Beckett's tragicomedies. Lest one think, then, that the noir ethos mirrors purely the dark and never the lighter gray side of existentialism, consider the banter between Neff (Fred MacMurray) and Keyes (Edward G. Robinson) in *Double Indemnity* (Billy Wilder, 1944), or the wit and even laughter of no less a hard-boiled type than Sam Spade (Humphrey Bogart) in *The Maltese Falcon* (John Huston, 1941). For those who consider the right tone, mood, or atmosphere a crucial part of noir, *Twin Peaks* is a plausible candidate.

Why Not Noir?

So far we have identified a number of noir elements woven into the fabric of *Twin Peaks:* the crime storylines, iconic characters, stylistic elements, and broodingly existential atmosphere. Are these elements, taken together, sufficient to peg *Twin Peaks* as noir? It might seem so. We should consider, then, some preliminary objections to the notion that *Twin Peaks* is noir. First, it might be observed that noir has not only a typical subject, crime, but also a typical setting, the city. Noirs are characteristically urban crime stories; it is the vicissitudes of urban, not rural, life that private eyes and femmes fatales must skillfully negotiate. One could view *Twin Peaks* as noir displaced from its proper home, and all the more unnerving, then, apropos of noir. One could also acknowledge that while noir, even classic noir, is typically urban, it is not essentially so. Consider the rural setting of *The Postman Always Rings Twice* (Tay Garnett, 1946), whose Twin Oaks Diner tellingly prefigures both the RR Diner and the very title *Twin Peaks.*

In "A Darker Shade: Realism in Neo-Noir," I argue that one of the essential elements of noir is realism, not in the technical philosophical sense that one is a realist *about* something, taking that kind of thing to be real, but rather in the more common sense of the term, being realistic about the way the world is, seeing things as they are.[5] I also suggest that a significant dimension of such realism is presenting characters that are evil in some cases and morally ambiguous in others.[6] In his "Moral Clarity and Practical Reason in Film Noir" in the same volume, Aeon J. Skoble argues, correctly in my view, that noir heroes such as Sam Spade, rather than being morally ambiguous, are, or at least can be, good people in, and trying to negotiate their way out of, bad situations.[7] From a certain perspective, my view and Skoble's are compatible. Spade certainly *appears* shady throughout most of *The Maltese Falcon,* not only because he flouts conventional morality, but also because it is not until near the end that he fully reveals himself to be the gritty, noble hero that he is. Such appearances are not just compatible with Spade's underlying nobility, they also, as he himself remarks, help him do his job.

Here it seems we run into a snag for the notion that *Twin Peaks* is noir, for some characters come off as obviously morally good, sullied at most by eccentricity. Although this concern would be largely assuaged by Skoble's characterization of noir characters, Agent Cooper, on the surface, does not fit the mold of a true noir hero. Further, whereas Cooper declined, Spade probably would have bedded Audrey (Sherilyn Fenn). Still, although Agent Cooper gleams knightlike, without even a trace of tarnish, in many scenes, the complete picture suggests that he is far from pristine. For one thing, he has a troubled past, in step with other noir heroes, having previously fallen in love with his partner's wife, a federal witness, who died in his custody. He similarly fails in the Black Lodge in attempting to rescue Annie (Heather Graham), his fear, his failure of nerve, makes him susceptible to BOB and, in the end, turns him evil. On the whole, although Cooper's apparent moral ambiguity is less obvious than that of typical noir detectives, it is still there, if not in spades. He passes the noir moral litmus test.

The Reification of BOB

The question whether noir constitutes a proper genre certainly is a vexing one, and I will not engage it here. But *Twin Peaks* is such a mishmash, crossing over the boundaries of so many genres, categories, and styles, as befits its postmodern status, that suggesting it is noir in any straightforward sense is bound to raise some hackles, and rightly so. This is not to say that the notion of postmodern noir is incoherent. Far from it: Films like *Reservoir Dogs* (Quentin Tarantino, 1992), *The Usual Suspects* (Bryan Singer, 1995), *L.A. Confidential* (Curtis Hanson, 1997), *Bound* (Andy Wachowski and Larry Wachowski, 1996), and Lynch's own *Blue Velvet* (1986) and *Lost Highway* (1997) are excellent candidates for the label.[8] Much as it incorporates noir elements, sensibility, iconography, and style, however, *Twin Peaks* seems less like a postmodern noir and more like a hodgepodge with noir as merely one among a host of other ingredients. Leaving out categories closely related to noir, including crime, thriller, and mystery, in *Twin Peaks* we have also elements of horror, fantasy, drama, soap opera, comedy, romance, and even western. This cross-fertilization of genres is pivotally reflected in the metaphysical status of BOB. The uncertainty of his status not only lies at the very heart of why the series is not noir but also, more important, is of independent interest vis-à-vis the interpretation of art. To this we now turn.

It would be helpful at this point to reintroduce the notion of noir metaphysics. As noted earlier, realism is arguably essential to noir. In other words, the world of film noir is a realistic one, a naturalistic one. A general sense of noir is sufficient to establish this claim, and an extensive survey of examples would strengthen it. The noir world is our world, noir metaphysics our metaphysics. The same could be said for noir epistemology, although this is not a central claim, considering my focus. In a discussion of methods of detection in *Twin Peaks,* Angela Hague provides a historical perspective on the matter. She notes that hard-boiled fiction inherited from the classical detective story, originating with Edgar Allen Poe and Sir Arthur Conan Doyle, a naturalistic worldview, ruling out all "supernatural or preternatural agencies."[9] We may add that the legacy continues, from noir fiction (that of Hammett, Chandler, Cain, and Woolrich, in particular) to noir film, from noir film to noir TV. Of course there were other influences on the development of film noir—German expressionism, Freudian psychology, and French surrealism, to name a few—but these can be viewed as stylistic expressions, logical extensions, and symbolic manifestations of what, at base, is a naturalistic outlook, as we shall see.

It may be controversial to interpret *Twin Peaks* naturalistically, but it is by no means out of the question. From a metaphysical point of view, the decisive issue is the metaphysical status of BOB and, similarly, where he comes from, the Red Room/Black Lodge/White Lodge. BOB can be interpreted symbolically, and there are many cues in the series and aesthetic inducements for doing so. BOB can be reduced, or deflated, to no more than Leland's and later Cooper's dark side, a representation of the psychopathology that in Leland's case leads to long-term abuse that culminates in the rape and murder of his own daughter. Similar observations can be made about the Red Room, which might plausibly be interpreted symbolically. Granted, symbolism on this scale and of this type is rather uncommon in noir, except in cases of dream and hallucination imagery. But the strangeness in *Twin Peaks* may in fact come to that. Witness the references in virtually every episode to life in Twin Peaks being, or being like, a dream. That aside, there is nothing wrong with distinguishing seemingly non-noir surface data from an underlying naturalistic realm, in which case *Twin Peaks* might be labeled "deep noir" or "psychological noir." Cooper's intuitions and visions, the paranormal informativeness of his dreams, of his sleep-deprived and possibly hallucinatory states, might be chalked up to little more than coincidence in some cases, subliminal perception and unconscious reasoning in others—the latter two, common analogues of a well documented condition known as "blindsight."[10] At almost every turn, in fact, *Twin Peaks* provides its viewers with enough raw material for a naturalistic reading.

But a naturalistic reading of *Twin Peaks* runs up against pretty stiff competition from precisely those supernatural appearances it works hard to reconfigure by reducing them to symbols. Viewing *Twin Peaks* supernaturalistically is at least as defensible as, and certainly no less plausible than, a naturalistic reading. BOB seems to be a malevolent spirit capable of possessing different human hosts, one attracted especially to those who fear him, whose weakness and moral turpitude make them particularly suitable hosts. BOB also emanates from, and returns to, the Red Room/Black Lodge/White Lodge, a spiritual realm accessible to gifted and altered states of consciousness as well as—at the right time and place, and with the right emotional keys ("Fear and love open the door")—physically. On this tack, we cannot reduce Cooper's intuitive procedures, synchronistic insights, "Tibetan method," or invocation of magic to mere implicit reasoning, subtle perceptiveness, and luck. BOB is taken not as symbolic or fictional but as real, on this reading, no less real in the realm of *Twin Peaks* than Cooper himself or the RR's cherry pie. BOB is *reified* (from the Latin *re*, for thing), a real entity, a bona fide being. Such metaphysics and methods are naturally anathema to a naturalistic reading, and as such, anathema to noir.

Which is the better interpretation here, the naturalistic or the supernaturalistic? This is a difficult question. There is a legitimate sense in which, focusing on the viewer's aesthetic pleasure as the sole criterion, whichever (if either) interpretation better fosters a person's aesthetic experience of an artwork, that is the preferred, the better interpretation (for that person).[11] A naturalistic reading might work better for me, a supernaturalistic one for you, without contradiction. If, however, we have reason to want something more, some intersubjective standard, an interpretation that provides a best explanation of the data (details, elements) provided by the work, *Twin Peaks* leaves us with a dilemma. To reduce or reify? That is the question. Notice how this interpretive dynamic is at work in the discussion that occurs immediately after resolution of the Laura Palmer case. Sheriff Truman opens with a comment on the recently deceased Leland:

> Truman: He was completely insane.
> Cooper: Think so?
> Albert: But people saw BOB. People saw him in visions—Laura, Maddy, Sarah Palmer.
> Major: Gentlemen, there's more in heaven and earth than is dreamt of in our philosophy.
> Cooper: Amen.
> Truman: Well, I've lived in these old woods most of my life. I've seen some strange things, but this is *way* off the map. I'm having a hard time believing.
> Cooper: Harry, is it any easier to believe a man would rape and murder his own daughter, any more comforting?
> Truman: No.
> Major: An evil that great in this beautiful world. Finally, does it matter what the cause?
> Cooper: Yes, because it's our job to stop it.
> Albert: Maybe that's all BOB is, the evil that men do. Maybe it doesn't matter what we call it.
> Truman: Maybe not. But if he was real, if he was here, and we had him trapped, and he got away, where's BOB now?[12]

As viewers, we have a relative epistemic advantage in that we see more of what goes on in Twin Peaks than the characters do, or could. Owing to this and particularly to what viewers discover in the final episode, we may be tempted to lean slightly toward a supernatural reading. But it ultimately remains unclear which reading is better, or whether either is, whether BOB, vis-à-vis the official list of things in the Twin Peaks universe, should be penciled in or crossed off. Perhaps, then, after all, the dichotomy is a false one. As Diane Stevenson writes:

> The strange case of the killing of Laura Palmer can be accounted for either by paternal psychopathology or by demonic possession. The universe of *Twin Peaks* alternates between the psychological and the phantasmal, the physical and the metaphysical, and the boundaries between these realms are blurred. Such confusion of realms, such

transgression of limits, such hesitation between a natural and a supernatural frame of reference, characterize . . . *the genre of the fantastic.*[13] (emphasis mine)

It is not just that *Twin Peaks* can be read either way but that the truth, how it should be read, lies between the two readings. The best interpretation seems to rule out neither reading, yet falls short, on pain of clear contradiction, of wholly affirming either. Whether works of this kind constitute a definite genre, and whether this genre, if it is one, is aptly called "the fantastic" is a matter we may leave aside. The point is, aesthetically speaking, the dichotomy is a false one.

Open Interpretation

These considerations suggest an obvious question: Is it a good thing for an artwork to be interpretively open? We will now consider whether, and to what extent, the interpretive openness excluding *Twin Peaks* from the noir class is aesthetically desirable, and what, if so, this means for noir. So far we have engaged predominantly descriptive questions. It is time to address the evaluative side of the relationship.

Let us start by taking up some of the aesthetic and moral qualms we might have about interpretive openness. Generally, it might seem that we do a work, or ourselves, a disservice by failing to narrow down possible interpretations to a precise, closed, best one. But while this tack is plausible in connection with a scientific account of certain aspects of the world, the notion that artworks always—if ever—yield single, univocal interpretations, irrespective of permissibly variable purposes and standards, is easily countered.[14] Instead of such general misgivings about interpretive openness, we may have specific moral concerns about such interpretive openness as *Twin Peaks* exhibits. (Reread Cooper's disturbing line in the dialogue above, and see note 10.) Even if we do not reify BOB outright, keeping him in limbo between reduction and reification might seem to overshadow, diminish the significance of, aestheticize, and, worse, mitigate the horror of father-daughter abuse and murder.[15] From a consequentialist perspective, this might be a legitimate concern, although it is not clear how a BOB-inclusive aesthetic would transfer to our view of other works, much less make the leap—as BOB himself fictionally does—into the real world, tranquilizing or blinding us to such harsh truths. We know better. We know too much. It would seem more realistic, less evasive, to address the matter, and in a negative light, as *Twin Peaks* does, than to fail to broach it at all.

Some doubt might linger that interpretive openness of the sort in *Twin Peaks* is aesthetically desirable, and so it might be helpful to take another illustrative case. While there are many such across the arts, it seems best to use another breakthrough television series exhibiting strong interpretive openness and noirishness to boot. I have in mind *The Prisoner,* which has a number of crucial, yet interpretively open, elements. Throughout the series, it is unclear which side in the Cold War controls the Village, where Number 6 (Patrick McGoohan) is imprisoned. In the series finale, Number 6 finally meets Number 1, the mysterious, previously unseen agent in charge of his imprisonment, an apparently insane version of himself. This revelation invites us to read the series as a psychological allegory and yet falls short of establishing, as merely symbolic, the unreality of all the preceding events composing almost the entire series. Similarly, the finale's final shot, Number 6 in his sports car zipping down a sun-drenched highway, suggests a variety of possible interpretations: a loop back to the start of the series, a metaphor for freedom regained—or perhaps for freedom possessed all along—optimistically that all psychosis leads to freedom, or pessimistically, given the loop, that freedom leads to psychosis. These elements force the interpretation here wide open, and the provocative aesthetic appeal of the series is clearly enhanced, not compromised, as a result. Such interpretive openness most strikingly distinguishes series like *The Prisoner* and *Twin Peaks* from those less aesthetically rewarding.

This might seem, by implication, to undermine the aesthetic quality of noir, casting it in a pale light, too pale a light, really, since such works as *The Maltese Falcon,* which would be corrupted by the kind of interpretive openness in *Twin Peaks,* are hardly of inferior grade. It could be that, aesthetically speaking, interpretive openness is simply desirable without being strictly necessary. Admittedly, *The Maltese Falcon* is not interpretively open in the same way, or to the same degree, as *Twin Peaks.* It is naturalistic, thoroughly so. But this does not mean that it is not, even significantly, interpretively open. The aesthetic appeal of *The Maltese Falcon* arguably depends on a kind of interpretive openness, psychological indeterminacy. Consider the prime example of the values that guide Sam Spade through the noir labyrinth. Beyond self-preservation via solving the mystery, there seems to be far more to Spade's motivation than we may initially suspect. Yet it is not clear whether he is moved by stoically silent compassion for his dead partner, a desire to avenge his partner's death, sexual desire for the prototype femme fatale, a cruel wish to punish her, wealth in the wake of finding the Falcon, an intrinsic desire to crack the case, the principled aim of trying to redress the injustices and have the wrongdoers held accountable, the practical aim of avoiding what would be bad for business, or preventing on a wider scale what would be "bad for every detective everywhere." All are plausible; none is clearly and decisively his. Spade's is a kind of existential project, to be sure, but his psychologically uncertain status remains, and remains piquant, even in his fainthearted attempts to explain himself (citing, in turn, the last three reasons in the list above). These may be convincing enough on their own, but they do not at all seem to strike Spade himself that way. Even if we accept Spade's explanations, however, it is not without legitimate doubt. Less aesthetically satisfying noirs leave much less open. Note the unnecessary, irksome expatiations on personal motives and poetic justice in *The Postman Always Rings Twice.* While interpretive openness is a good thing to have in art, the degree of appropriate openness is contextually variable. For obvious reasons, the fantastic, like *Twin Peaks,* is more open than the realistic, noir included, which limits without eliminating openness per se.

The Omissive Aesthetic

As a last remark, it seems appropriate to highlight the connection between interpretive openness and what might be called the "omissive" aesthetic, the poignancy of *leaving out,* of letting some things remain unsaid, undepicted, unshown, which is quite possibly a characteristic of all artwork. Good artwork, moreover, seems to have it more than most. Leaving things out opens up interpretation. The less left unsaid, the more clumsy, telegraphed, artless the work. The other extreme, except in rare cases (some abstract and conceptual art), is likely equally insufficient for the purposes of art. Enough content and structure must be given to prompt, and delimit within manageable bounds, an audience's engagement. Having to read between the lines, bringing, as an appreciator, something *to* the work, and doing some work oneself, is an irreplaceable part of an ideal, perhaps of any *real,* artistic transaction. Work that allows enough space for this, that elicits rewarding intellectual contemplation in tandem with deep emotional response, is valuable as such, precisely for that reason. By leaving the metaphysics, hence the interpretation, open as it does, *Twin Peaks* exhibits the omissive in art and affords such aesthetic rewards.

Notes

I am most grateful to Steven M. Sanders and Aeon J. Skoble for invaluable comments and criticisms, from the initial framing of this paper to revising it for print, and to Marc Ramsay and Ami Harbin for enjoyable shared viewing and provocative discussion of *Twin Peaks*.

1. Specifically, in Timothy Egan, "Northwest Noir: The Art of the Seriously Goofy," 14 July 1991, B1, B20; and Jeremy Gerard, "A 'Soap Noir' Inspires a Cult and Questions," 26 April 1990, C22.

2. The name "BOB" is given in capital letters in the subtitles shown during scenes in the Red Room, and most commentators and theorists follow this convention. The identification of the Red Room with the Black Lodge is straightforward. While it is less clear whether the White Lodge is yet another descriptive name for the same thing, there are several clues in the series suggesting that this additional equivalence holds.

3. Jason Holt, "A Darker Shade: Realism in Neo-Noir," in *The Philosophy of Film Noir*, ed. Mark T. Conard (Lexington: University Press of Kentucky, 2006), 24.

4. Angela Hague, "Infinite Games: The Derationalization of Detection in *Twin Peaks*," in *Full of Secrets: Critical Approaches to* Twin Peaks, ed. David Lavery (Detroit, MI: Wayne State University Press, 1995), 130–43.

5. Holt, "A Darker Shade," 24–25, 37–39.

6. Ibid.

7. Aeon J. Skoble, "Moral Clarity and Practical Reason in Film Noir," in Conard, *Philosophy of Film Noir,* 41–43.

8. A recent discussion of themes, styles, and narrative patterns of postmodern film noir can be found in Andrew Spicer, *Film Noir* (Harlow, England: Pearson Education, 2002), chapter 8. Steven M. Sanders identifies postmodernist epistemological and aesthetic theses and describes how they are exemplified in episodes of *Miami Vice* in "Sunshine Noir: Postmodernism and *Miami Vice*," in *The Philosophy of Neo-Noir*, ed. Mark T. Conard (Lexington: University Press of Kentucky, 2007), 183–201.

9. Hague, "Infinite Games," 130, quoting Ronald Knox, "A Detective Story Decalogue," in *Detective Fiction: A Collection of Critical Essays,* ed. Robin W. Winks (Woodstock, CT: Foul Play, 1988), 200–201.

10. For more on this counterintuitive, philosophically provocative condition, see Jason Holt, *Blindsight and the Nature of Consciousness* (Peterborough, ON: Broadview, 2003).

11. Jason Holt, "The Marginal Life of the Author," in *The Death and Resurrection of the Author?* ed. William T. Irwin (Westport, CT: Greenwood, 2002), 74–75.

12. *Twin Peaks,* episode 17 (following Lavery, Full of Secrets, 233, listed as 16 in video releases, which do not include the pilot). Director: Tim Hunter; writers: Mark Frost, Harley Peyton, Robert Engels. Original airdate: Dec. 1, 1990. Notice that Albert, the noir patter specialist, takes a decidedly uncharacteristic stance on BOB at first, only

later returning to a more hard-boiled point of view. Note also the Major's paraphrase of the famous line from Hamlet (I.v.166–67), Cooper's disturbing equation of epistemic justification with psychological comfort (which fuels the moral concerns mentioned later), and the unwitting irony of Truman's answer, "No." The right answer is clearly "Yes," because the naturalistic explanation is much more justified, hence easier to believe in that sense, and more comforting, too, for in a naturalistic framework, the evil, horrible as it is, dies with Leland, but in a supernaturalistic one, BOB is free to go on wreaking havoc, death, and suffering.

13. Diane Stevenson, "Family Romance, Family Violence, and the Fantastic in *Twin Peaks*," in Lavery, *Full of Secrets*, 70. Stevenson appeals to Tzvetan Todorov, *The Fantastic*, trans. Richard Howard (Ithaca, NY: Cornell University Press, 1975).

14. Holt, "Marginal Life," 75–76.

15. See Christy Desmet, "The Canonization of Laura Palmer," in Lavery, *Full of Secrets*, 93–108, and Diana Hume George, "Lynching Women: A Feminist Reading of *Twin Peaks*," in the same volume, 109–19.

CONTRIBUTORS

JEROLD J. ABRAMS is associate professor of philosophy at Creighton University. His essays appear in the *Modern Schoolman, Philosophy Today, Human Studies,* the *Transactions of the Charles S. Peirce Society,* and *James Bond and Philosophy* (Open Court, 2006), *Woody Allen and Philosophy* (Open Court, 2004), *Star Wars and Philosophy* (Open Court, 2005), and *The Philosophy of Film Noir* (University Press of Kentucky, 2005).

SHAI BIDERMAN is a doctoral candidate in philosophy at Boston University. His research interests are philosophy of culture, philosophy of film and literature, aesthetics, ethics, existentialism, and Nietzsche. His publications include articles on personal identity, language, determinism, and aesthetics. He has also written about the television shows *Seinfeld* and *Star Trek* and the films *Minority Report, Kill Bill, Down by Law,* and *Rope.*

ERIC BRONSON is a visiting professor in the Division of Humanities at York University in Toronto. He coedited *The Lord of the Rings and Philosophy* (Open Court, 2003) and edited *Baseball and Philosophy* (Open Court, 2004) and *Poker and Philosophy* (Open Court, 2006). His research interests include philosophy and religion, Asian philosophy, and existentialism.

ELIZABETH F. COOKE is associate professor of philosophy at Creighton University. She researches in epistemology, philosophy of science, and American pragmatism, especially the logic of inquiry in Charles S. Peirce. She has published articles in the volumes *Star Wars and Philosophy* (Open Court, 2005) and *Peirce's Pragmatic Theory of Inquiry: Fallibilism and Indeterminacy* (Continuum Press, 2006) and journals including *Contemporary Pragmatism* and *Philosophia Mathematica.*

WILLIAM J. DEVLIN is assistant professor of philosophy at Bridgewater State College. His fields of interest are philosophy of science, theories of truth, Nietzsche, and existentialism. His publications include articles on Nietzsche, metaphysics, aesthetics, and on such films and television series as *Twelve Monkeys, The Terminator, Lost,* and *South Park.*

ROBERT E. FITZGIBBONS is professor of philosophy at Bridgewater State College and is the author of textbooks on ethics and philosophy of education.

JASON HOLT is assistant professor at Acadia University, where he teaches communication in the School of Recreation Management and Kinesiology. He specializes in aesthetics and philosophy of mind. His *Blindsight and the Nature of Consciousness* (Broadview Press, 2003) was shortlisted for the 2005 Canadian Philosophical Association Book Prize. His work in philosophy and popular culture includes essays on *Seinfeld, The Simpsons, The Matrix,* Woody Allen, film noir, Stanley Kubrick, and Alfred Hitchcock.

DEBORAH KNIGHT is associate professor of philosophy at Queen's University. Her primary research is in the philosophy of art, with particular interest in the narrative arts, including film and film genres. Her papers appear in volumes such as *Literary Philosophers: Borges, Calvino, Eco* (Routledge, 2002), *The Oxford Handbook of Aesthetics* (Oxford University Press, 2003), and *Film Theory and Philosophy* (Oxford University Press, 1999), as well as such periodicals as the *Journal of Aesthetics and Art Criticism, Philosophy and Literature,* and *Film and Philosophy.*

SANDER LEE is professor of philosophy at Keene State College. He is the author of *Eighteen Woody Allen Films Analyzed: Anguish, God, and Existentialism* (McFarland, 2002) and *Woody Allen's Angst: Philosophical Commentaries on His Serious Films* (McFarland, 1997). He has also written numerous essays on issues in aesthetics, ethics, Holocaust studies, social philosophy, and metaphysics.

GEORGE MCKNIGHT is associate professor of film studies in the School for Studies in Art and Culture, Carleton University. He edited *Agent of Challenge and Defiance: The Films of Ken Loach* and has published articles on British cinema. With Deborah Knight, he has coauthored papers on *American Psycho, The Matrix,* Hitchcock's use of suspense, and detective narratives.

JENNIFER L. MCMAHON is chair of the English, foreign language, and humanities departments at East Central University in Ada, Oklahoma. Her research interests include existentialism, philosophy and literature, aesthetics, nonwestern philosophy, and biomedical ethics. She has published articles in journals including *Asian Philosophy* and the *Journal of the Association for Interdisciplinary Study of the Arts.* She has also published essays on philosophy and popular culture in *Seinfeld and Philosophy* (2000), *The Matrix and Philosophy* (2002), *The Simpsons and Philosophy* (2001), and *The Lord of the Rings and Philosophy* (2003), all with Open Court Press.

MICHAEL VALDEZ MOSES is associate professor of English and a founding member of the Gerst Program for Political, Economic, and Humanistic Studies at Duke University. He is the author of *The Novel and the Globalization of Culture* (Oxford University Press, 1995), editor of a collection of critical essays, *The Writings of J. M. Coetzee* (Duke University Press, 1994) and coeditor of *Modernism and Colonialism: British and Irish Literature, 1900–1939* (Duke University Press, 2007). He is currently at work on *Nation of the Dead: The Politics of Irish Literature 1890–1990*.

R. BARTON PALMER is Calhoun Lemon Professor of Literature at Clemson University. Among his many books on film are *Hollywood's Dark Cinema: The American Film Noir* (Second revised and expanded edition, University of Illinois Press, forthcoming), *Joel and Ethan Coen, Twentieth Century American Fiction on Screen* (University of Illinois Press, 2004), and (with David Boyd) *After Hitchcock: Imitation/Influence/Intertextuality* (University of Texas Press, 2006).

STEVEN M. SANDERS is professor emeritus and former chair of the department of philosophy at Bridgewater State College. His publications in philosophy and film include essays on Alfred Hitchcock, Martin Scorsese, and Stanley Kubrick, and *The Philosophy of Science Fiction Film* (University Press of Kentucky, 2007), which he edited. He has written widely on topics in ethics and is coeditor (with R. Barton Palmer) of the forthcoming *Hitchcock as Moralist*. He writes a blog, *Sunshine Noir,* at www.misternoir.blogspot.com.

AEON J. SKOBLE is associate professor of philosophy and chair of the philosophy department at Bridgewater State College. He is the coeditor of the anthology *Political Philosophy: Essential Selections* (Prentice-Hall, 1999) and author of the forthcoming *Deleting the State: An Argument about Government* (Open Court, forthcoming), as well as many essays on moral and political philosophy in both scholarly and popular journals. In addition, he writes widely on the intersection of philosophy and popular culture—including such subjects as *Seinfeld, Forrest Gump, The Lord of the Rings,* superheroes, film noir, Hitchcock, science fiction, and baseball—and coedited and contributed to *Woody Allen and Philosophy* (Open Court 2004) and the best-selling *The Simpsons and Philosophy* (Open Court, 2000).

KEVIN L. STOEHR is assistant professor of humanities at Boston University. He is the author of the forthcoming *Nihilism in Film and Television* (McFarland, 2006), and coeditor of the forthcoming *John Ford in Focus: Essays on the Filmmaker's Life and Art* (McFarland, 2008). He has also edited a volume entitled *Film and Knowledge* (McFarland, 2002), and he has written widely on the intersections between philosophy and popular culture.

INDEX